Where Extremes Meet: Rereading Brecht and Beckett

The Brecht Yearbook 27

Guest editor
Antony Tatlow

Managing Editor
Stephen Brockmann

Editorial Board
Sigfrid Hoefert, Karen Leeder, Marc Silberman, Antony Tatlow, Carl Weber

The International Brecht Society
Distribution: University of Wisconsin Press

Produced at Carnegie Mellon University, Pittsburgh, Pennsylvania, USA. Distributed by the University of Wisconsin Press, 114 N. Murray, Madison, WI 53715, USA.

ISSN 0734-8665
ISBN 0-9718963-0-5

Cover Illustration: Andrew Johnson (2002).

Photographic material courtesy of the Brecht Archive, Berlin.

Layout: Alicia C. Nawrocki.

Printed in Canada

Officers of the International Brecht Society:

Alexander Stephan, President, Department of German, 314 Cunz Hall, 1841 Millikin Road, Ohio State University, Columbus, OH 43210-1229, USA. Email:stephan.30@osu.edu

Erdmut Wizisla, Vice-President, Chausseestr. 125, 10115 Berlin, Germany. Email: bba@adk.de

David W. Robinson, Secretary/Treasurer, Department of Literature and Philosophy, Georgia Southern University, Statesboro, GA 30640, USA. Email: DWROB@gasou.edu

Gudrun Tabbert-Jones, Editor, *Communications,* Department of Modern Languages, Santa Clara University, Santa Clara, CA 95053, USA. Email: gtabbertjone@scuacc.scu.edu

* * *

Internet Website address: http://polyglot.lss.wisc.edu/german/brecht

* * *

Membership:

Members receive *The Brecht Yearbook* and the biannual journal *Communications of the International Brecht Society.* Dues should be sent in US$ to the Secretary/Treasurer or in Euro to the Deutsche Bank Düsseldorf (BLZ 300 702 00, Konto-Nr. 76-74146):

Student Member (up to three years)	$20.00	☐ 20
Regular Member,		
annual income under $30,000	$30.00	☐ 30
annual income over $30,000	$40.00	☐ 40
Sustaining Member	$50.00	☐ 50
Institutional Member	$50.00	☐ 50

* * *

Submissions:

Manuscripts should be submitted to *The Brecht Yearbook* on hard copy (double-spaced) and/or diskette. They may also be sent as email attachments. Endnote or footnote format should be internally consistent, preferably following *The Chicago Style Manual.* Address contributions to the editor:

Stephen Brockmann, Department of Modern Languages, Carnegie Mellon University, Baker Hall 160, Pittsburgh, PA 15213-3890, USA. Email: smb@andrew.cmu.edu

Inquiries concerning book reviews and conference participation should be addressed to:

Marc Silberman, Department of German, 818 Van Hise Hall, University of Wisconsin, Madison, WI 53706, USA. Email: mdsilber@facstaff.wisc.edu

The International Brecht Society

The International Brecht Society has been formed as a corresponding society on the model of Brecht's own unrealized plan for the Diderot Society. Through its publications and regular international symposia, the society encourages the discussion of any and all views on the relationship of the arts and the contemporary world. The society is open to new members in any field and in any country and welcomes suggestions and/or contributions in German, English, Spanish or French to future symposia and for the published volumes of its deliberations.

Die Internationale Brecht-Gesellschaft

Die Internationale Brecht-Gesellschaft ist nach dem Modell von Brechts nicht verwirklichtem Plan für die Diderot-Gesellschaft gegründet worden. Durch Veröffentlichungen und regelmäßige internationale Tagungen fördert die Gesellschaft freie und öffentliche Diskussionen über die Beziehungen aller Künste zur heutigen Welt. Die Gesellschaft steht neuen Mitgliedern in jedem Fachgebiet und Land offen und begrüßt Vorschläge für zukünftige Tagungen und Aufsätze in deutscher, englischer, spanischer oder französischer Sprache für *Das Brecht-Jahrbuch*.

La Société Internationale Brecht

La Société Internationale Brecht a été formée pour correspondre à la société rêvée par Brecht, "Diderot-Gesellschaft." Par ses publications et congrès internationaux à intervalles réguliers, la S.I.B. encourage la discussion libre des toutes les idées sur les rapports entre les arts et le monde contemporain. Bien entendu, les nouveaux membres dans toutes les disciplines et tous les pays sont accueillis avec plaisir, et la Société sera heureuse d'accepter des suggestions et des contributions en français, allemand, espagnol ou anglais pour les congrès futurs et les volumes des communications qui en résulteront.

La Sociedad Internacional Brecht

La Sociedad Internacional Brecht fué creada para servir como sociedad corresponsal. Dicha sociedad se basa en el modelo que el mismo autor nunca pudo realizar, el plan "Diderot-Gesellschaft." A través de sus publicaciones y los simposios internacionales que se llevan a cabo regularmente, la Sociedad estimula la discusión libre y abierta de cualquier punto de vista sobre la relación entre las artes y el mundo contemporáneo. La Sociedad desea, por supuesto, la participación de nuevos miembros de cualquier área, de cualquier país, y accepta sugerencias y colaboraciones en alemán, inglés, francés y español para los congresos futuros y para las publicaciones de sus discusiones.

Contents

BOOK REVIEWS

Editorial

In his editorial to volume 21 of the Yearbook, Maarten van Dijk wrote: "On behalf of the IBS and the other editors I would here like to thank Marc Silberman warmly for his devoted and gifted work as editor of the Yearbook for so many years. He created and is creating continuity. He is a hard act to follow, and we are most grateful for his further back-stage presence." I would like now to use Maarten van Dijk's own words to thank him for his excellent work on the Yearbook for the last six years. He and Marc Silberman are both difficult acts to follow, and the legacy that they and others have created imposes a burden of duty on any managing editor who succeeds them. I will do my best to try to live up to this legacy and to carry this burden. And of course I hope that I will continue to benefit from the "further back-stage presence" of both Maarten van Dijk and Marc Silberman. I would also like to express my thanks to Sigfrid Hoefert, who is stepping down from the editorial board this year, for his many years of service to the Yearbook. Sigfrid Hoefert's place on the editorial board will be taken by Vera Stegmann of Lehigh University.

This volume of the Yearbook is devoted to a conference on Brecht and Samuel Beckett that took place in Dublin, Ireland in the spring of 2001. That conference was organized by Antony Tatlow, a long-time member of the editorial board of the Yearbook, and I am grateful to Tatlow for his hard work on both the 2001 conference and the present volume. Tatlow has brought the same erudition and creativity to rethinking the Brecht-Beckett connection that Linda Kintz, in a review in this volume, finds in Tatlow's recent book *Shakespeare, Brecht, and the Intercultural Sign*. Indeed, Kintz's assessment that "Tatlow's work might provide a way to assess Buddhist and Asian conventions in Brecht that can counter New Age misappropriations of Eastern thought in U.S. culture" could just as easily be applied to his essay "Saying Yes and Saying No: Schopenhauer and Nietzsche as Educators" in this volume.

I would like to dedicate my own work on this volume, and as managing editor of the Yearbook now and in the coming years, to the memory of my dear friend and mentor Ruth Limmer, the literary executor of Louise Bogan, one of the major American poets of the twentieth century. Ruth Limmer died in New York City at the end of October, 2001, and I miss her greatly; it was from her that I learned much of what I know about writing, editing, and the literary life more generally. I can only hope that my work can begin to live up to the very high standards she set.

In the past decade Brecht scholarship has continued to generate controversy and polemic. As managing editor of the

Yearbook, I am committed to allowing as many voices as possible to be heard. Whatever one's stance on Bertolt Brecht himself, and to whomever one chooses to give credit for his achievements, it is indisputable that the body of work designated by Brecht's name is a central part of twentieth century literary and theatrical culture, and that it continues to play an important role in the twenty-first century. I want to maintain the high standards of the Yearbook as the central forum for discussion and scholarship about the life and work of Brecht. In addition, I wish to open the Yearbook to issues and problems that Brecht himself was interested in, especially the politics of literature and theater nationally and internationally. It seems to me that these issues have only become more important in the wake of the terrorist attack on the United States in September of 2001 and the resulting and ongoing military actions. Brecht was committed to literature and theater that had a political and social use value, and scholars of literature and theater might do well to apply some of the same commitment to their own work. I particularly welcome submissions that explore the work of Brecht specifically, and the politics of theater more generally, in a global context. Volume 28 of the Yearbook is an open issue, and I look forward to a wide variety of perspectives. The deadline for submissions to volume 28 is November 20, 2002.

Stephen Brockmann, Pittsburgh, April 2002

Introduction

Antony Tatlow

With the exception of the last contribution, whose reading of feminism and Brecht is affiliated with topics in the other papers, the contributions to this volume 27 of *The Brecht Yearbook* all originated in a Symposium, *Where Extremes Meet: Rereading Brecht and Beckett.* It was held in the University of Dublin's Samuel Beckett Theatre on 4 and 5 May 2001 by the Graduate Centre for Arts Research and the School of Drama, headed by the Samuel Beckett Professor of Drama and Theatre Studies, Dennis Kennedy. The Symposium, open to the general public, consisted of four lectures, one of which, delivered by Herbert Blau, constituted *The Sixth Annual Samuel Beckett Lecture,* as well as two Panels on *Brecht and Beckett in the Theatre.* Given the more "formal" position of the annual Beckett Lecture, special time was allocated for response to questions. The panelists presented position statements and discussed among themselves and with the audience.

These discussions have been shortened and, I hope, judiciously edited. This proved necessary when, on occasion, they turned on unhelpful rather than productive misunderstandings, stemming from insufficient knowledge of one or the other of the authors' work or person. There was no *a priori* intention or demand on the part of the organizers, nor any *a posteriori* editorial compulsion to employ a comparative or double focus in the topics, merely an expectation that the work of Brecht and Beckett, or its effect on later writers, could be usefully discussed in some kind of resonance with each other. Given that deliberately broad context, it was interesting to observe how arguments made solely in terms of one can be, as it were, silently and productively extrapolated in respect of the other. Another quality of information in these discussions has been retained for its intrinsic interest, as when the director of the Gate Theatre in Dublin and producer of the recent, successful and controversial filmings of all of Beckett's plays explains something of his response to this historic project.

The contributions address different aspects of these conjunctures. They speak for themselves and I shall not try to summarize them. I do, however, wish to revisit the whole project, briefly suggesting further reasons why juxtaposing Brecht and Beckett, a topic that once appeared accomplished to the point of exhaustion, either when interpreting their work or tracing its effect on other writers, still paradoxically almost seems as if it had never been seriously addressed, and hence should lead to more differentiated readings. Is it

Where Extremes Meet: Rereading Brecht and Beckett / Begegnung der Extreme. Brecht und Beckett: Eine Re-interpretation
Stephen Brockmann et al., eds., *The Brecht Yearbook / Das Brecht-Jahrbuch*
Volume 27 (Pittsburgh: The International Brecht Society, 2002)

possible, for example, to think of two modern writers whose work so encourages comparative discussion, both in terms of its global influence and of its transgeneric range? Heiner Müller is only one of a number of artists whose personally acknowledged debt to both is evident. It would be interesting to extend such study of absorption and transformation into other art forms and outside Western cultures and, for example, to compare the effect, also personally acknowledged, which both their work had on artists like Philip Glass and Gao Xingjian.

Though monographs make one-on-one comparisons, one reason why there has not yet been more wide-ranging comparative study must surely be the tenacious supposition that Brecht and Beckett have been so exhaustively juxtaposed and read against each other that nothing more can possibly be said about the relative positions of their work. Scores of books, hundreds of chapters, thousands of articles have investigated and above all contrasted their positions. What one had in abundance, the other seemed to lack, so between them they bestrode the global stage. For this reason advocacy was, and to a degree still is, often partisan, such that if you held to one, you could not logically or emotionally embrace the other. Their advocates frequently employed differently allusive discursive styles, communicating in conceptual shorthand, and even developed distinctive body languages. Equally, one offered the antidote or counterpoison which would protect against the other's enticement.

The word "dichotomy" might have been invented to describe their relative positions, in the dictionary sense of a division into two parts or classes, especially when these are sharply distinguished or opposed, and reinforced by its use within biology, where such a division establishes two equal parts. Yet in astronomy the moon is dichotomous when half of the surface is illuminated. And here we find a metaphorical image which suggests that appearances can be very deceptive, that at their best at least half of what is substantial may be concealed from superficial inspection. All is perhaps not as clearcut or as transparent as it may once have seemed to be.

Let us consider some of these dichotomies in the light of what they conceal. It is as if Brecht had anticipated the difference between his own project and Beckett's when he set out the fundamental distinctions in the *Notes for Mahagonny* under the headings "epic" and "dramatic" theater, concluding with the subsequently removed because too reductive opposition between "feeling" and "reason."[1] If man is

---

[1] Bertolt Brecht, *Werke, Große Berliner und Frankfurter Ausgabe* (Frankfurt: Suhrkamp 1991), v. 24, p. 79 (GBA 24, 79); John Willett, ed. & trans., *Brecht*

regarded as "unalterable" in the dramatic and "alterable and able to alter" in the epic theater, there would seem, on the surface, no doubt who belongs in which category. Then we juxtapose Beckett's static sets and minds with Brecht's kinetic flow of things and history. Yet there is plenty of evidence that both believed in the fluidity of the ego.

There are as many parallels as differences in their use of metaphor, in personal behavior and attitudes, and in the responses these invoked from others. The coldness of the earth is a founding metaphor for both and can be given a convergent as well as a divergent reading. They shared a sensitivity to music, and no matter how differently it resonates in their work, were affected by the fear that it might overwhelm them, and so, even as they needed it, they kept it at a distance. In 1947 Brecht wrote an outline for a pantomime, *From Circus Life* (GBA 20, 184), and gave it to Lotte Goslar, who later remarked how this story of a "silent subject" was comparable to Beckett's *Act without Words*.[2] Though Beckett worked in isolation, and Brecht through collaboration, both meticulously documented their innovative but comparable practice in the theater. With quite different personalities in charge, the behavior of their Estates in believing that these practices had to be protected was virtually identical. Beckett is a sharp observer of class-specific behaviour, and survival is at the center of Brecht's project. They both focused on the small and the ordinary. When power confronts the powerless, Beckett recourses to a flawed detective, Brecht to a flawed judge. They both invoked intense loyalty among their advocates and followers who stylized them as paragons: Beckett as secular saint, Brecht as embodied practical friendliness.

If one asks who has written most persuasively about both writers, near if not at the top of most lists must be Martin Esslin. He worked in particular sympathy with Beckett as a consequence of his position as Head of Drama in the BBC. Though not emotionally or politically close to Brecht, he nevertheless had a lively sense, evident in *Brecht: A Choice of Evils*,[3] of his extraordinary talents and the capacity of his work. But he contrasted them, and where we might have expected more searching comparisons, for example in the book that

---

on Theatre: The Development of an Aesthetic (New York: Hill & Wang 1964), p. 37.

[2]   See James K. Lyon, *Bertolt Brecht in America* (Princeton: Princeton University Press 1980), p. 195.

[3]   Martin Esslin, *Brecht: A Choice of Evils. A Critical Study of the Man, his Work, and his Opinions* (London: Eyre Spottiswoode 1959).

bears both their names in its title, they are again taken separately.[4] Yet in respect of doubleness, or that other side of the self or work, of what needs to be illuminated in order to achieve a better appreciation of the whole, Esslin did produce a reading of Brecht that at least cut him in two, even if this was radical surgery with its own postoperative complications. He proposed a personal "subconscious" totally at odds with Brecht's surface public politics and with what Esslin construed as necessary party discipline. Because he read Brecht as riven by violent contradictions, he saw his work as infused, if not directly produced, by guilt over the suppression both of the emotions or instinct and also of reason. Given the tenor of the times, it would not have been easy, and was maybe impossible, to produce readings in the 1950s that advanced beyond such binary oppositions, no matter where you located them. But it must be said that splitting Brecht even in this too schematic way into epistemological or political, and personal incompatibilities was certainly preferable to hagiography and at least pointed towards a source of the complexity of his writing.

But we have left "Beckett and the Absurd" or "Brecht and Behaviorism" behind us. Two recent books, which engage with their subjects from very different critical, professional, and cultural perspectives, nevertheless reveal surprising congruities, but then compatibilities of this kind never happen by accident. As his publisher, John Calder had unique access to Beckett, and he offers unusual perspectives and insight into the person and his work.[5] The German translation of Fredric Jameson's *Brecht and Method* is aptly entitled *Lust und Schrecken der unaufhörlichen Verwandlung aller Dinge: Brecht und die Zukunft*.[6] Yet it might just as well have been called *The Philosophy of Bertolt Brecht*, because Jameson reads Brecht's work as an articulation of a fundamental attitude that depends on triangulating language, narrative, and thought. Attempts to derive abstract meanings or to extrapolate particular political positions out of that work respond to it below the level of its complexity. Both books affirm for their subjects the importance of a particular kind of philosophical reflection

---

[4]   Martin Esslin, *Mediations: Essays on Brecht, Beckett, and the Media* (London: Eyre Methuen 1980). The chapter "The Mind as a Stage—Radio Drama" (171-187) also passes up the opportunity for comparison.

[5]   John Calder, *The Philosophy of Samuel Beckett* (London: Calder Publications 2001).

[6]   Fredric Jameson, *Brecht and Method* (London: Verso 1998). I describe and situate Jameson's response to Brecht in an article, "For and Against Method: Jameson, Brecht, and the Dao," in *Colloquia Germanica* v. 34, n. 3/4, 2001, pp. 287-316.

upon the conditions of existence, upon ways of living, which we could describe as ethical and which touches upon stoic values. They show how such reflection informs both this writing as well as perspectives upon it, and why all of this should be taken seriously. Jameson suggests that both of them draw on archaic experience and develop their own forms of minimalism—seeing in Brecht a "reduction of the object world...to the few poor items...a poverty and singularity of objects which, as in Beckett, empty the stage out and leave the surviving items ready for their definite article: *the* tree, *the* leaf, *the* rope, and so on."[7]—such that the use of the definite article in both "therefore proposes a kind of peasant history," which draws exploitation down to cyclical and perennial animosities, pitting oppressors and oppressed against each other.[8] Jameson sees in Brecht's reflections on the nature of identity, given the inescapable flow of time, "a Beckett-like drift scarcely held in place by the afterthought of a situation and response framework." He adds that this may "from a post-contemporary position, seem a mode of containment, and a way of managing the otherwise frightening chaos of psychic flux that threatens individuality's dissolution." [9]

It can also be no accident that both Calder and Jameson draw attention to Buddhist philosophy, and in the case of Brecht also to Daoism, so that we are invited to reflect on the importance of the concept of "nothing" for both their work, though I suspect that Beckett's "nothing" is maybe closer to Sartre's "néant" than any Buddhist nirvana, which, if the relationship is properly expounded, is indeed pertinent to Brecht, for whom the term "Nichts" is just as suggestive, if not more so, than it is for Beckett. Calder traces Beckett's "nothing" from Geulincx through to Buddhism. Brecht's "nothing" resonates with Nietzsche. If, as Calder reminds us, Beckett held that the key word in his writing is "perhaps," can we not see a Brechtian equivalent to this in his call to actors to embody in their performance what the character does not do, which he called "fixing the 'not/but'" (Fixieren des *Nicht-Sondern*, GBA 22.2, 643), provided we do not read this as advocating a loaded binary opposition between right and wrong, but rather, as Jameson suggests, as an opportunity to reflect on the construction of a restrictive "identity" that is confronted by multiplicity?[10] Both Brecht's and Beckett's work is infused by paradox,

---

7   *Brecht and Method*, 134.

8   *Brecht and Method*, 137.

9   *Brecht and Method*, 78.

10   *Brecht and Method*, 58.

doubleness, and contradiction, and that accounts for the importance of laughter to them both, though Beckett's laugh is the *risus purus*, the laugh which laughs at laughter.

In the shape of a specific allusion, we can observe another intriguing non-coincidence in their work. Both employ the image of a "vulture" to metaphorize a complex, overdetermined response to the conditions of life. This "vulture" suggests something of the contiguity and discompatibility of their imaginations, since the images radiate beyond their particular contexts into the rest of their work. Beckett's *The Vulture*, said to have derived from a reading of Goethe's poem, *Harzreise im Winter*, is the first poem in the collection *Echo's Bones*, published in 1935.[11] Esslin holds that Beckett's poem anticipates "the future argument of Beckett's complete *oeuvre*."[12]

Compared with Brecht, Beckett wrote very little poetry, but, just as can be said of Brecht, a powerful poetic imagination infuses all his work. Brecht's "vulture" figures in an extraordinary verse of the *Hymn of the Great Baal* which opens his first play, *Baal*, the only verse then repeated within the play itself (GBA 1, 86). It too could well be considered fundamental to the project that is Brecht's work. These "vultures" metaphorize the imagination as a soaring, circling bird of prey, figuring the life of the mind which must nourish itself upon that of which it is itself a part, upon death in nature. They are all acts of exorcism, philosophical poems probing destiny, focusing loneliness; they are all close to the person of their authors. The self-identification with this insatiable, transcendent, immortal/mortal murdering force is as evident in Beckett's "dragging his hunger through the sky/ of my skull shell of sky and earth" as it is for Brecht's Baal, who, by shamming death in the form of its prey, then catches the swooping vulture in order to devour it, to swallow death, and internalize its

---

[11]   Samuel Beckett, *Collected Poems 1930-1978* (London: John Calder 1984), p. 9. Goethe, *Werke* (Hamburg: Christian Wegner Verlag, 1964), v. 1, p. 50. The German word employed by Goethe and then by Brecht is "Geier." This translates into English as "vulture." Beckett's use suggests he took it in the sense of vulture as eater of carrion, since the last word in his poem is "offal." But in German the word was often used for any large death-bringing "bird of prey," and associated with hawks and eagles. I doubt there is a connection between Brecht's use and Goethe's poem. For another reading of Brecht's poem see my article, "Gibt es neue Wege zum alten Brecht?" in *Dreigroschenheft* 3/2000, pp. 13-25. For pertinent information on Goethe's *Harzreise im Winter*, see James Boyd, *Notes to Goethe's Poems* (Oxford: Blackwell 1961), v. 1, pp. 134-147.

[12]   *Mediations*, 113.

soaring immortality. If you take your Brecht in English, the nuances of this passage are lost in the Methuen translation, sacrificed to an unfortunate rhyme.[13] When he has caught the vulture, Baal, in the last words of the verse, eats it "zum Abendmahl," a word which means both "dinner" and the Holy Sacrament that recalls the Last Supper. Both Beckett and Brecht materialize the spiritual or sacramental by facing, or facing up to, by ingesting death.

The Beckettian "perhaps" is a word that certainly applies to Brecht, and especially to his political and philosophical activity, since the physical/metaphysical flow of the "river of things" and of time will not cease. This "perhaps" surrounds his work like the discernible circle of the moon before its visible half is fully illuminated. And "perhaps" we can say that there is a "not/but" in Beckett too, a grimmer one, since he wanted to be both forgotten yet remembered and consciousness would not be obviated. In Clov's words, more affirmation perhaps than denial of this thought: "It's not certain."

---

[13]   "Baal watches the vultures in the star-shot sky/ Hovering patiently to see when Baal will die./ Sometimes Baal shams dead. The vultures swoop./ Baal, without a word, will dine on vulture soup." Bertolt Brecht, *Collected Plays* (London: Methuen 1970), v. 1, p. 4.

Ja sagen und nein sagen: Schopenhauer und Nietzsche als Erzieher

Tracing the relationships between Schopenhauer and Nietzsche, the evident and hidden parallels between Brecht and Beckett, and both writers' response to these philosophical mentors, allows us to isolate and deconstruct the dilemmas of their various discourses and to test the depth or shallowness of the ideological presuppositions that construct interpretation. Reading Beckett and Brecht through each other helps to uncover the repressions within their writing and suggests new readings. Attempts to embody, and escape from, the Schopenhauerian and the Hegelian dialectic inform both their work. The passage through East Asian thought, especially Buddhism, far from peripheral, is in fact substantial to their wider purpose and fascinating in its complexity. Visiting the philosophical and cultural 'periphery' yet again shifts our sense of the center.

Gehen wir den Beziehungen zwischen Schopenhauer und Nietzsche und den offensichtlichen wie versteckten Parallelen zwischen Beckett und Brecht sowie dem Grad der Einvernahme der jeweiligen philosophischen Lehren durch die späteren Schriftsteller nach, dann vermögen wir, sowohl die Dilemmas der verschiedenen Diskurse anzuvisieren und zu dekonstruieren, als auch die Tiefen oder auch die Seichtheiten der ideologischen Voraussetzungen auszumessen, die eine Interpretation ermöglichen. Wenn wir den einen durch den anderen lesen, sind wir eher in der Lage, das in ihren Werken teilweise Verdrängte zu entdecken, und sie daher neu zu lesen. Ihre Werke sind durch den Versuch gekennzeichnet, die Dialektik Schopenhauers bzw. Hegels sowohl zu verkörpern, als auch ihr zu entkommen. Daß ihr Weg gedanklich auch durch Ostasien, und besonders über buddhistische Gedankengänge führt, ist in Bezug auf den weiteren Horizont ihres Lebenswerks keineswegs peripher, sondern eher substantiell und so verwickelt wie faszinierend. Was am Rande zu liegen scheint, verändert wieder einmal die Vorstellung einer sonst unbefragt vorausgesetzten Zentrierung.

Saying Yes and Saying No:
Schopenhauer and Nietzsche as Educators

Antony Tatlow

I

Genealogies are problematic and certainly impure. Nietzsche also held that *endings* are *un*scripted. The Eternal does *not* return, not because what is unchanging cannot repeat itself within time, but because the idea of the same is a *verbal* illusion. *Eternal Return* means *process* never ends. What is eternal is recurrence itself: *life* everlasting. The challenge is not how to become strong and constant enough to overcome the world, but how to live in a world without end that never stays the same.[1] *Will to Power* means the act of accepting that everything changes, including yourself. The later Nietzsche also employs another rhetoric, of dominance and exclusivity, which is unconscionable. It influenced many artists and had a certain social effect but was historically limited compared with his other writing.

Since we speak of impure origins and repetitions, let me hazard: In the beginning was the lecture. Or rather: In the beginning were the lectures, and they clashed. The truth has already split in two. Perhaps we are into a dialectic. That still sounds more promising. But what lectures, and what truths? The story is well known. When Schopenhauer became a *Privatdozent* at the University of Berlin, he deliberately scheduled his lecture at the same time as Professor Hegel's, with predictable results. At the back of Hegel's class Bert Brecht could be heard *talking*. He called him one of the great comic writers because in his system everything kept changing into something else. Sam Beckett was definitely *listening* to Schopenhauer. But because nobody else came, he discontinued the course and, like his student, put academic life behind him: the essential step, according to Nietzsche, for a serious professional career.[2]

---

[1]   On the nature of Nietzsche's eternal return, see Ofelia Schutte: *Beyond Nihilism. Nietzsche wihout Masks*, University of Chicago Press, Chicago & London 1984, pp. 57-75.

[2]   Friedrich Nietzsche: *Schopenhauer als Erzieher. Sämtliche Werke, Kritische Studienausgabe* (KSA), Deutscher Taschenbuch Verlag, Munich 1988, vol. 1, especially pp. 393-404.

Where Extremes Meet: Rereading Brecht and Beckett / Begegnung der Extreme. Brecht und Beckett: Eine Re-interpretation
Stephen Brockmann et al., eds., *The Brecht Yearbook / Das Brecht-Jahrbuch*
Volume 27 (Pittsburgh: The International Brecht Society, 2002)

Foto einer ostasiatischen Plastik. Eingeklebt gegenüber dem Titelblatt
in: *Die Bibel oder Die ganze Heilige Schrift des Alten und Neuen*
Testaments. Nach der deutschen Übersetzung Martin Luthers. Berlin:
Britische und ausländische Bibelgesellschaft, 1924. (Nachlaßbibliothek
Bertolt Brecht)

It seems you had to choose between Hegel and Schopenhauer, and to do so from the start: either a rational, outward-looking, history-encompassing, and teleologically benign system, or the opposite to all of that. Brecht's and Beckett's work was and is routinely described as divergent, even incompatible. But those lectures clashed not because they were so different, and certainly not just because they were scheduled concurrently, but because they had so much in common. Nobody is so like me as my own worst enemy. *Constructing* oppositions means they can be thought together. Brecht and Beckett stood for antitheses. Dominating theater for decades, their work seemed to cover, without overlap, the range of possible expression. It was used to place, not deconstruct, its opposite, a sure sign that criticism was caught within the episteme as, at first, it always must be. Epitomizing opposed possibilities, they relativised anyone assigned to either camp: the theater of the absurd which, recognizing aspects of himself, Brecht disparaged;[3] the theater of political engagement or Schiller's moral institution, which Beckett rejected.[4] Sartre was eclipsed by Brecht, Ionesco by Beckett. It is scarcely any longer possible to imagine two artists and dramatists so dominating the cultural discourse.

There is a danger of talking at cross purposes. It is not easy to have the full range of their texts and interventions in mind. Then we use the same names but mean different authors. Brecht is perhaps half, maybe only a quarter, known in English, his prose virtually unopened, though it is as aesthetically, if differently, innovative in respect of identity construction as Beckett's. Brecht mostly stands for an aesthetically difficult corrective to dramatic conventions, and for a sharp focus on the politics of art. Yet that dramatic work, never mind the rest, is more differentiated than either the standard political readings appreciate, which I will not recapitulate, or those which seek to reverse them, taking his early writing as desirably pre-postmodernist but the rest as dustbin-of-history stuff.[5]

---

[3]   In *Bei Durchsicht meiner ersten Stücke*. Bertolt Brecht: *Werke, Große kommentierte Berliner und Frankfurter Ausgabe* (GBA). Aufbau-Verlag, Berlin & Suhrkamp-Verlag, Frankfurt 1988-, vol. 23, p. 239-40.

[4]   James Knowlson: *Damned to Fame. The Life of Samuel Beckett*. Simon and Schuster. New York 1996, p. 427; also in *Spectaculum* 6, 1963, p. 319.

[5]   Terry Eagleton's talk in the Abbey Theatre, Dublin, during a late celebration of Brecht's centenary in April 1999 exemplifies the first alternative and Elizabeth Wright's *Postmodern Brecht. A Re-Presentation*. Routledge, London 1989, the second. Neither grasp the complexities of the texts.

Beckett unfolds into a spread of language texts, self-fashioned or self-approved, producing culturally distinct resonances. A French or German Beckett is differently nuanced from his Irish namesake, though confusions can be creative. We may prefer one to the other, and can legitimately take sides, intellectually and emotionally, in any contest of excellencies, but a good holding assumption might be that we really don't know either Brecht or Beckett that well.

Of the two I suspect Brecht is less understood, naturally so in Dublin, London or Sydney, though perhaps also, for other reasons, in Berlin. I wonder, for example, how many who take their Brecht in English know why a German critic once said: "He feels chaos and putrefaction physically. Hence the incomparable vividness of his language. You feel this language on your tongue, in the roof of your mouth, in your ear, in your spine."[6] Most readers probably know one author better than the other. Hence detailed textual description would be only too familiar to at least half the readers, and risk either boredom or suffering, as Schopenhauer predicted, and Beckett feared. So I will say little about the texts themselves. The consequence may be the same.

Instead of reading Beckett, for example, as the last Essentialist and Brecht as the last Marxist, we could see both as deconstructing the dilemmas of their own discourses. Then Parmenides transubstantiates into Beckett's paradoxical Zeno—that impossible heap—and the Heraclitean flux of *Mann ist Mann* (GBA 2, 189)—we cannot step twice into the same river—is transformed into a Brechtian Zen or Dao. Beckett once spoke, in German, of passing through 'das Nichts' and, whether or not anyone could follow him, creating poetry on the other side.[7] We can say something similar of Brecht. But where does this come from and where does it lead us?

II

So with apologies, which I shall not repeat, now primarily to the Brechtians, I want to summarize some critical views. When they seem authorially indexable, but have been taken out of their contemporary discourse and thereby necessarily more abstractly placed in other contexts, the subtexts and overtones get lost. What was culturally astute suddenly looks much cruder. Words on their own are never enough. It is always a problem of cultural translation.

---

[6]   Quoted in Edith Krull: *Herbert Ihering*. Henschelverlag, Berlin 1964, p. 20.

[7]   A remark made in 1963, quoted in *Die Zeit*, 4.1.1980. See also Knowlson, p. 427.

If we set aside anxiety of influence, why did Howard Barker so scorn Brecht as "The One Who Knows," and why does this irascible rejection of a claim to knowledge still reverberate, as whoever followed the Brecht centennial will have noticed?[8]   That "knowledge" was grounded in political struggle: against Fascism, for Socialism and, finally, located within the deeply insecure East German state.   What may look, later and from outside, like a government policy statement was virtually always formulated in resistance to official dogma. I am not thinking of the unambiguous—"Would it not be simpler if the government dissolved the people and elected another?" (GBA 12, 310)—but rather of formulations within quieter theoretical writing.

If we have no ear for the language of resistance, we read naively, and take a stronger moral stand. "Creative realism in art can only be developed in conjunction with the rising classes..."[9]   Brecht hardly expresses a Broadway or a Beckettian ethos, yet every term here has a subversive meaning.   Read in the 1950s this amounts to a shrewd, prophylactic declaration of war against cultural policies. The East German government wanted a controllable, not a rising working class. It was terrified of creativity. Brecht's realism turned the official script upside down. Listen to his 1955 public description of Soviet art: "...inhuman, barbaric, superficial, bourgeois, that is to say petit-bourgeois, slipshod, irresponsible, corrupt, etc., etc."[10]   Enough said. English-speaking feminist dramatists and critics value Brecht's deconstructing of the subject but dislike what they see as his putting people in place, which they associate with a male authority reflex. These responses seem contradictory.[11] I will return to the subversive counter-knowledge of the one who knows.

Part of this adverse reaction may well be indirectly connected with perceptions of Brecht's response to *Waiting for Godot*. The play

---

[8]   Howard Barker: *Arguments for a Theatre*. Manchester University Press, Manchester 1997, p. 112. See Heiner Zimmermann: "Howard Barker's Brecht or Brecht as Whipping Boy," a paper presented at the Fifth Conference of the European Society for the Study of English (ESSE), Helsinki, 2000; also, in respect of the Brecht Centennial, my contribution, "Ghosts in the House of Theory," in *The Brecht Yearbook*, 24, 1999, pp. 1-13.

[9]   Written in 1940. See Werner Hecht: *Aufsätze über Brecht*. Henschelverlag, Berlin 1970, p. 117.

[10]   Bertolt Brecht: *Über die bildenden Künste*, ed. J. Hermand, Suhrkamp, Frankfurt 1983, p. 213.

[11]   This is well described in Elizabeth Sakellaridou, "Feminist Theater and the Brechtian Tradition: A Retrospect and a Prospect," in this volume.

was originally bad news in East Berlin and shunned by officialdom. "Without substance and without humour," was a typical critical comment.[12] Brecht recognized a challenge to his own project. I have looked at his papers. He began making changes to Beckett's text, but they are minimal and soon peter out: Vladimir, an intellectual; *von* Pozzo, a landowner, social concretizations which hardly move that far from Beckett.[13] Heiner Müller argues that it was only the start of what might have looked very different, had he pursued it.[14] But that was no longer possible, and would certainly have ended in disaster, had the idea communicated by one of his assistants prevailed. Clas Zilliacus quotes Rülicke-Weiler. Brecht was in hospital with four months to live. The "magnificently written" play, she observes, contradicted the purpose of Brecht's theater. So projected film scenes would show people changing the world, while Vladimir and Estragon wait for Godot.[15] I wonder about her account anyway. She never grasped the subtleties of Brecht's *Coriolanus* adaptation. But that is all part of a once socially authorized discourse. A counterplay was not then possible. One form comes later, when Heiner Müller amalgamates Brecht's dismembering the clown in the *Badener Lehrstück,* and the disappearing carafe and the prod on wheels from Beckett's two *Act without Words* in 'Nachtstück' from *Germania, Tod in Berlin.*[16]

Adorno thought Beckett the *greater* realist: but as the realist of *total* reification, for whom there is "no more nature." Beckett's absolute refusal of commodified language, exemplifying Adorno's negative dialectics, was the only possible post-Auschwitz political intervention. He opposed Beckett to what he saw as the positive dialectics of both Lukács and Brecht, about whom he held contradictory views, not based on any real understanding of his work, which Brecht reciprocated. Since Lukács was the greater enemy for Brecht, it is both not surprising and fascinating that the Marxist Lukács objected to Beckett in language virtually identical to conservative West

---

[12]   *Aufsätze über Brecht,* p. 123.

[13]   Bertolt-Brecht-Archiv 1061/ 1-52. The few emendations are made to the First Act of the German edition published by Suhrkamp in 1953.

[14]   *Der Dramatiker und die Geschichte seiner Zeit. Ein Gespräch zwischen Horst Laube und Heiner Müller,* in *Theater 1975, Sonderheft der Zeitschrift Theater Heute,* p. 120.

[15]   Clas Zilliacus: "Three Times Godot: Beckett, Brecht, Bulatovic." In *Comparative Drama* 1970, vol. 4, No. 1, p. 8.

[16]   Heiner Müller: *Germania, Tod in Berlin.* Rotbuch-Verlag, Berlin 1977, p. 113.

German academic criticism of Brecht. Beckett, Lukács complained, reduces human beings to the state of animality, exactly the charge against Brecht. The political extremes meet in aesthetic conservatism, marking political regression more accurately, as Adorno also once argued, than abstract statements of social intent.[17]

If Lukács and Brecht represented what Adorno designated an unattractive "official optimism,"[18] Beckett mythologized disenchantment, offering "realism...minus reconciliation" (127). Using Schopenhauerian language, Adorno argues that communication rests on the principle of sufficient reason, but Beckett alone shows that reason masks interest (139f.). In effect, Adorno argues that Beckett's play is the *Endgame* of the subject, and therefore parodies the master/servant dialectic. When history has been annulled, what is left is compulsive repetition. Because Beckett does not mention the specific historical danger, the nuclear threat, Adorno calls him the "simplifier of horror," adding however that, "unlike Brecht he refuses simplification."[19] But Adorno also maintains that they were "not so dissimilar...insofar as [Beckett's] differentiation becomes sensitivity to subjective differences, which have regressed to the 'conspicuous consumption' of those who can afford individuation. Therein lies the social truth."[20] Beckett's images also represent the historical form of his society: "Because there was no other life than the false one, the catalogue of its defects becomes the mirror image of ontology." (133) Adorno saw Beckett within the post-Second World War, post-Holocaust balance of terror, but had himself described the consequences of instrumentalizing nature in *Dialectic of Enlightenment*. In such a reading Beckett offers the vision not of local but of total catastrophe, and becomes the realist of planetary destruction.

---

[17] Adorno cites Lukács's criticism of Beckett in "Trying to Understand Endgame," in *New German Critique*, vol. 26, p. 125. Helmut Koopmann points to the animal-like anti-intellectuality of Brecht's first plays, which "reverse" the Enlightenment's human ethic mediated through the theater. "Baal ist not so much the expressionist individualist, who determines his own law of life out of his animality without bothering about any alien morality, he is rather the predatory animal." "Brecht—Schreiben in Gegensätzen," in Helmut Koopmann und Theo Stammen (eds.): *Bertolt Brecht—Aspekte seines Werkes, Spuren seiner Wirkung*. Ernst Vögel Verlag, München 1983, pp. 9-29, esp. p. 16.

[18] *Trying to understand Endgame*, p. 125.

[19] Theodor W. Adorno: *Gesammelte Schriften*. Suhrkamp, Frankfurt 1974, vol. 2, p. 289.

[20] *Trying to understand Endgame*, p. 125.

III

It is relatively easy to construct a Beckettian Brecht from the early work. This passage in Foucault could apply to either:

> From within language experienced and traversed as language, in the play of its possibilities extended to their furthest point, what emerges is that "man has come to an end," and that, by reaching the summit of all possible speech, he arrives not at the very heart of himself but at the brink of that which limits him; in that region where death prowls, where thought is extinguished, where the promise of the origin interminably recedes. [21]

Beckett could have written this dialog from *Baal*:

> Baal: What's wrong with you?
> Gougou: Bronchitis. Nothing bad. A little inflammation. Nothing serious.
> Baal *to Bolleboll*: And you?
> Bolleboll: Stomach ulcers. Won't kill me!
> Baal *to the beggar*: There's something wrong with you too, I trust?
> The Beggar: I'm mad.

He would have underwritten what follows:

> Baal: Here's to you! We understand each other. I'm healthy.
> The Beggar: I knew a man who said he was healthy too. He believed it. He came from the forest and one day he went back there as there was something he had to think over. He found the forest very strange and no longer familiar, he walked for many days. Always deeper into the forest, because he wanted to see how independent he was and how much endurance there was left in him. But there wasn't much. *He drinks...*
> Ekart: Did it cure him?
> The Beggar: No. He had an easier death, though.
> Maja: I don't understand that.
> The Beggar: Nothing is understood. But some things are felt. If one understands a story it's just because it's been told badly. (GBA 1, 121-22)[22]

Where Brecht conventionally stands for political and Beckett for ontological metaphor, we can construct a Brechtian Beckett. The

---

[21]   Michel Foucault: *The Order of Things. An Archaeology of the Human Sciences.* Vintage Books, New York 1973, p. 383.

[22]   Bertolt Brecht: *Collected Plays*, Methuen, London 1970, vol. 1, p. 42f.

master/servant dialectic may be parodistic, but is still in use. No matter what Beckett may have said, some plays are open to directly political readings—*Catastrophe, Rough for Theatre II, What Where.*

But much in the *later* Brecht also undoes Adorno's political "simplification": his dislike of "Weltbildhauer" or world systematizers (GBA 21, 349); his suspicion of the "myth" of a continuous ego (GBA 26, 476 & 682); his rejection of correspondence in favor of relational or coherence theory (GBA 21, 428; 22/1, 458);[23] his questioning of rational art, when asking whether he really wanted "to do away with the space where the unconscious, half conscious, uncontrolled, ambiguous, multipurposed could play itself out" (GBA 22/1, 468), and the unstated answer is obviously: No!

I wish to dehistoricize readings whereby Beckett's ontology becomes an expression of frozen history, of the historically created malaise of the bourgeoisie, of an immobility and functionalization closer to Max Weber than Karl Marx, but also Brecht's Marxist solution for historical problems. I then wish to rehistoricize the emerging conjunctures on another level of analysis. The trajectory through Schopenhauer and Nietzsche is necessarily roundabout. But we need to understand why there are such contradictory movements in their work: a strong disintegrative undertow in Brecht, and a powerful integrative desire in Beckett. Before I get into these central arguments, I first want to inspect what we might call their parallel lives. The method is partly anecdotal, like Plutarch's, but the information interesting, though readers may find some of this reviewing distasteful.

IV

Hans Mayer, Professor of Literature in Leipzig, worked with Brecht, though he was never part of the theater's inner circle. Beckett liked him enough to present him a poem in French written in 1976, which Mayer only let go when he published it in 1995.[24] He found them both "very lonely men." In respect of Brecht, this observation may have been retrospectively constructed after understanding the disproportion between Brecht's hopes and the realities of his last years. But it connects with an aspect of Brecht's mind which Mayer knew less about, and does not describe, but is apposite to our topic: what I would

---

[23] See also W. F. Haug: *Philosophieren mit Brecht und Gramsci.* Argument, Berlin 1996, pp. 21-27.

[24] Hans Mayer: *Beckett und Brecht. Erfahrungen und Erinnerungen. Ein Vortrag.* Berliner Ensemble, Drucksache 15, 1995, p. 559.

term the *longue durée* of Brecht's thought.[25] Brecht spoke in Berlin of "Chinese exile,"[26] not meaning, as some have thought, that he wished he were in China, but rather that he felt shunted aside, his views not welcome. Bai Juyi, the Tang dynasty poet Brecht translated, had been physically exiled.

Beckett told Mayer that he knew Brecht's work. Since there seems no very obvious response to it, all the more reason, we might think, for sticking to those handy antitheses. Then Brecht's "interventionary thought" is set against Beckett's epiphany: man is the "non-knower, non can-er."[27] But there is a "non-knower, non can-er" in Brecht as well. Siegfried Unseld published both and tells a story that bears on *longue durée*.[28] During one of their meetings in Paris, Beckett quoted a poem—en face/ le pire/ jusqu'à ce/ qu'il fasse rire—and described it as continuing the spirit of Goethe's *Xenien* or his *Chinesisch-Deutsche Jahres- und Tageszeiten*. (These are philosophical-satirical, or short late lyrical poems loosely but interestingly connected with China.) Beckett then offered a German version. Unseld later brought him another translation, by Tophoven, improved by Karl Krolow, a poet Beckett admired: "bis zum Äußersten/ gehn/ dann wird Lachen entstehn." According to Unseld, Beckett agreed this recalled a perception in Laozi (Lao Tse): "Eh' nicht das Äußerste erreicht ist, kehrt sich nichts ins Gegenteil." (Only when the extreme is reached, will something turn into its opposite.) Even the longest encounters will turn in the end. Brecht certainly absorbed that Daoist dialectic early on, and it remained fundamental to his work.

The record of Beckett's second conversation with Georges Duthuit, on the painter Masson, ends when Duthuit asks if he really can "deplore the painting that admits 'the things and creatures of spring, resplendent with desire and affirmation, ephemeral no doubt, but immortally reiterant'... B: – (exit weeping)."[29] What interests me here is the emotional load thereby uncovered, the depth of the

---

[25]   Haug also speaks of Brecht's knowledge, "which is not for the day and must last a long time." Haug, p. 159.

[26]   Werner Hecht: *Brecht Chronik 1898-1956*. Suhrkamp, Frankfurt 1997, p. 1021.

[27]   Knowlson, p. 320.

[28]   Siegfried Unseld: "Bis zum Äußersten. Samuel Beckett zum 80. Geburtstag—1986" In: *Theater Heute*, 2, February 1990, p. 23.

[29]   Samuel Beckett: *Proust and Three Dialogues with Georges Duthuit*. John Calder, London 1965, p. 113.

repression. Brecht's counterpart was to ask what terrible times he lived in when, in spite of the beauties of spring, only the horrors of history drove him to his writing desk (GBA 14, 432)?

Both had uncomplicated fathers, and a tortured relationship with their complex mothers. Both endured psychosomatic trauma, including real fear of heart failure. Both led complicated emotional lives with tangled relationships. Beckett to Pamela Mitchell in 1954: "Be fond of me but not too fond, I'm not worth it, it'll make you unhappy, you don't know me."[30] Brecht, in a poem: "Here you have someone on whom you can't rely."[31] Beckett to his wife: "As we both know that [love] will come to an end, there is no knowing how long it will last."[32] Brecht, in *The Threepenny Opera*: "For love will endure or not endure/ Regardless of where we are."[33] Both simultaneously stage-managed a wife and two mistresses in Berlin.

Both were musical, rejected Wagner, admiring students of Schönberg. Both preferred blackbirds to nightingales. They disliked Rilke, praised Breugel, used Rimbaud, found German acting too emotional, disapproved of empathy and psychologizing. Both loved detective stories, especially Edgar Wallace, though Beckett also read Agatha Christie. Both were wary of Aristotle: for Beckett, "the master of those who know" (Watt).[34] Brecht's anti-Aristotelian theater was not really anti-emotional, or even anti-naturalist, but ultimately anti-teleological. Brecht once remarked that in the interest of socialism, somebody should make a list of the questions they could not answer. Me-ti, Brecht's Chinese persona, "was against constructing too complete images of the world" (GBA 18, 60). Both loved music hall and popular theater, beds disintegrating on stage: Brecht's *Die Kleinbürgerhochzeit*; in Beckett's case, affection for O'Casey's *The End of the Beginning*, when the two characters lie "in an agony of callisthenics, surrounded by the doomed furniture."[35]

---

[30]   Knowlson, p. 360.

[31]   Bertolt Brecht: *Collected Poems*, Methuen, London 1976, p. 107 ; "In mir habt ihr einen, auf den könnt ihr nicht bauen." GBA 11, 120.

[32]   Knowlson, p. 271.

[33]   Bertolt Brecht: *Collected Plays*, Methuen, London 1979, vol. 2/2, p. 26; "Die Liebe dauert oder dauert nicht/ An dem oder jenem Ort." GBA 2, 254.

[34]   Richard Kearney: "Beckett: The Demythologising Intellect," in Richard Kearney (ed.): *The Irish Mind. Exploring Intellectual Traditions*. Wolfhound Press, Dublin 1985, p. 286.

[35]   Anthony Cronin: *Samuel Beckett. The Last Modernist*. Flamingo, London 1997, p. 58.

Both drew extensively on the Bible. The index of Biblical quotations in Brecht is in double columns thirty pages long (GBA Registerband, 647-680). Knowlson speaks of Beckett's "grafting technique, and at times it almost runs wild."[36] He stitched St. Augustine into *Dream of Fair to Middling Women*, and Knowlson observes: "It is not that he plagiarizes; he makes no attempt to hide what he is doing."[37] Apart from remarking that you cannot show quotation marks in the theater, Brecht's best comment on borrowing comes in a description of Zhuangzi in a Keuner story, *Originality*:

> "Nowadays," Mr. K complained, "there are countless people who boast in public that they can write large books all by themselves, and this meets with general approval. As a grown man, the Chinese philosopher Zhuangzi composed a book of 100,000 words, nine tenths of which consisted of quotations. We can't write such books any more, we haven't the intelligence..." (GBA 18, 18)

All writing is plagiarism, says Derrida. Thank goodness they both plagiarized. Chateaubriand has the last word on that topic: "An original writer is not someone who imitates nobody, but someone whom nobody can imitate."[38]

Both thought of working with Eisenstein. Brecht met him in Moscow in 1935. There are fascinating parallels within their work based on comparable mediations of Japanese aesthetics. Beckett wrote to Eisenstein.[39] What if he had answered? In Berlin Beckett said *Waiting for Godot* was "a game in order to survive."[40] Brecht's early work is an encyclopaedia of survival strategies. Of course they permeate what follows. As reported by Benjamin, he answered a question about political content in 1934, when formal variations of the allegedly doctrinaire, so-called didactic plays still preoccupied him: "I'd have to admit, I'm not entirely serious."[41] Beckett met Karl Valentin in Munich and watched him in performance.[42] Brecht performed with

---

[36]   Knowlson, p. 112.

[37]   Knowlson, p. 114.

[38]   *Penguin Dictionary of Quotations*, Jonathan Cape, London 1962, p. 106.

[39]   Knowlson, p. 212.

[40]   Knowlson, p. 536.

[41]   Walter Benjamin: *Versuche über Brecht*. Suhrkamp, Frankfurt 1981, p. 154. Conversation on 6 July 1934.

[42]   The actor who introduced him to Valentin, Josef Eichheim, had himself played in Brecht's *Life of Edward II*. See Knowlson, pp. 241 & 666.

Valentin. They also made a short film in 1923. Brecht wrote the script, and helped Erich Engel direct *Mysterien eines Frisiersalons.* Engel worked in many later productions but said he had never had so much fun in his whole life.[43] In this short film Valentin, the barber's assistant, inadvertently cuts off a customer's head but smartly tapes it on again. In a duel shortly afterwards the head falls off, to the astonishment of the customer's opponent. The Great War had just industrialized slaughter. In this graphic deconstruction, the individual cannot command his own body. Somebody else slips up, and you lose your head. The sovereign subject is comically decapitated.

Beckett loved Chaplin too, and made that film with Buster Keaton. There is a strange parallel in what look, on the surface, like two quite different films, with Beckett's focused on the impossibility of any escape into silence and invisibility, of hiding from self-perception, as the camera's eye closes on the protagonist's: *esse est percipi,* to be, quoting Berkeley, is always to be perceived.[44] There is no escaping consciousness, if not the individual's, then God's. Yet both films show the paradox of an essentialist claim to individuation, which can neither determine nor escape the conditions of existence. Both figure ultimate absence of control. There is a counter aesthetic, and ethic, in Brecht, often expressed through material from East Asian culture, which resist pre-arranged hierarchical constraints, whether social or theoretical, in favor of a looser, more pragmatic relationalism. That is why Brecht's favorite Chaplin scene is when he closes the suitcase, picks up a scissors, and cuts off everything left sticking out, whatever does not suit the case, a graphically reductive *découpage* of the discourse.

Beckett remarked that Valentin was "reduced here and there to knockabout," but even if the Munich accent was hard to grasp, he records: "I was very moved."[45] And indeed there is much in Valentin's work that feels like Beckett, far more than the Laurel and Hardy act or the Irish and English music-hall repartee, to which he is assimilated in respect of any effect he had on Beckett.[46] Brecht said that Valentin

---

[43]   Wolfgang Gersch: *Film bei Brecht.* Henschelverlag, Berlin 1975, p. 23.

[44]   Beckett followed this conventional reading. David Berman argues Berkeley only ever said of "unthinking things.. Their *esse* is *percipi.*" He maintained neither God nor anyone else could perceive the workings of a mind which could only be construed analogically from observed effects. See David Berman: "Beckett and Berkeley," in *Irish University Review. A Journal of Irish Studies.* Spring 1984, Special Issue, pp. 42-45.

[45]   Knowlson, p. 241.

[46]   Knowlson makes these analogies, loc., cit.

enabled him to see "the inadequacy of all things including ourselves" (GBA 21, 101). This is one reason why some of Brecht's early writing, including part of the one act plays of 1919, sounds so like Beckett. When Brecht was directing *Life of Eduard II* in Munich, Valentin showed up at the rehearsal, a highly unusual thing for him to do. Brecht asked him what the soldiers going into battle should look like. Valentin replied in his Munich accent: "Furcht hams, blass sans." (They're scared, they're pale.)[47] They got white face masks, in this defining production for the development of Brecht's theater.

Since Valentin is not well known outside Germany, I'll say something about his methods which carry through into Brecht and Beckett, whether or not anyone transported them. You can read him, if you know German, or listen to him on recordings, if you understand Bavarian, or watch him on video. His stage was local accent, popular comedy sketches which he wrote himself. He was phenomenally talented and completely neurotic. He told Beckett he'd like to come to London, only the propeller would probably drop off the plane.[48] He also made a few half-hearted attempts to go to Berlin by train, but had to get off shortly after leaving Munich. Lucky the country whose popular culture can accommodate a parody of Zhuangzi's *Butterfly Dream*: Valentin's *Ententraum (Dream of a Duck)*.

He offered a form of physical farce in the sense that the scenes or stories were often physically ridiculous, but in Valentin this was guided, not by clowning but by an eccentric and impeccable logic, hence mostly by language, and language did not make sense of the world. In *Moving House (Der Umzug)*,[49] he is asked why the wheels on the cart he is pulling are still chained, and replies: so that nobody can steal it. The fish bowl is problematic. He pours the water from one receptacle into another, can't find a drain, and finally drinks it. When a long lost document falls out of a drawer, he reads it: "Birth certificate, 1783, Greatgreatgrandmother, Catholic - kann uns nichts mehr passieren." That means both "this is the last straw," and "nothing more can go wrong after this." The predictions reinforce and contradict each other and neither is correct. Actions are circular, mystifying, funny, leading nowhere in terms of goal-directed behaviour. Arguing about pronounciation, Valentin says the word is "Katástrophé." His companion insists on the normal German "Katastróphe." I think of

---

[47] See Antony Tatlow: *The Mask of Evil*. Peter Lang, Berne 1977, p. 222.

[48] Knowlson, p. 241.

[49] Karl Valentin: *Die Raubritter von München. Szenen und Dialoge*. Deutscher Taschenbuch Verlag, Munich 1964, pp. 147-157.

désert and desért in *Endgame*. He also discovers a flea and hammers it with a rolling pin, and his companion immediately smothers everything with insecticide. The whole catastrophe, however you pronounce it, reiterates continuously, and when they reach the end, the script goes back to the beginning again. This is definitely a case of Hegelian "bad infinity," rather than a Nietzschean "eternal return."

Maybe this helps to explain how "A dog came in the kitchen," at the start of the *da capo* Second Act of *Waiting for Godot*, also appears, for the same circular reason, when Kragler sings it in the Fourth Act of *Drums in the Night*, the first of Brecht's plays to be performed, in 1922 (GBA 1, 217). The Act begins with Glubb, the bar owner, singing *Ballad of the Dead Soldier*, the song that supposedly put Brecht at the top of the Nazi list of arrestees, in which the recruitment commission digs up the already dead and sends them off to a second death. Both songs are circularities, doomed attempts at survival, in which execution, burial, enforced resurrection, execution continue forever. This is a reason why Beckett's and Brecht's work is haunted by ghosts from beginning to end. That would be another essay.

Finally, in respect of these strangely parallel lives, they both read Fritz Mauthner, who in 1901 advanced positions we associate with Wittgenstein. Sweeping aside most of the tradition of Western thought, and following Nietzsche, he argued that philosophy was only possible as a *critique* of language.[50] Mauthner concluded that identity was caught up in the play of language and fragile. He therefore also wrote on Buddhist philosophy. Brecht knew that, and Beckett read him for and presumably to the nearly blind Joyce. Words are all we have. Reality lies beyond them.

Wolfgang Haug, Professor of Philosophy in Berlin, calls Brecht the poet among the philosophers, perhaps even that poet-philosopher Nietzsche spoke of.[51] Because of its thorough critique of linguistically suggested essentialisms, Brecht engaged with Buddhism. If you do not believe it, just look at his own copy of Luther's Bible. Opposite the

---

[50] "So ist jedes geschlossene System eine Selbsttäuschung, so ist die Philosophie als Selbsterkenntnis des Menschengeistes ewig unfruchtbar, und so kann Philosophie, wenn man schon das alte Wort beibehalten will, nichts weiter sein wollen, als kritische Aufmerksamkeit auf die Sprache." Fritz Mauthner: *Beiträge zu einer Kritik der Sprache*. Vol 1, p. 648. J. G. Cotta'sche Buchhandlung Nachfolger, Stuttgart 1901. For Beckett, see Knowlson, p. 267, & 327, also Kearney, p. 290; for Brecht, see Tatlow: *Brechts Ost Asien*, Parthas, Berlin 1998, p. 41.

[51] Haug, pp. 103 & 10.

title page he pasted in a Song dynasty boddhisatva. I take this Buddhist figure as a metaphor of the alternative to a Western mind-set which would therefore be defined, and circumscribed, by this very opposition. Against the revealed and written word, he sets aesthetic gesture; against language's guarantee of substantiality and its promise of ultimate and personal redemption, he implies the refusal of an absolute self; against a belief in God the Father and a paternalistic state, he offers relational thought, consciousness of process. In Buddhist terminology, having (in Chinese: *you*) cannot exist without nothing (*wu*). There can be no fullness without emptiness. Let me leave it for now at this mythopoeic level.

What about Beckett on Buddhism? Apart from that very Buddhist observation about passing through "nothing" and coming out on the other side, there is an interesting complication, which I believe both derives from Schopenhauer and is also a *definer* of his philosophical position, but for the moment let us hold onto a comment of Beckett's whose implications really take us into Brechtian territory: "Gautama...disait qu'on se trompe en affirmant que le moi existe, mais qu'en affirmant qu'il n'existe pas on ne se trompe pas moins."[52] The problem is how to live under these circumstances.

V

In *Untimely Reflections III: Schopenhauer as Educator,* Nietzsche does not describe Schopenhauer's philosophy; instead he offers a coruscating critique of contemporary cultural life against which he then projects his intellectual autobiography.[53] He observes, for example: "The Schopenhauerian person accepts voluntary suffering for truthfulness, and this suffering helps to stifle self-willing and to prepare for that total overturning and reversal of his being to which the real purpose of life leads us." (371) "Many people," he notes, "see in negation the sign of evil. But there is a way of negating and destroying which emanates from a powerful longing for sanctification and deliverance, and Schopenhauer was its first philosophical teacher among us disenchanted and thoroughly secularized human beings." (372) And he concludes: "A happy life is impossible: the highest we can achieve is a *heroic life*..." at the end of which, following Schopenhauer, "the will, mortified throughout a whole life by strain

---

[52]   Samuel Beckett: *Disjecta, Miscellaneous Writings.* Calder, London 1983, p. 146.

[53]   *KSA* 1, pp. 337-427. Nietzsche also acknowledges this rereading of Schopenhauer in *Ecce Homo, KSA* 6, p. 320.

and work, by failure and lack of gratitude, is extinguished in nirvana."
(373)

Since Nietzsche could not have written as he did without Schopenhauer, since Brecht absorbed a great deal of Nietzsche, and since Beckett unquestionably found in Schopenhauer a loadstone for his life, it is worth asking some questions about these interrelationships. Nietzsche transvalued Schopenhauer. Did Beckett do something similar, or did he rather take his Schopenhauer straight? Is there perhaps even a Schopenhauer in Brecht? That is not so fantastic as it may seem. An argument has been made, and the particular difficulty I have with it loops back into that defining complication in Schopenhauer.

Because Schopenhauer said "No" to the *World as Will*, and Nietzsche first embraced negation and then radically transvalued it into a "Yes" for the *Will to Power*, my title seems to imply that these educators animate the projects behind the masks of Beckett and Brecht, that Schopenhauer's Beckettian No is transvalued by Nietzsche's Brechtian Yes. Yet that would bring us close to Adorno's simplifications. To understand these processes, I therefore need to re-complicate them. The best way is through a defamiliarizing trajectory out of Western, into Asian culture. This is not a detour because it is substantial within their writing, no matter to what extent they were aware of it.

To ask what Schopenhauer meant for Beckett, or Nietzsche for Brecht, involves getting forensic in respect of texts and then stepping behind the discourses. By way of introduction, here are three short examples of more complex genealogies:

1. Negation, says Nietzsche, is taken as a sign of evil, a word which Brecht internalized—in German, "böse"—, provocatively stylizing himself as: "B. B. REIN, SACHLICH, BÖSE" (GBA 13, 266; "pure, matter of fact, evil"). For Nietzsche, however, "evil" was the only possible moral position in the face of what society considered to be "good." To choose "evil" is, therefore, to embrace the pathos of opposition to a world on the path to the disasters he so clearly predicted. Hence he preferred the new and evil to the old and good, and Brecht followed here too in praising the "bad new" of any innovation. According to Nietzsche, Christ was crucified because he was "evil, " since he opposed the good, that is to say, those who ruled.[54] So

---

[54] Friedrich Nietzsche: *Also Sprach Zarathustra*. Kröner-Verlag, Stuttgart 1956, p. 235f., *Von alten und neuen Tafeln*, #26. On Nietzsche and 'evil,' see also Schutte, p. 135.

Nietzsche's "evil" was a *pharmakon* or counterpoison to what Schopenhauer had described as the "evil" world, though he used a less theological word—"Übel"—to define it.[55] One evil can only be fought by another. Schopenhauer seeks to counter his "evil" with equally strong medicine, and although it may be substantially different in Beckett's and Brecht's apothecary, the countermove is structurally analogous and no less difficult.

2. At the close of *Endgame*, Hamm replaces the handkerchief on his reddened face: "Old stancher, you remain." Surely he seeks, no matter how calculated the verbal echo, "to staunch the eternal wound of Being," something Kafka's *Country Doctor* fails to do for his patient Rosa's life wound. It is a Schopenhauerian wound of course, but the passage occurs in *The Birth of Tragedy*.[56] For Nietzsche the first of three illusions or beguilements is that knowledge can stay the pain of this wound. Did Beckett take some of his Schopenhauer through Nietzsche?

3. Saying "Yes" was Zarathustra's, and the child's, sacred "Yes" to Life.[57] But the child in Brecht's *Der Jasager*, whose *title* clearly suggests Nietzsche, since the play adapts a Japanese plot, chooses self-*sacrifice*. The schoolchildren in the original production objected to this conclusion, thereby provoking a *Neinsager*, who rejects suicidal affirmation and so refuses a political metaphysics. Events took a hand in re-transvaluing Brecht's transvaluation of Nietzsche. I doubt if he forgot that lesson.

But what about the Schopenhauerian presence in Brecht? Friedrich Dieckmann attributes a fundamentally melancholic personality structure to Brecht, a secret desire for self-extinction. This reading assumes repressed psychological trauma, which other critics have also supposed, loss of unity, fear of abandonment, and guilt.[58]

---

55   Arthur Schopenhauer: *Parerga und Paralipomena*, Sämtliche Werke, Brockhaus, Mannheim 1988, vol. 6, #149, p. 309f.; *Essays and Aphorisms*, trans. R. J. Hollingdale. Penguin, Harmondsworth 1970, p. 41f.

56   Friedrich Nietzsche: *The Birth of Tragedy*. Trans. Francis Golffing. Doubleday, New York 1956, p. 108; *KSA*, 1, p. 115. 'Beguilement' translates 'Reizmittel.'

57   Echoed at the end of Joyce's *Ulysses*. *Also sprach Zarathustra*, p. 27; see also Schutte, p. 39f.

58   See also Carl Pietzcker: *"Ich kommandiere mein Herz."* Brechts *Herzneurose - ein Schlüssel zu seinem Leben und Schreiben*. Würzburg 1988.

The only way of banishing this fear of chaos is to redirect the truncated sense of personal protection into hope and belief in a protecting system. Such unconscious conflicts are, of course, the source of poetry. Dieckmann therefore reads Brecht's poem *Gleichnis des Buddha vom brennenden Haus* (GBA 12, 36; *The Buddha's Parable of the Burning House*), as a direct expression of a desire for "redemption from the burning will to live," which is sought in a "Schopenhauerian-Buddhist nirvana."[59] Here, however, everything turns on the meaning of nirvana.

Apart from the analogy, and it may be more, with Beckett's personality structure, I think here of a comment that denial of self and life is an expression of resentment against time.[60] That is Nietzsche, of course, so hypersensitive a psychologist that Freud, who destroyed all his notes three times, saying he wanted to make things difficult for his biographers, simply took over his theories, themselves reactions to Schopenhauer, so that passages in Freud map straight onto Nietzsche. Freud once told his friend Wilhelm Fließ that he was "not at all a man of science, not an observer, not an experimenter, not a thinker. I am by temperament nothing but a conquistador—an adventurer." [61]

Reaction to this fear of the flux of time passes from Schopenhauer, through Nietzsche and then Freud, to Brecht, who quotes from the just published *Civilization and its Discontents* in his 1930 *Notes to Mahagonny* that set out the differences between the old dramatic and the new epic theater (GBA 24, 83); the image of a destructive (Dionysiac) flow that now must be contained recurs time and again within his later work, for example in the *Short Organon* (GBA 23, 73). Perhaps we can speak, mixing Hegel's and Nietzsche's terminologies, of a sublated transvaluation, whereby what is apparently transformed continues to affect all thought in the new formulation which must therefore, through the act of reworking, be beholden to what it believes to have refuted.

Though a recent book on Schopenhauer and the arts does not mention Beckett, Schopenhauer's importance to him is well known, yet

---

[59]   Friedrich Dieckmann: "Brechts Utopia," in Wolfgang Heise (ed.): *Brecht 88. Anregungen zum Dialog über die Vernunft am Jahrtausendende.* Henschelverlag Kunst und Gesellschaft, Berlin 1987, pp. 69-108, here p. 92; see also *Brechts Ost Asien*, p. 40.

[60]   *Also sprach Zarathustra*, p. 154; see also Schutte, p. 43f.

[61]   Jeffrey Mason (ed.): *The Complete Letters of Sigmund Freud to Wilhelm Fließ, 1887-1904.* Harvard University Press, Cambridge, Mass. 1985, p. 398.

I wonder about some readings.[62]   In the only full study of Schopenhauer and Beckett, Ulrich Pothast considers his Proust essay the equivalent of *The Birth of Tragedy* for Nietzsche, meaning that it summarizes or projects his later aesthetic.[63]   Yet if Nietzsche's essay drew extensively on Schopenhauer, and reads like performance notes for *Tristan and Isolde*, he later transvalued the positions, whereas the essay on Proust does indeed anticipate Beckett's later attitudes, and when they seem to differ, that is thinkable in terms of an even stronger reading of Schopenhauer.   Nietzsche's celebrated essay not only glosses a Schopenhauerian Wagner, it also contains an uncanny anticipation of Brecht's aesthetic practice.   Pothast reminds us that Wittgenstein noted that Schopenhauer distinguished what can be said from what can be shown.[64]   Where philosophy cannot go, art begins. One could argue that in the Proust essay art, as a metaphysical activity, is stronger than philosophy because, in defamiliarizing reality, it captures the quality of "astonishment" (Verwunderung) which Schopenhauer sought.

That Beckett drew on Schopenhauer is incontrovertible; not only does he name him, he also uses Schopenhauerian language. Yet we must differentiate the Schopenhauerian effect.   If habit dulls perception, there are moments, Beckett argues, when "the boredom of living is replaced by the suffering of being."[65]   We suffer when facing "the spectacle of reality," because "the mortal microcosm cannot forgive the relative immortality of the macrocosm." (21) This obviously embodies Nietzsche's observation of resentment against time.   If Proustian involuntary memory is the expression of an unconscious desire to be taken out of the intrinsic flux (17) and unified with past experience, we then breathe the air of the only Paradise available: Paradise Lost (74).   Significantly at that moment, "Time is not recovered, it is obliterated." (75) *Krapp's* experience of time falls short of the Proustian invocation of unity, because of a *closer* reading of Schopenhauer.   But in the Proust essay, the desire is still for an *achieved* stasis, the "exaltation of a brief eternity." (75)   Where "the classical artist assumes omniscience and omnipotence" (81), allegory

---

[62]   Dale Jaquette (ed.): *Schopenhauer, Philosophy, and the Arts*. Cambridge University Press 1996.

[63]   Ulrich Pothast: *Die eigentlich metaphysische Tätigkeit. Über Schopenhauers Ästhetik und ihre Anwendung durch Samuel Beckett.* Suhrkamp, Frankfurt 1982, p. 24f.

[64]   Pothast, p. 386. He cites Wittgenstein's Diaries for 1916.

[65]   *Proust*, p. 19.

moves towards anagogy (80), and here we glimpse a distrust of all systematizers. Proust, however, "does not deal in concepts, he pursues the Idea, the concrete." (79) After a Schopenhauerian invocation of the power of music, Beckett concludes "the Proustian stasis" is—and he uses these German words—"holder Wahnsinn," let us say "beautiful madness" (91). He also cites a Spanish quotation in Schopenhauer: the original sin is the sin of having been born. (67) [66]

When glossing Schopenhauer once again, Beckett invokes "the wisdom of all the sages, from Brahma to Leopardi, the wisdom that consists not in the satisfaction but in the ablation of desire." (18) There is a slip here, in one sense trivial, except that it highlights a crucial divergence. Beckett names two *sages*. Yet Brahma is a not a sage, but a *god*, personifying creation, often confused with *Brahman*, Hinduism's ultimate, universal principle into which *atman*, or individual soul, is finally absorbed. Beckett probably confused Brahma with Buddha, the enlightened one, as Gautama indeed a sage, one of the greatest. My point is not just that Schopenhauer also confused Buddha and Brahma, but that this misapprehension was not accidental, because it reveals that impossible, unconscious agenda: not just a Buddhist ablation of desire, but the Hindu cessation of consciousness, as soul, or mind, and universe become an undifferentiated One, a possibility which philosophical Buddhism rejected.

Extinction of consciousness, not just the ablation of desire, guarantees the dancer's perfect gracefulness in Kleist's "Über das Marionettentheater," which Beckett so admired.[67] The invocation of such perfection, impossible to any human figure, if we accept the modalities of this thought, occurs in a passage where the angel ejects humanity from the gate of Paradise. We must travel round the world to see if there is perhaps a back door. Likewise, from the same text of Kleist, the bear as perfect fencer, also mentioned by Beckett, stands for that unselfconsciousness now forever lost, at least to Western culture.[68] It seems the ablation of desire will not alone suffice, and that the necessary loss of (self-)consciousness is impossible. How did Schopenhauer address this problem?

---

[66] Arthur Schopenhauer: *Die Welt als Wille und Vorstellung (WWV),* *Sämtliche Werke,* Brockhaus, Mannheim 1988, vol. 2, #51, p. 300; in *Endgame,* "Our revels now are ended," probably because Schopenhauer quotes from that passage too: 'We are such stuff as dreams are made of'—*WWV,* #5, p. 20.

[67] Knowlson, p. 517 & 558.

[68] Knowlson, p. 558.

"I owe what is best in my own development to the impression made by Kant's works, the sacred writings of the Hindus, and Plato."[69] Schopenhauer stressed the importance of the *Upanishads,* the final stage of the *Vedas.*[70] The teaching based on them, the *Vedanta,* in the first and most important school, promulgated *Advaita,* or Nondualism. Atman was identical with Brahman, the Absolute, though the *empirical* ego reincarnates. The world, apart from Brahman, is *Maya* or illusion. For the main teacher of this school, Sankara, there are two levels of insight: for the lower, the world and objects in space and time are real; for the higher they are illusory, as a result of a mystical experience of release and identification with Brahman, the undifferentiated One of ultimate reality. Kant's *Thing-in-Itself* is unknowable, only the phenomenal world is given to consciousness.

The title of Schopenhauer's main work, *Die Welt als Wille und Vorstellung,* is misleading, if taken to imply a Kantian dichotomy between idea, or representation, of the knowing subject and the separate, unknown and unknowable metaphysical life force called Will. Schopenhauer sets up a contradiction in which Beckett, probably as no other writer, lived and had his being. For Schopenhauer: "we ourselves are the thing-in-itself," because we are not merely "knowing subjects," constructing the outside world according to the principle of sufficient reason, but also *willing* subjects, since everything in the world is an expression of Will. Hence "a way *from within* stands open to us to that real inner nature of things to which we cannot penetrate *from without.*"[71] If the Will is, therefore, not absolutely impenetrable and unknowable, Schopenhauer nevertheless held the best course of action was, where possible, to suppress it. There are two ways of doing this, even when the results are temporary: through art and through a religious-philosophical intellectual mortification. These paths culminate either in the work of the "genius," or in the behaviour of the "saint."

---

[69] Arthur Schopenhauer: *World as Will and Representation (WWR),* trans. E. F. J. Payne. Dover Publications, New York 1966, vol. 1, p. 417; *WWV,* p. 493. See also the Preface to the first edition of *WWV;* also Moira Nicholls: "The Influence of Eastern Thought on Schopenhauer's Doctrine of the Thing-in-Itself." In: *The Cambridge Companion to Schopenhauer,* ed. Christopher Janaway. Cambridge University Press 1999, p. 179.

[70] *WWV,* #1, p. 4; see Nicholls, p. 180.

[71] *WWR,* vol. 2, ch. 18, p. 195; *Sämtliche Werke,* vol. 3, Kap. 18, p. 218. See also Dale Jacquette: "Schopenhauer's metaphysics of appearance and Will in the philosophy of art." In Jacquette (ed.): *Schopenhauer, philosophy, and the arts.* Cambridge University Press, Cambridge 1996, p. 4-5.

His description of the genius reads like a version of Beckett's position, provided we do not take it literally, the problem being the extent of the dilemma, as I will explain:

> That pure, true, and profound knowledge of the essence of the world now becomes for him an end in itself; at it he stops. Therefore it does not become for him a quieter of the will, as...in the case of the saint who has attained resignation; it does not deliver him from life forever, but only for a few moments. For him it is not the way of life, but only an occasional consolation in it.[72]

Unlike the genius, the saint can deny the Will. Schopenhauer says: "The Buddhist faith calls that existence Nirvana, that is to say, extinction."[73] He equates nirvana with "the phenomenon of non-volition" or "denial of the will to live."[74] But nirvana means something else. Schopenhauer, in effect, aligns the Buddhist concept of nirvana with the Hindu obliteration of difference, or attainment of absolute identity between atman and brahman, and also equates Kant's Thing-in-Itself, the Will, and brahman as sustainer of the world. Only Schopenhauer's is not a holy, it is a *catastrophic* monism: "...the origin of the world (this Samsara of the Buddhists) is itself based already on evil; that is to say, it is a sinful act of Brahma. Now we ourselves are again this Brahma, for Indian mythology is everywhere transparent."[75]

What Schopenhauer proposes could be called a negative ontology of substance, which we cannot but affirm yet must try to deny: "That which in us affirms itself as will-to-life, is also that which denies this will and thereby becomes free from existence and the sufferings thereof."[76] Surely the effect is to place the empirical individual in a non-classic, because not primarily psychological, double bind that is nevertheless infrangible, from which there is no

---

[72] *WWR*, vol. 1, #52, p. 267; *WWV*, #52, p. 316. See also John E. Atwell: "Art as liberation: a central theme of Schopenhauer's philosophy." In: Jacquette, p. 94.

[73] *WWR*, vol. 2, ch. 41, p. 508; *Sämtliche Werke*, vol. 3, Kap. 41, p. 583. See also Nicholls p. 192.

[74] *Essays and Aphorisms*, p. 61.

[75] Arthur Schopenhauer: *Parerga and Paralipomena*, trans E. F. J. Payne, Clarendon Press, Oxford 1974, vol. 1, p. 62; *Sämtliche Werke*, vol. 5, p. 66. See also Nicholls, p. 184, who misquotes.

[76] Arthur Schopenhauer: *Manuscript Remains*. Trans. E. F. J. Payne, Berg, Oxford 1989, vol. 3, p. 376; see also Nicholls, p. 193.

escape. For if consciousness is itself an expression of the will, it cannot then deny itself, since the act of denying is an intervention of what is to be denied. One consequence must be to create an ineradicable sense of guilt. The absolute unavoidability of this impossibility is also why Schopenhauer and Beckett recourse to music.

Schopenhauer, famously, found music not just an "adequate objectification of the will," like the Platonic ideas reproduced in the other arts, but an image or reproduction of the Will itself: "Abbild des Willens selbst." Therefore the world could just as well be called "embodied music as embodied will."[77] Leibniz called music "an unconscious exercise in arithmetic in which the mind does not know it is counting," and Schopenhauer changes this into "an unconscious exercise in metaphysics in which the mind does not know it is philosophizing."[78] But Schopenhauer reveals a *repressed* rationalism when he argues: since perfect pitch is impossible—a problem when tuning keyboard instruments, as no tuning system is mathematically impeccable—"a perfectly correct music cannot even be conceived, much less worked out; and for this reason all possible music deviates from perfect purity."[79] Here I see a significant parallel, when Beckett, explaining to Duthuit why he admires Bram van Velde's paintings, says that, instead of embracing it, most painting tries "to escape from this sense of failure...in a kind of tropism towards a light...as though the irrationality of pi were an offence against the deity, not to mention his creature."[80] This programatic explanation probably needs a psychoanalytic reading since underneath it surely lies a repressed desire for the disparaged rationality or purity, because Beckett continues, in respect of approaching van Velde's fidelity to "failure": "I know my inability to do so places myself...in what I think is still called an unenviable situation, familiar to psychiatrists." We can call that situation a double-bind.

But music, as embodied Will, could not, did not indeed have to be explained, just listened to. Because it was not phenomenal, it was also painless. For Schopenhauer the bass notes embody the lowest form of the will's objectification, and the melody, corresponding to

---

[77]   *WWV*, #52, p. 310.

[78]   *WWV*, #52, p. 313. See also Lydia Goehr: "Schopenhauer and the musicians." In: Jacquette, p. 209.

[79]   *WWR*, #52, p. 266; *WWV*, #52, p. 314, see also Jacquette, p. 209.

[80]   *Proust*, p. 125-126.

human intentionality, sets its course towards its own goal.[81] So music seems to offer a way out of that double bind, as if the will somehow came to an awareness of itself through goal-directed melody, rising over the lower music which, as embodied will, has no end or goal. Yet surely this double bind is merely displaced, becoming the source of a philosophically ambiguous, and temporary, aesthetic pleasure, though the transaction relieves language of its burden of expression. Perhaps that explains why, in Beckett, music takes over where language cannot go, as in *Ghost Trio* or *Nacht und Träume*.

As for other Schopenhauerian constructions, Beckett's novels show the progressive collapse of the principle of sufficient reason, which secures the relationship between constructing subject and observed object. Murphy, seen from outside, may disintegrate, but the narrative does not. Moran, in *Molloy*, offers, in Schopenhauer's language, a "window to the real," as his body collapses. In *The Unnameable*, the Will is in dialog with itself: "If only the voice would stop, the meaningless voice which prevents you from being nothing."[82] Though Schopenhauer could never have imagined the plays—after all Rossini was his favorite composer—they are visual translations of what he called "the essential nature of life," oscillating between boredom and suffering, where happiness is only contemplated as an abatement of suffering. In *Waiting for Godot*, Valdimir and Estragon both deny and affirm their existence, embodying what Schopenhauer called "the duplicity" of our being.[83] For Pothast this exemplifies Schopenhauer's metaphysical perception that individuality is denied, but I argue perception is here double: the will knows the will; the subject is trapped. The conclusion must be that Beckett's double bind is consciousness. His avowed inability to express, together with the compulsion to do so, is hardly the mark of aesthetic incompetence for Beckett, if words mean anything, was a master of his art, but is rather the effect of a displacement of the necessary, impossible self-suppression of the Will.[84]

This contradictory rhetorical figure, when the music of the world as Will comes to consciousness of itself in melody, suggests why Schopenhauer's and Hegel's lectures clashed. Hegel secularized an

---

[81] *WWV*, #52, p. 306ff. See also Cheryl Foster: "Ideas and Imagination: Schopenhauer on the Proper Formulation of Art." In: Janaway, p. 241.

[82] Quoted in Kearney, p. 285. The divergence from Brecht's 'nothing' is obvious.

[83] *WWV*, #54, p. 327. See also Pothast, pp. 366-377.

[84] For Beckett's statement on the dilemma of expression, see *Proust*, p. 103.

eschatological teleology. History, revealing the World Spirit, though conflictual, is the image and deed of Reason. The Schopenhauerian dialectic, however, sees the World Spirit as *malign*. Yet a blind Will is *also* self-divided, driven into ever new, competing forms of self-existence. Although it produces, in human intelligence, a higher form of itself, the ultimate *telos* is negative, and that intelligence must turn against it. Both Hegel and Schopenhauer theorize time, the emergent problem of their 19th century episteme, by developing new metaphysical teleologies. For one, the ultimate process is good; for the other, it is evil. In Schopenhauer, Spirit goes underground and turns into *libido* or Drive. Then the enigma is no longer outside and above us, it is within and below. This is how Schopenhauer describes the dilemma of his dialectic:

> Every individual is on the one hand the subject of knowledge, ie., the supplementary condition of the possibility of the whole objective world and, on the other hand, an individual appearance of the will, of that which objectifies itself in every thing. But this duplicity of our being does not rest in a separate unity: otherwise we would be able to become conscious of our selves through our self and independently of the objects of knowledge and of the will: yet this we simply cannot do, but rather as soon as we try to, and turn knowledge inwards to really reflect upon ourselves, we lose ourselves in a bottomless void, we are like a hollow sphere of glass out of which a voice speaks, but whose cause cannot be found inside it, and as we try to lay hold on ourselves, we grasp, shuddering, nothing but an insubstantial ghost.[85]

Beckett turns Schopenhauer's metaphysic, the impossibility of escape, into the *form* of his art. Brecht sought to escape from an ontologized Hegelian Marxism. Other concepts of time and process become evident in his writing. This takes us back to Nietzsche.

VI

Brecht absorbed much from Nietzsche and he transvalued, only possible because of what they had in common. In *The Birth of Tragedy* Nietzsche seeks to explain why the extraordinary Greek form declined so suddenly. Fusing Dionysian intoxication and Apollonian illusion, tragedy was destroyed by their mutual opponent: Socratic rationality. But destructive reason also found its voice *within* the theater: the voice of Euripides. Here Nietzsche's analysis sounds like a description of Brecht's Epic Theater:

---

[85]   *WWV*, #54, p. 327. My translation.

What in Euripidean, as compared with Sophoclean tragedy, has been so frequently censured as poetic lack and retrogression is actually the straight result of the poet's incisive critical gifts, his audacious personality. The Euripidean prologue may serve to illustrate the efficacy of that rationalistic method. Nothing could be more at odds with our dramaturgic notions than the prologue in the drama of Euripides. To have a character appear at the beginning of the play, tell us who he is, what preceded the action, what has happened so far, even what is about to happen in the course of the play—a modern writer for the theatre would reject all this as a wanton and unpardonable dismissal of the element of suspense. Now that everyone knows what is going to happen, who will wait to see it happen?...But Euripides reasoned quite otherwise. According to him, the effect of tragedy never resided in epic suspense, in a teasing uncertainty as to what was going to happen next. It resided, rather, in those great scenes of lyrical rhetoric in which the passion and dialectic of the protagonist reached heights of eloquence.[86]

Euripides...lays his plan as Socratic thinker and carries it out as passionate actor. So it happens that the Euripidean drama is at the same time cool and fiery, able alike to freeze and consume us. It cannot possibly achieve the Apollonian effects of the epic, while on the other hand it has severed all connection with the Dionysiac mode; so that in order to have any impact at all it must seek out novel stimulants which are to be found neither in the Apollonian nor in the Dionysiac realm. Those stimulants are, on the one hand, cold paradoxical ideas put in the place of Apollonian contemplation, and on the other fiery emotions put in the place of Dionysiac transports. (78f.; KSA 1, 84)

Some such combination of cold control and fiery emotions, of passion and dialectic, energizes Brecht's theater where, as in East Asian art, aesthetic strength in representing emotions depends upon intellectual control over the structures which contain them. I am reminded of Brecht's comment: "Meier-Graefe says of Delacroix that here was a warm heart beating in a cold person. And when you come down to it, that's a possible recipe for greatness." (GBA 26, 215)[87] Nietzsche had roots in the Enlightenment, visible in his identification with Voltaire,[88] in his absolute disdain for anti-Semitism, in his disgust with German nationalism, in his alarm over the destruction of personality in modern culture, over what he called the

---

[86]   *The Birth of Tragedy*, 79f.; *KSA* 1, p. 85.

[87]   Bertolt Brecht: *Diaries 1920-1922*. Methuen, London 1979, p. 98.

[88]   *Ecce Homo, KSA* 6, p. 322.

"*Un*persönlichkeit des Arbeiters" (depersonalization of the worker) in industrializing society, over the falsity of the economy (KSA 6, 316).

His impact on Brecht was considerable: elements of self-stylization; the early Wagner infatuation; the metaphor of coldness in the early poetry; the rejection of religion in favor of a "strong" philosophy (GBA 26, 272); the whole "deconstructive" metaphysic contained in Nietzsche's remark—"Since Copernicus man has been rolling from the centre toward X." [89]—which is picked up in *Mann ist Mann* (GBA 2, 206). There are countless echoes of Nietzsche's love of paradox and contradiction: "Only someone who changes is compatible with me." (KSA 5, 243: "Nur wer sich wandelt, bleibt mit mir verwandt.") Brecht's version is in the *Geschichten vom Herrn Keuner*: 'A man, who hadn't seen Mr. K. for a long time, greeted him with the words: "You haven't changed a bit." "Oh!" said Mr. K. and grew pale.' (GBA 18, 21)

But beyond all these echoes, and there are many others, one strand of thought stands out, especially since Nietzsche transvalued Schopenhauer. When ideas and metaphors are transvalued, and sometimes they are just unproblematically integrated, what has apparently been changed is retained as the unconscious of the discourse. Coming out of the house in the Augsburg street, *Am Rain*, where Brecht was born, you step onto an iron grill between door and pavement beyond. Looking down, water races past under your feet, an unforgettable image: the grid of our systems projected over a mill race. I think of Nietzsche's observation about building a cathedral of concepts on flowing water.[90] Zarathustra rejects what the soothsayer preaches: "'Oh, where is redemption from the flux of things and the punishment of existence?' Thus preached madness."[91] That recalls Beckett's "holder Wahnsinn" and its Proustian stasis, the impossible heap.

Nietzsche embraced what Schopenhauer sought to escape. Images of flux abound in Brecht's work, forming its central metaphor:

---

[89]   Friedrich Nietzsche: *The Will to Power*. Trans. Walther Kaufmann & R. J. Hollingdale. Weidenfeld & Nicholson, London 1968, #1, p. 8; see also *Zur Genealogie der Moral*, KSA 5, p. 404, where 'X' is significantly equated with 'Nichts' or 'the void.'

[90]   KSA 1, p. 882: 'Man darf hier den Menschen wohl bewundern als ein gewaltiges Baugenie, dem auf beweglichen Fundamenten und gleichsam auf fliessendem Wasser das Aufthürmen eines unendlich complicirten Begriffsdomes gelingt...'

[91]   *Also sprach Zarathustra* II, *Von der Erlösung*, p. 154.

from body-dissolving rivers in the early poetry to later rivers of history. They link what some critics categorize as incompatible. This particular term, 'flux of things' (Fluß der Dinge), occurs in many places. In Me-ti it refers to the Marxist dialectic (GBA 18, 73 & 113). But that begs the question of its other connotations (GBA 18, 73; Über den Fluß der Dinge). An autobiographical poem, The Doubter, written in dialog with a splendid Chinese painting, which hung at the head of his bed, asks: "Are you truly in the stream of happening?" (im Fluß des Geschehens, GBA 14, 376) This has been taken as implying a Nietzschean temptation to say 'Yes' to the world in all its cruelty, meaning in 1937 only one thing: to accept Stalinism.[92] But this poem, as well as that painting, is about the problematics of practice. So it opposes perfect theories, political ontology, and pseudo-scientific determinism. This flow of events is a critique of such "theory."[93]

VII

Schopenhauer's evocation of nirvana as extinction is another form of self-assertion, the only one left in a monist system of thought. In philosophical Buddhism, however, what is annihilated is not the self, but the illusion of an independent self. There is no absolute, no essential self, therefore we cannot hold it in the form of perfect consciousness, neither can we fear its loss. Nirvana is not achieved after death, but in this world by embracing samsara, by relating to all that is and helps to shape us. Everything is relational. The goal of nirvana is therefore the road itself. In Brecht's poem about the Buddha, as in many popular stories, Buddha falls silent, refusing to describe or define nirvana when pressed by his disciples, because his questioners seek impossible verbal abstractions and theoretical certainty, instead of responding to urgent real situations: to get out of the burning house.

Adorno read Endgame as equating the totality invoked by Clov with nothing, and the play's negative ontology as the negation of ontology, undermining "the absolute claim of what merely is."[94] There are no more absolutes. If we speak of rehistoricizing, perhaps Beckett and Brecht represent two sides of the problem when essentialism, no matter how metaphorized, is replaced by field theories of knowledge.

---

[92] Reinhold Grimm: Brecht und Nietzsche oder Geständnisse eines Dichters. Suhrkamp, Frankfurt 1979, p. 235. Grimm first documented Brecht's wide use of Nietzsche. 'Fluß des Geschehens' is another term in Nietzsche. Here I disagree with Grimm's reading; see Brechts Ost Asien, p. 13-16.

[93] Brechts Ost Asien, pp. 13-16.

[94] Trying to Understand Endgame, p. 148.

What I have argued could be summarized thus: Brecht's supposed preoccupation with the rational and Beckett's with the irrational needs qualification, since the repressed of each discourse unfolds within the other. The unconscious haunts Brecht's texts from start to finish—that would be another essay—and Beckett's topic is the ghost of consciousness.

The historian Fernand Braudel proposed three ways of counting time: as individual life time, as the time of societies and social groups and, sustaining these, as the longer rhythms or *longue durée* of bio-geographical time. In Schopenhauer's philosophy, the Will, as blind force, realizes itself in consciousness and thereby produces its own double bind. If we rehistoricize this metaphysical trajectory, it figures the justifiable fear of an inability to control the forces, guided by a perceived and immediate, but limited self-interest, which now operate through us and may well lead to our destruction. Such thoughts become possible in the early nineteenth century, as the uncontrollable monster created by Mary Shelley's Dr. Frankenstein reminds us. So we could perhaps say that an older theology of fear has been unconsciously historicized by Schopenhauer, and simultaneously dehistoricized into a metaphysic. In this sense we could say that Schopenhauer's metaphysic socialized the ontological. Beckett shows us how the individual can experience this as unredeemable failure.

That vital strand in Brecht's thinking, related to Nietzsche's *flux of things*, dehistoricizes revolutionary time but then rehistoricizes it in terms of *longue durée*, because it does not abandon but rather stretches the process of change. When 'das Nichts' or nirvana is equated with acceptance of samsara, or the flux of things, identity is relationalized. Our fate, as the fate of humanity, lies outside and within us. As Gautama, the Buddha, observed: the self both exists and does not exist. Because this fate becomes an inescapable, collective responsibility, we could say that Brecht ontologizes the social.

Maybe that is why he said of his own work: "My plays and theories are applicable in bourgeois and capitalist societies, in socialist, communist and classless societies and in all subsequent social formations."[95] And maybe that is also, since problems are not solved by thinking alone, why one of his very last poems is entitled:

---

[95]   Quoted by Reinhold Grimm, "Der katholische Einstein: Brechts Dramen- und Theatertheorie." In: *Brechts Dramen, Neue Interpretationen*, ed. W. Hinderer, Stuttgart 1984, p. 30.

Dauerten wir unendlich

If we lasted forever
Everything would change
But since we don't
Many things stay the same. (GBA 15, 294)

BIBLIOGRAPHY

Adorno, Theodor W. *Gesammelte Schriften.* Suhrkamp, Frankfurt 1974.

Adorno, Theodor W. *Trying to Understand Endgame, New German Critique,* vol. 26, p. 119-150.

Atwell, John E. *Art as liberation: a central theme of Schopenhauer's philosophy.* In: Jacquette, pp. 81-106.

Barker, Howard. *Arguments for a Theatre.* Manchester University Press, Manchester 1997.

Beckett, Samuel. *Disjecta, Miscellaneous Writings.* Calder, London 1983.

Beckett, Samuel. *Endgame.* Faber & Faber, London 1958.

Beckett, Samuel. *Proust and Three Dialogues with Georges Duthuit.* John Calder, London 1965.

Beckett, Samuel. *Waiting for Godot. A Tragicomedy in two acts.* Faber & Faber, London 1956.

Benjamin, Walter. *Versuche über Brecht.* Suhrkamp, Frankfurt 1981.

Brecht, Bertolt. *Collected Plays.* Methuen, London 1970, vol. 1.

Brecht, Bertolt. *Collected Plays.* Methuen, London 1979, vol. 2/2.

Brecht, Bertolt. *Collected Poems.* Methuen, London 1976.

Brecht, Bertolt. *Diaries 1920-1922.* Methuen, London 1979.

Brecht, Bertolt. *Über die bildenden Künste,* (ed.) J. Hermand, Suhrkamp, Frankfurt 1983.

Brecht, Bertolt. *Werke, Große kommentierte Berliner und Frankfurter Ausgabe (GBA).* Aufbau-Verlag, Berlin & Suhrkamp-Verlag, Frankfurt 1988-.

Cronin, Anthony. *Samuel Beckett. The Last Modernist.* Flamingo, London 1997.

Dieckmann, Friedrich. *Brechts Utopia.* In: Heise, pp. 69-108.

Foster, Cheryl. *Ideas and Imagination: Schopenhauer on the Proper Formulation of Art.* In: Janaway, pp. 213-251.

Foucault, Michel. *The Order of Things. An Archaeology of the Human Sciences.* Vintage Books, New York 1973.

Gersch, Wolfgang. *Film bei Brecht.* Henschelverlag, Berlin 1975.

Goehr, Lydia. *Schopenhauer and the musicians.* In: Jacquette, pp. 200-228.

Grimm, Reinhold. *Der katholische Einstein: Brechts Dramen- und Theatertheorie.* In: Hinderer, pp. 11-32.

Grimm, Reinhold. *Brecht und Nietzsche oder Geständnisse eines Dichters.* Suhrkamp, Frankfurt 1979.

Haug, W. F. *Philosophieren mit Brecht und Gramsci.* Argument, Berlin 1996.

Hecht, Werner. *Aufsätze über Brecht.* Henschelverlag, Berlin 1970.

Hecht, Werner. *Brecht Chronik 1898-1956.* Suhrkamp, Frankfurt 1997.

Heise, Wolfgang (ed.). *Brecht 88. Anregungen zum Dialog über die Vernunft am Jahrtausendende.* Henschelverlag Kunst und Gesellschaft, Berlin 1987.

Hinderer, W. (ed.). *Brechts Dramen, Neue Interpretationen,* Reclam, Stuttgart 1984.

Janaway, Christopher (ed.). *The Cambridge Companion to Schopenhauer.* Cambridge University Press, Cambridge 1999.

Jaquette, Dale (ed.). *Schopenhauer, Philosophy, and the Arts.* Cambridge University Press, Cambridge 1996.

Kearney, Richard (ed.). *The Irish Mind. Exploring Intellectual Traditions.* Wolfhound Press, Dublin 1985.

Kearney, Richard. *Beckett: The Demythologising Intellect.* In: Kearney, pp. 267-291.

Knowlson, James. *Damned to Fame. The Life of Samuel Beckett.* Simon and Schuster. New York 1996.

Koopmann, Helmut und Theo Stammen (eds.). *Bertolt Brecht – Aspekte seines Werkes, Spuren seiner Wirkung.* Ernst Vögel Verlag, München 1983.

Krull, Edith. *Herbert Ihering.* Henschelverlag, Berlin 1964.

Mason, Jeffrey (ed.). *The Complete Letters of Sigmund Freud to Wilhelm Fließ, 1887-1904.* Harvard University Press, Cambridge, Mass. 1985.

Mauthner, Fritz. *Beiträge zu einer Kritik der Sprache.* J. G. Cotta'sche Buchhandlung Nachfolger, Stuttgart 1901.

Mayer, Hans. *Beckett und Brecht. Erfahrungen und Erinnerungen. Ein Vortrag.* Berliner Ensemble, Drucksache 15, 1995.

Müller, Heiner. *Der Dramatiker und die Geschichte seiner Zeit. Ein Gespräch zwischen Horst Laube und Heiner Müller.* In: Theater 1975, Sonderheft der Zeitschrift Theater Heute, pp. 119-123.

Müller, Heiner. *Germania, Tod in Berlin.* Rotbuch-Verlag, Berlin 1977.

Nicholls, Moira. *The Influence of Eastern Thought on Schopenhauer's Doctrine of the Thing-in-Itself.* In: Janaway, pp. 171-212.

Nietzsche, Friedrich. *Also Sprach Zarathustra.* Kröner-Verlag, Stuttgart, 1956.

Nietzsche, Friedrich. *Sämtliche Werke, Kritische Studienausgabe* (KSA), Deutscher Taschenbuch Verlag, Munich 1988.

Nietzsche, Friedrich. *The Birth of Tragedy*. Trans. Francis Golffing. Doubleday, New York 1956.

Nietzsche, Friedrich. *The Will to Power*. Trans. Walther Kaufmann & R. J. Hollingdale. Weidenfeld & Nicholson, London 1968.

Pothast, Ulrich. *Die eigentlich metaphysische Tätigkeit. Über Schopenhauers Ästhetik und ihre Anwendung durch Samuel Beckett*. Suhrkamp, Frankfurt 1982.

Schopenhauer, Arthur. *Die Welt als Wille und Vorstellung. Sämtliche Werke*, vol. 2.

Schopenhauer, Arthur. *Essays and Aphorisms*, trans. R. J. Hollingdale. Penguin, Harmondsworth 1970.

Schopenhauer, Arthur. *Manuscript Remains*. Trans. E. F. J. Payne, Berg, Oxford 1989.

Schopenhauer, Arthur. *Parerga and Paralipomena*, trans E. F. J. Payne, Clarendon Press, Oxford 1974.

Schopenhauer, Arthur. *Sämtliche Werke*. Brockhaus, Mannheim 1988.

Schopenhauer, Arthur. *The World as Will and Representation*, trans. E. F. J. Payne. Dover Publications, New York 1966.

Schutte, Ofelia. *Beyond Nihilism. Nietzsche wihout Masks*, University of Chicago Press, Chicago & London 1984.

Tatlow, Antony. *Brechts Ost Asien*, Parthas, Berlin 1998.

Tatlow, Antony. *Ghosts in the House of Theory*. In: *The Brecht Yearbook*, 24, 1999, pp. 1-13.

Tatlow, Antony. *The Mask of Evil*. Peter Lang, Berne 1977.

Unseld, Siegfried. *Bis zum Äußersten. Samuel Beckett zum 80. Geburtstag - 1986*. In: *Theater Heute*, 2, February 1990, p. 23.

Valentin, Karl. *Die Raubritter von München. Szenen und Dialoge*. Deutscher Taschenbuch Verlag, Munich 1964.

Wright, Elizabeth. *Postmodern Brecht. A Re-Presentation*. Routledge, London 1989.

Zilliacus, Clas. *Three Times Godot: Beckett, Brecht, Bulatovic*. In *Comparative Drama* 1970, vol. 4, No. 1, p. 3-17.

Brecht and Beckett in the Theater I

Hans-Thies Lehmann, Walter Asmus, and Carl Weber
Chair: Moray McGowan

* * *

Hans-Thies Lehmann
B, B, and B. Fifteen minutes to comply.

I

If someone has to write about the oriental world, the young Brecht noted, it is no good if he has the feeling of sitting between Persian carpets; it is better if he has the feeling of sitting in front of paper. Each in his way, Brecht and Beckett, separates himself from the theater of convention. They both insist on the theatrical moment as a poetic and artistic reality in its own right. Creating theater is not creating an illusion, the realm of Persian carpets. Theater is not transmission of a text and the fiction it signifies. It is a text in itself, a practice in space and time, here and now, an artistically meaningful moment, which therefore participates in the whole range of ambiguity, self-reflection, doubt, and retreat of meaning which characterizes the modern and/or postmodern text and artwork in general. If we have difficulty bringing B and B together, this is only in part caused by the differences between their artistic stances. It is mainly due to difficulties we introduced ourselves by the strong tradition of reductive reading of both Bs. Neither is Brecht a didactic simplifier who trades in ready-made political options, nor Beckett an author of the absurd in the sense of absence of sense. But both realize in fact a theater/text where the discourse of identification, the discourse of self-identical meaning is broken, not repeated. Both "suspend" meaning in an undecidable ambiguity between seriousness and the artistic use of literary forms like the parable. Both question even the possibility of identity.

Yes, there are profound differences between B and B. But there are also great and deep differences between Bertolt and Brecht, between Samuel and Beckett. The point must be: thinking the field in between; between difference and similarity; between the Bs; within the Bs; asking for a theater, and for thinking about the theater. And here is the beginning: B is not B; S is not B. We must read beyond the signatures. Arrive (better: start) at a point where ideally the discourse would be able to avoid even the names. Speak to B and B, and about B and B, where each B is at least two Bs and probably three, or more. I will not arrive there, not even come close to this point in fifteen minutes. Instead I go back, to have a look at the landscape where both

Where Extremes Meet: Rereading Brecht and Beckett / Begegnung der Extreme. Brecht und Beckett: Eine Re-interpretation
Stephen Brockmann et al., eds., *The Brecht Yearbook / Das Brecht-Jahrbuch*
Volume 27 (Pittsburgh: The International Brecht Society, 2002)

Bs find themselves in an equally political and absurd situation. There is this dialog in *Fatzer* by B, which could well be by B:

> "Hallo!—Ist jemand hier? Wie nach der Sintflut—Was ist da?—Nichts. Kommt heraus.—Was sagt er?—Hier ist nichts.—Kommt ruhig heraus, hier ist/ Kein Mensch—Nichts/ Wie nach der Sintflut—Kein Feuer? In der Luft kein Eisen? Wir sind/ Falsch gesteuert. Seid froh, es ist/ Eine falsche Gegend."

II

I name, tentatively, starting points: B teaches; B does not teach. But how, if Adorno was right in speaking about the didactic element in B as an artistic principle ("das Lehrstück als artistisches Prinzip")? B stands for a theater of gestures, and, more precisely, Walter Benjamin compared B to Kafka, who presents, as he observed, "gestures out of context" so that they lose, open up, obscure, shift, and displace their readability. Yes, the theater of B and B is essentially a theater of "pure gesture" in the sense Giorgio Agamben gave to this notion in one of his essays on the political.[1] And I insist on one of the contradictions, which are only rarely taken into consideration: within B there is a lifelong fight between a theater of gesture (Gestus) and a theater of story (Fabel).[2] One is normally said to be the harmonious and logical completion of the other. In fact there is a discrepancy beyond the apparent unity of the signature. It is the theater of gesture which brings him close to B. It is the theater of fable which at first sight supports the view of the teacher B who is worlds away from B.

III

It is common to oppose the alleged social optimism of B to the non-social or asocial pessimism of B, who always presents failure. But from *Baal* and *Dickicht* to the learning plays, to *Galilei*, *Courage*, and *Der gute Mensch von Sezuan*, B's is a theater of failure. But we say theater of failure more often in respect of the theater of B. The objection to emphasizing these parallels is bound to be raised: does not B give answers, historical, political answers, while B never does?—Certainly, in a certain way. But then: does anybody, including

---

[1]   Giorgio Agamben, "Notes sur le geste," in *Moyens sans fins. Notes sur la politique* (Paris, 1995), pp. 59-72.

[2]   Hans-Thies Lehmann, "Fabel-Haft," in Virginia Cisotti and Paul Kroker, eds., *Poesia e Politica. Bertolt Brecht a 100 anni dalla nascita* (Milan, 1999), pp. 13-26.

B himself (or in which of his selves as B), purely and simply "believe" in the wisdom and truth of the answers his plays seem to give or to imply?[3] Does Shakespeare believe in Fortinbras? And if both doubted, are their answers then answers?

IV

B, the radical detractor of bourgeois *Einfühlung*, and B, the author of the great Absurd ("das große Absurde", as the late B wrote), stand close together also in the view of common adversaries—enemies, to be sure, in different ways and of very different kinds: Georg Lukács, common sense, realist ideology, moralism. For these enemies, both Bs represent a not-theater, a marginal theater, an inhumanly cold theater, a theater that makes no sense, or nothing but sense, a theater for intellectuals, neglecting the desires of the fabled "normal" spectator. On the other hand, in the eyes of these enemies, both Bs are guilty, although in different ways, of a naïve, terrible simplification of social and political reality.

B and B stand close together by the fact that in this moment, at least in Germany, Italy, and France, neither of them attracts great passion in theater people. Both are rarely staged—and staged more or less as repertoire plays. They are considered to be entertaining under certain conditions, but not regarded as enlightening for any new dimensions of theater or human existence—let alone politically motivating truth about society. This situation, which we have to face without illusion, does not take away anything from B and B as authors of great literary works and as monuments of theater history. But apart from our love, and our interest in investigating these works, we must ask the question: what might be the theatrical prospects for B and B? Only, this is my contention, if they are both read, brought together, and subjected to a transferral of the concepts of theater which to all appearances separate them.

V

With both Bs we associate a theater of abstraction which, in consequence, brings about a certain *désinvolture*, a distanciation of the spectators. The latter can easily regard the action on stage as very distant proceedings—like a piece of music or a story *here*, which, even as it is narrated and reflected upon now, took place *there* a long

---

[3]   A serious treatment of this question could start with rereading the conversations of Brecht and Benjamin in the 1930s. For a commentary, see Werner Hamacher, "The Gesture in the Name," in *Premises* (Harvard University Press, 1996), pp. 295-298.

time ago. For quite some time now the focus of interest in the theater has shifted to the specifically physical aspect and to the very special spiritual experiences rendered possible by the real presence of the performing body, by the tension in the act of looking at the body while being a body.

In the age of the media the expectations, the hopes (insofar as they still exist), and possibilities of the art of theater have changed profoundly, and in ways we are far from understanding in their scope. If we leave aside the legitimate function of theater as a kind of museum, then we are left with the aesthetic, ethical, and political implications of the basic structure of performance as physical reality, co-presence.

Obviously the role, the place, and time-structure of the act we call "understanding" in the theatrical process is deeply affected by this development. As Heiner Müller insisted: theater is not something that you understand in the first place. It is first of all a specific experience. Understanding, perhaps, may come later. This seems to favor B rather than B. However, the latter wrote: "The relations between human beings in our times are incomprehensible. It is the task of art to show this incomprehensibility." Yes, this is a quote from B. And if we read the short prose piece by the same B about the man who reads about Apfelböck and becomes crazy from hypertrophic meaning, and in the end runs through the streets, "psalmodierend"—we have difficulty bringing together in our mind this image of the destruction of meaning with B, the alleged teacher of rationalism. But again, we have little difficulty dreaming of a theater which would be able to play games between the serious and the artistic, between answering and the lack of answers, between commitment and fun.

Can we arrive *there*, overcoming the problem of often feeling compelled to draw a dividing line between the Bs? By now, at least, we have learned much about Brecht and Nietzsche, about Brecht and the formalist Asian theater. This should provide us with new starting points. We take into consideration that none other than Adorno called *Mahagonny* the first surrealist opera. We have had a different reading of Brecht from Heiner Müller, and we have acquired a different view of the learning plays, which long seemed to forbid any attempt to think of B and B together. Now we can see: the *Lehrstücke* intensify rational contradictions to a point where the very principle of calculating rationality—of political rationality—itself is not simply affirmed, but thoroughly and fundamentally questioned in the scenic process. Not the political mistake is on trial, but the calculation itself that may, by being too clever, miss the way out, which cannot be forseen but could happen through acts which cannot be calculated in advance, through acts that are perhaps absurd.

Hans-Thies Lehmann, Walter Asmus, and Carl Weber
Chair: Moray McGowan

"You were clever..." Fatzer says to his comrades, who gave up on him for very rational reasons: "Ihr wart recht klug/ Aber vielleicht zu klug?/ Standet ihr da und hattet eure Muskeln in der Hand?/ Solchen kann es nicht übel gehen./ So kluge Leute brauchen niemand zum Beistand./ Höchstens könnte man sagen, euch fehlte es/ (Nur um ein Geringes)/ An impulsiver Zuneigung/ Törichtem Aufbrausen/ Vielleicht hättet ihr euch durch solche/ Unbeherrschtheit hineingeritten und/ Vielleicht wärt ihr auch wieder herausgekommen/ Vielleicht durch euren/ Von soviel Zuneigung gerührten Fatzer..."

In a lecture (or better a causerie) with the title "Brecht and Beckett" in 1995, a few months before the death of Heiner Müller, Hans Mayer pointed out how much esteem Beckett had for Brecht, that he had read his plays.[4] Even if the common ground of parable (mentioned by Mayer), the common negation of a direct influence of art on society, the common *dégout* for realist illusion, in short, the common roots in modernity, are not enough for us to see them as neighbours, there is a curious closeness between them, which has still to be fully uncovered. Theodor Adorno did not really like Brecht, but if we consider the many remarks and discussions of Brecht in his *Aesthetic Theory*, we nevertheless find a constant mark of deep respect. In the last instance, however, Adorno saw in Beckett, and perhaps in him alone, the very small field left over for authentic artistic expression. Brecht, on the other hand, sinned by way of three interrelated positions—all of them deeply wrong in the eyes of Adorno: communication, didactic structure, and consciousness. Radical art must shy away from communiciation which is rotten to the core. While the plays of Beckett are closed, hermetic, and self-sufficient, Brecht's writing participates in the ideology of influencing the audience/reader. However, we may ask today, from the viewpoint of theatrical practice, if it may not be exactly these sins which suggest a future of new performance practices (in the sense of performance art or postdramatic strategies) which would then include not an alternative— B or B—but rather a space open to Brecht as well as to Beckett, provided the theater is free enough for new dealings with Plays, Endgames, Learning plays and merely "invented works" like Mahagonny.

***

---

[4]   Hans Mayer, *Beckett und Brecht. Erfahrungen und Erinnerungen. Ein Vortrag* (Berliner Ensemble Drucksache 15, 1995).

Berliner Ensemble, 1951: Proben zu *Biberpelz und Roter Hahn* von Gerhart Hauptmann. Foto: Gert Schaefer.

Carl Weber
Beckett and Brecht: Comparing their "Scenic Writing"

Brecht began to direct early in his life and later regarded none of his texts as completed until he had translated the text on the page into the text's "scenic writing" on the stage.

Beckett didn't begin to direct until late in his life, after he had been established as one of the great playwrights of his century. But then, wherever and whenever possible, he directed his own texts, which he had already inscribed with precise instructions for their scenic writing.

Some aspects B & B texts have in common:

Both Beckett and Brecht used objects or props constituting visual metaphors that embody or anchor the play's fable or meaning. For example:

Beckett:
The tree in *Godot*
The cell, wheelchair, ladder, and trash bins in *Endgame*
The table, tape deck, and banana in *Krapp's Last Tape*
The mound, parasol, purse, and cosmetic utensils in *Happy Days*
The urns in *Play*
The rocker in *Rockaby*

Brecht:
The railway canteen car in *Man Equals Man*
The boxing ring in *Little Mahagonny*
The fishing net and oven in *Senora Carrar's Rifles*
The wagon in *Mother Courage*
The telescope(s) and globe in *Galileo*
The large tables in *Puntila* (first, third last, and last scene)

Beckett liked to insert quotations from the Bible into his texts. So did Brecht, for whom the Luther Bible (and especially its language) was his favorite source text. There is, as far as I know, no other twentieth-century playwright who shared to a similar degree Brecht's and Beckett's predilection for biblical quotations.

Another, quite amusing propensity they shared was for the ditty "A dog came to the kitchen..." Beckett used it in *Waiting for Godot*, and it certainly was much liked by Brecht.

Beckett admired clowns and comedians, as did Brecht. Beckett's favorite was Buster Keaton, Brecht's Charlie Chaplin.

There is a text by Brecht that in an uncanny way anticipated Beckett's *Godot*: *Flüchtlingsgespräche*, written in 1941 in Finland.

Two characters, Kalle and Ziffel, whose relationship is comparable to Estragon's and Vladimir's in *Godot*, meet every day in the restaurant of Helsinki's railway station and ponder the ways of the world, while they keep waiting for the papers that would permit them to emigrate to a safer country. Such papers never seem to arrive.

Some preferences B & B shared as directors:

Many critics have observed—though others dispute this—that Beckett's productions had many things in common with those of Brecht:

Beckett used powerful V-effects in his texts and their staging. As, of course, did Brecht, who had theorized the V-effect and applied it—to varying degrees—throughout his directorial practice, beginning with the white-faced soldiers in the first production he staged, *Das Leben Eduard II von England*, in 1924.

Walter Asmus, Beckett's long-time assistant director, has pointed out several aspects of their work where they both employed V-effects.

About Beckett, several Berlin actors (Bernhard Minetti and Ernst Schroeder, for instance, who have both played Krapp) remarked that he had an "anti-theater" attitude. They seem to have meant his noticeable contempt for the conventional theater of the time—the 1950s and 1960s. Brecht, of course, posited his theater, from his very beginnings in the 1920s, as a project against the conventional performance practice of the German theater, even if he selectively employed some of those practices.

Beckett once remarked, in a letter to Alan Schneider, in reference to a London production of *Godot* that was mooted: "If they did it my way, they would empty the theater." This reminds us of Brecht's reported remark after the final dress rehearsal of his adaptation of *The Tutor*, the eighteenth-century play by J. M. R. Lenz: "Tomorrow the audience may very well flop."

The director Beckett frequently corrected the author B. in rehearsal, cutting and changing text. Asmus has commented: "When directing his early plays, he got rid of a lot of redundancies."

Brecht also habitually reworked his texts in rehearsal, eliminating text, sequencing lines in a different order, adding text, etc. Before a dress rehearsal, actors at the Berliner Ensemble became used to finding in their dressing room notes by Brecht that instructed them to replace a certain line with a rephrased or newly written one.

Beckett, when staging *Endgame* in Berlin, brought to rehearsal a small story book with sketches drawn by himself, as the production's assistant, Haerdter, has told us.

Brecht, of course, always asked his designers (Caspar Neher and Karl von Appen, for instance) to provide him with numerous sketches of the key moments in each scene, sketches that amounted to a play's story book, and he used them when he began staging the text. He called them "Arrangements-Skizzen," i.e. blocking sketches. For the Charles Laughton production of *Galileo* in Beverly Hills in 1947, Brecht asked an animation designer of the Disney Studio to create a story book.

Walter Asmus has commented on Beckett rehearsing: "The *movement* structure tells the *story*." (And the American director Carey Perloff pointed out: "Language and gesture are intricately related in Beckett.") That is exactly what Brecht aimed for with his "Erzählendes Arrangement," i.e. *the narrative was to be told through the blocking/choreography.*

Beckett took enormous care in rehearsal to achieve the most appropriate, "correct" position of objects, props, etc. As, for instance, with Hamm's wheelchair in *Endgame*, according to Beckett's assistant Haerdter. Brecht also paid extremely close attention to scenic detail and to the precise positioning of crucial props, for example the wagon in *Mother Courage*; the size and look of the bundle representing the baby that Grusha carries across the mountains in *The Caucasian Chalk Circle*; the number of bank notes and their slow and careful counting out when a small farmer pays his debts to another farmer in *Katzgraben*. (This play by Erwin Strittmatter was the only text dealing with contemporary life in the German Democratic Republic that Brecht staged.)

Beckett had a strong predilection for the color gray, as has often been remarked, though Walter Asmus points out that he was "very happy when color creeps in, as long as it is the right color, the true color." The same has been observed of Brecht's preference for gray. There is a remark credited to him: "All colors are fine as long as they are gray." Of course he too eventually used color, for instance in his production of *The Caucasian Chalk Circle*, where von Appen's sets and costumes employed a wide range of colors.

Beckett was deeply interested in certain painters, among them Pieter Bruegel and, as Jonathan Kalb has pointed out, Caravaggio. A painterly influence can certainly be seen in many of his stagings, especially the influence of Caravaggio in the productions Beckett directed for German television. Brecht was also a great admirer of Bruegel, as is evident from his essay on the painting *The Fall of Icarus* and its narrative aspects. The *Dulle Griet* was often mentioned by Brecht as an inspiration for the gestus of Grusha, and there were many details that offered evidence of Bruegel's influence in Brecht's staging of *The Caucasion Chalk Circle*. Walter Asmus has said that Beckett's plays are written images. One might very well describe Brecht's plays in the same way.

The insistence on directorial control which B & B shared:

The German critic Helmut Karasek once noted: "When Beckett stages Beckett, there won't be anything that is accidental. Every cross, every gesture, every pause expresses precisely what it wants to express and is supposed to express." The actor Horst Bollmann, who performed Clov for Beckett in *Endgame* and Estragon in *Waiting for Godot*, observed: "As a director, Beckett remains the controlling author of the piece, controlling dialog, rhythm, choreography, stage set, lights, costumes, props—the totality of the performance." (Bollmann also claimed, in contrast to his colleagues mentioned earlier, that Beckett loved the theater.)

Both of these statements about Beckett could literally have been made about Brecht's directing. For example, Brecht insisted on a rigid control of playing time. A three-hour performance like *Mother Courage*, for instance, that deviated by more than three minutes from the original running time was promptly checked with a stop watch so that those scenes could be spotted where additional time had crept in and where specific lapses in the actors' performance had caused this. If deemed necessary, rehearsals were scheduled to restore the original timing of the performance.

Comparable rehearsal practices of B & B:

At the beginning of rehearsal for *Endgame* at Berlin's Schiller Theater, Beckett told the actors, according to the critic Georg Hensel: "Let's *not talk about philosophy but about situations*." A similar statement could easily have been made by Brecht in rehearsal.

According to his assistant Haerdter, Beckett worked first for the accurate gestus and afterwards developed the intonation of a given text based on the gestus. For Brecht, too, the definition of a character's gestus by the actor was a priority in rehearsal.

Beckett excelled in demonstrating line-readings and the concomitant physical behavior to the actors, as Walter Asmus has frequently mentioned: "I haven't experienced one play [with Beckett directing]...where somebody wouldn't say: 'Why don't you play this part?'"

Brecht was also extremely impressive when demonstrating, though he preferred the use of gibberish when indicating tonal values and rhythms, so as to avoid the actors' parrotting his line readings. Actors, who loved to goad Brecht into demonstrating, often asked: "Couldn't you show me the way you'd like it?"

Beckett refused to discuss any psychological interpretation of their parts with the actors, as many of his collaborators have pointed out. So did Brecht, who always worked with actors toward the performance of behavior and rarely, if ever, discussed its likely psychological motivation.

Beckett: "The way it is written or said *is* the meaning. There is no meaning beyond that." (According to Walter Asmus.) This sounds like a quote of Brecht talking to his actors, something I heard him say many times.

B & B demanded that the author's performance model ought to be respected:

Beckett insisted that directors follow his precise stage directions. He tried to intervene and even stop productions where his wishes were spurned. (The most notorious example might be JoAnne Akalaitis' 1984 production of *Endgame* at the American Repertory Theater of Cambridge, Massachusetts, where she had changed Beckett's required "cell" into a wrecked New York subway station, hinting at its destruction by a nuclear war.)

Brecht rarely inscribed directions in his texts. He regarded any play as merely a tentative version until he had occasion to stage it and thus did arrive at its final definition. That is, until he did another production and redefined a text's shape and wording, as he did with *The Mother* when staging it again in 1951, nineteen years after his original production of 1932. However Brecht wanted other directors to follow the visual performance pattern he had created, which was minutely recorded in model books. On the other hand, he encouraged directors to improve on his model after they had carefully explored the model book. (Only once, in my experience, did he try to stop a production, namely Joan Littlewood's *Mother Courage*, in 1955. After its opening at Barnstaple, Devon, no permission was granted to move the production to London. One of several reasons was that Littlewood had refused to consider the model at all.)

When we compare the published *Regiebuch* of Beckett's staging of *Krapp's Last Tape* with Brecht's model books, we notice a fundamental difference. The Beckett model traces the production moment for moment, down to minute recordings of the actor Martin Held's gestures and facial expressions. (Of course, this particular play depends greatly on such performative detail.) Brecht's model books, on the other hand, present simply a sequence of key moments, "turning points" as Brecht used to call them, with a caption providing the apposite text. Nearly all the photographs, up to 600 per production, show the complete stage picture so that the blocking pattern can be ascertained clearly.

From all available evidence, Beckett appears to have been much more insistent on ultimate control of his texts in performance than Brecht was.

The fundamental difference between B & B:

In spite of the many traits of their theatrical practice that they shared, there remain, of course, profound differences between the two playwright/directors. I don't think I need to elaborate here, but let me mention one instance where their attitudes differed sharply: Brecht held that, as a playwright and director, he was obliged to enlighten his audience about their position with respect to society, and to advocate social change, i.e. the improvement of society, which, in his view, was most likely to be attained through socialism. Beckett, on the other hand, had no avowed intention to educate anyone or to change the world in the least. When the critic/scholar Katherine Worth mentioned to him that Edward Bond "wanted to change the world" with his plays, Beckett commented: "Let it turn!"

Some of the lessons we can learn from B & B:

Walter Asmus: "What I learned foremost from working with Beckett was: to strive for precision, to strive for simplicity, to encourage actors to be simple with their means, to trust simplicity, to dare not to act, to act concretely and functionally."

This was also one of the most valuable lessons I learned from working with Brecht. Others were: the importance of creating a precise and easily readable visual narrative and of defining a concrete and sharply profiled gestus of characters when working with the actors. Most of all, to strive in the scenic writing for the clearest possible articulation of the fable as it has been derived from the text.

***

Walter Asmus
B&B

There is almost nothing left to tell, to quote Beckett. We are marrying them! I get the feeling B&B are now more or less synonomous. The only thing I can do is carry on in this vein. But I can't refrain from remarking that there were times when Beckett was a *persona non grata* on one side of the world, and Bertolt Brecht had a very hard time in the 1960s on this side of the world. So there are implications which we have forgotten about more or less, or which we put totally aside, which we should at least keep in mind without moralizing. It is an irony of history that this marriage can take place, and it is an image almost of what has taken place in the world over the last twelve or thirteen years. Willy Brandt said: "What belongs together, comes together." There must be such a togetherness, which has its origin in the twentieth century.

I tried to do my homework and browsed through some of Brecht's theoretical writing, *The Short Organon* among others. And when I read that, it was a reminder of my own remarks about Beckett's directing of *Godot* in 1975. May I quote?

> "To give confusion shape," Beckett said, when he arrived in Berlin, a shape through repetition of themes, not only themes in the script, but also themes of the body. When, at the beginning, Estragon is asleep, leaning on the stone, that is a theme that repeats itself a few times. There are fixed points of waiting, where everything stands completely still, where silence threatens to swallow everything up. Then the action starts again. Stefan Wigger, who played Vladimir, said: "But in spite of everything, it is at odd moments quite a cheerful game." Beckett: "Yes, of course. But that should be done very accurately. The splitting up of Vladimir and Estragon is such a point. They are in fact inseparable." Wigger: "Like a rubber band, they come together time after time." Beckett: "The principle is they have to come together step by step." Beckett walks on the stage, his eyes fixed on the ground, and shows the movement as he speaks Estragon's lines— "You had something to say to me?...You're angry? Forgive me. Come Didi. Give me your hand." With each sentence Beckett takes a step toward the imaginary partner. Always a step, then the sentence. Beckett calls this a step-by-step approach, a physical theme which comes up five or six or seven times and has to be done very accurately always in the same way. This is the balletic side of the story. Lucky falls twice and this musn't be done realistically but very cleanly. Wigger: "Does that mean there is no natural reason left whatsoever?" Beckett demonstrates. He goes down on his knees and his arms, first upwards, then, stretching forward, lets himself slide onto the ground. Wigger: "But how can one prevent the loss of all human consideration? How can one prevent it from becoming sterile?" Beckett: "It is a game. Everything is a game. When all four of them are lying on the ground, that cannot be handled naturalistically. That has got to be done artificially, balletically. Otherwise everything becomes an imitation, an imitation of reality." Wigger: "Are you implying a certain dryness?" Beckett stands up: "It should become clear and transparent, not dry. It is a game in order to survive."

In the *Short Organon for the Theatre* Brecht remarks:

> The most important thing in the theatre is the "Fabel" [the story], that is to say, the overall composition of all gestural events, which contain the communications and impulses that are meant to contribute to the pleasure of the audience. Every single event has a basic gesture...In blocking the characters on the stage and in the movement of the groups, the necessary beauty has to be achieved through the elegance with which the gestural material is presented...Since the audience is not invited to throw itself into the fable as into a river, to be carried hither and thither, the separate events have to be joined in a way that draws attention to the links. The events must not follow each other unnoticed, but in a way that allows us to interpose our judgment...The single parts of the fable have to be carefully placed against each other in order to give them their own structure as parts within the whole play. (GBA 23, 92)

Both Beckett and Brecht tried to leave generations after them a guide to their work by directing themselves in model productions: Brecht in his model books, Beckett in detailed production notebooks. Brecht was often misunderstood because of his theoretical writings on theater and acting, and especially in letters in which people agreed with his theories as far as the artistic side was concerned. He said: "I feel like a mathematician, who gets a letter saying, I quite agree with you that 2 by 2 is 5." He went on: "I cannot refrain from giving insight to the reader or spectator into my techniques, and they take revenge. I am a sinner at least in theory against the old rule, one of my favourite by the way, 'the proof of the pudding is in the eating'." Beckett couldn't have agreed more. And to one other conclusion of Brecht's, Beckett might have agreed: "The lightest way of existence is in art."

***

Discussion

Moray McGowan: I am struck in all the presentations by this tension between the whole question of the crisis of the subject and these writers, who as directors knew exactly what they wanted, and who had both a very strong authorial presence and authorial intention in the work. I wonder if you want to comment.

Carl Weber: I read an interview where you, Walter Asmus, said that one of Beckett's remarks was that the movement structure tells the story. This has something to do with what Brecht called *erzählendes Arrangement*, which means narrative blocking. As I mentioned, the sketches were done by his designers, but in the beginning of that process. Then he spent an enormous amount of time refiguring scenes and moving objects around, which I believe Beckett did too, by ten or even five centimeters, only to decide: no, that's not right. And then it was moved in the other direction another ten centimeters, until finally the right position was arrived at, in the context, of course, of the movement pattern the actors created on stage. When I first came to Berlin, even before I had a chance of working in the *Ensemble*, I talked to a designer at the *Deutsches Theater*, at the time when Brecht and Neher were rehearsing *Puntila*. And Kilger, who found this excessive, told me that one day they stopped rehearsal for two and a half hours just to figure out which of twenty-five or more chairs would be the right one for Puntila to sit on as the last scene of the play begins. The actor had to try out all these chairs. After two and a half hours they felt that none of them would do, and said: "Let's get another thirty chairs tomorrow. If necessary, we can then start again and try out some more." Such was the precision in the visual composition of scenes they were aiming for in rehearsal. Not only how the chair looked, or where it was positioned, but also, what it did to how the actor could sit on it, how he could get up from it. A difference of one half of a centimeter was decisive in their opinion. Very often Brecht had chairs cut that much [*shows a short length*], and then tried them again, and then cut a little more, and then again, and would finally say: "Well that's all right, now the actor can work with that chair."

Walter Asmus: But with an empty stage it is essential to work out precisely where the tree has to stand, to see the rectangle. Beckett makes it a theme in *Endgame*, after the tour around the world. Clov puts the chair in the center and Hamm says, it's not in the center, bang in the center. And this fight starts between the two of them about precision and being in the center.

Hans-Thies Lehmann: I would like to add a comment. If we look at theater practice nowadays, we could perhaps say that the *empty* stage is, so to speak, a transient point to *no* stage. There's one remark, where Brecht really says—it's rarely quoted—that the way of acting he is trying to develop is, so to speak, a colloquium of the actors with the audience. That is quite extreme. It would be a point of discussion between the model character of Beckett's and of Brecht's directing. There is also the problem that Brecht was thinking of a theater that would go beyond all conventional limits, for example in *Fatzer*, to a point where he could not even create, as in *The Measures Taken*, a play out of it. It drew apart into chapters. He wrote commentaries and the like. You have the feeling in 1929 and 1930 that he was at the point of thinking a theater which, not only as "*Thaeter,*" we would not be able to call theater anymore, that the whole intention of the theater would have to be transformed into something somehow in between celebration, discussion, communication, demonstration, and fiction. As a director, also by the way as the person commenting on theater, he was in a lifelong situation of compromise. I think it is very important— Carl, you always insisted on this—not to read Brecht as an authority on Brecht. Because most of his commentaries on the theater are just notes for himself, and were to be continued later. They were always written in a pragmatic situation. I think we have to go back to the extremes of Brecht's thinking on theater, to find the meeting point with this extreme other that Beckett was. Let us take, for example, the poems of Beckett, or his *Textes pour rien*, these were somehow where the power of language to articulate a "self" reaches a vanishing point. We find also in Beckett this empty stage, this moment of a theater that tends to disappear, a kind of silent communication, of gesture beyond what can be put into words. I think it is important and not contradictory to say that Brecht is a model, perhaps I should not use so strong a word, but his texts, like Heiner Müller's, are much more radical and point to a possible future of theater practice in terms of performance, also in terms of text, if you think of contemporary authors like Sarah Kane. We could have a long discussion whether this is more Beckettian or more Brechtian.

Carl Weber: I agree with you. The one great difference between them was that Beckett, finally, when he began to direct in Berlin and eventually in Stuttgart, for televsion, was in the enviable position of not having to compromise any more. Brecht *never* in his life could *ever* stage *anything* which was not a compromise. Be it in the 1920s in the regular, normal, conventional German state theater system, when he directed *Man is Man* and *Edward II*, or later, of course, on the few occasions he had a chance at all to direct in exile, *Galileo* with Laughton, of course a compromise to make it possible for Broadway. And then in East Berlin he had a constant fight with the authorities about his aesthetics. All his productions were compromises. He tried to get through as much as he could without provoking closure. It was always threatened. And it happened, with *Urfaust*, for instance, the most famous example.

Walter Asmus: I would go further. I think Beckett had to compromise.

Carl Weber: He did? OK!

Walter Asmus: Yes, of course, Beckett had to compromise. Not as an everyday director. He was very privileged. But Beckett himself compromised in a clearly visible way, especially during television and film. There's this terrible thing. You go home and have it in the can, and you can't change anything any more. Theater rehearsals are heaven compared to that. You go back next day and say: "Oh there's a mistake, can't we try it this way?" Which he did, by the way, though he had a very clear conception of his directing and so on. But in television he had to compromise as far as details are concerned, and he was absolute in his dissatisfaction. You could feel that. He would never say it, but you could feel it. By sitting next to him in the canteen, you knew what was going on inside him.

Carl Weber: Brecht, of course, probably for the same reason, never wanted to do film, except in his very young years, when film seemed to be good business. You know, when he did the famous film with Valentin. Later he was not really interested in doing film. And one of the things, I think, was exactly that: he felt the technical apparatus was so dominant that, although he does in a certain way have complete control, which Beckett had of course for his television productions, when it's done, it's done. And there is no way to improve it any more, whereas on stage you always can. On the other hand, Brecht had the other dissatisfaction or frustration with stage productions: that actors changed, of course, from performance to performance, which I think is wonderful. But Brecht wasn't absolutely convinced of that. He felt they should be able to repeat as closely as possible the once set pattern, which is very different from what Heiner Müller wanted from performance.

Moray McGowan: There's a question from the audience.

Question: This morning we were told that both men had tangled roots, and also that Beckett tried to give confusion shape. I wonder if the panel can see a relationship between their notional states and their obsession with detail and also with the precision in which they steeped their work.

Walter Asmus: There are experiences during rehearsals. I think Beckett had to be cheated by the actors to a certain extent. He told them exactly what to do, the blocking and all the props and everything, the line readings and so on, but he knew exactly: everything had to be filled. There is, for example, in *Waiting for Godot* a scene where they fight about the two thieves, a very fierce dialog. It's very, very fast and when actors do it in rehearsals, it tends to become very mechanical, because they want to be fast, they have been told it must be very fast, and it must go on and on and on, very mechanically. But the moment when it is filled by the actors, and they are really in it with their hearts, and feelings, and bodies, Beckett would sit there like a schoolboy in the first row and watch them. It was like a game between two boys, and he was enchanted. He was really moved and touched by that. There's a difference, and it must have been similar with Brecht, between the man and the director, the writer, the artist. I experienced a situation where somebody played Lucky, a young man from Chicago, and he did everything precisely to the spot in Lucky's monologue. But he was there with his heart and his soul, and Beckett sat for at least two minutes, *stunned*. I was sitting next to him. He didn't speak. I don't know, I didn't dare to turn around, whether he was about to cry or not. Perhaps this answers some of your question.

Carl Weber: To add something in answer to the question, I don't remember that Brecht brought personal feelings into rehearsal. There were moments when certain events happened in rehearsal, which provoked his anger or his frustration. And then he could blow up. He was notorious for screaming at times, at technicians for instance, or at actors who were sloppy. It was the prevailing mode of directing in Germany in those days. Directors shouted and bullied actors. That's how it was in the early 1950s. Fehling, for instance, a great director, was a model of that. Sometimes Brecht could explode. But usually it was a kind of acted explosion. He directed his anger at a particular person—let's say a technician who made a stupid blunder in carrying on a piece of furniture in a scene change—and he shouted at him for five minutes. Then he smiled and looked at us, and said: "Well I hope he learned his lesson." It was a created performance of anger. On the other hand, regarding what Walter said about Beckett's loving actors, if they really did something wonderful, Brecht really loved actors. And actors adored him for that, of course. That was why actors were extremely devoted to him and to his work. He could listen to actors sometimes for minutes and minutes when they said not very intelligent things about their role, just to find out what they were aiming at. Usually, however, if an actor said: "Well, Brecht, don't you think at this moment, this character would do this or that," he said: "Show me. Don't tell me. Show me." So he always encouraged actors to act out what they wanted to tell him, to demonstrate what they meant about a particular moment in a scene. I remember the very first time I saw Brecht rehearsing. I was already hired by the Ensemble but not yet in the company. I asked Weigel if I could watch a rehearsal, and she said, of course you can, everybody can, if there's a reason. So I went to a rehearsal for *Urfaust*. They were rehearsing the scene in

Auerbach's Keller, the drinking scene of students in Leipzig, when Faust and Mephisto enter, and Mephisto tries to entertain Faust by making him part of this drunken group of students. Brecht was sitting there in his armchair, and four actors were on stage trying to fall off the table. For nearly two hours. Always in a different fashion, and Brecht was laughing and amusing himself. And I really thought: they are on a break. This is just horseplay. Then I realized, no, this was rehearsal! What he tried to find was, as you said about Didi and Gogo falling in *Godot*, the most precise, the most effective, the best possible way to show this drunken behaviour of these students in Leipzig. So every actor tried at least fifteen to twenty different ways of falling off a table. Until they finally arrived at the solution they felt was possibly the best, and Brecht agreed to it and said, that's how we should do it. There was an endless playfulness in Brecht's rehearsals. That's one of the great things I remember about Brecht rehearsing. It was always playful. And the moment in rehearsal when it stopped being playful, and became tedious or laborious, he stopped and went to another scene, because he felt the atmosphere for rehearsal had become sterile.

Question: My question is directed towards Hans-Thiess Lehmann and your point about the actors and the audience as a colloquium. In a play like *The Good Person of Szechwan*, the issue that emerges can't be resolved by the actors. They play it out for the audience. Do you see any relationship between such ideas of Brecht and the work of Augusto Boal?

Hans-Thies Lehmann: Yes, certainly. I would like to continue your point. For me it is not so much this seeming, only apparent openness of the discussion at the end of the play: "Es muß ein guter Schluß gefunden werden, muß, muß, muß." I would say that is only the compromise again. What I'm thinking of is the tendency Brecht had to create, as in the Learning Plays, a kind of structure—not for audiences, but as a practice of gesture—which would develop into something different from the theater of fiction in general, an effort which he could not pursue. It is interesting to compare this with the tendency of performance. Such an attempt was, of course, neither institutionally nor politically possible. But it is, I think, the most creative point. And there is a kind of *dépense*, how do you translate this term of Bataille, I don't know what you would say, *Verausgabung*? There is a kind of *dépense* of the theater, which starts there, that people give only in the theatrical moment. They would give a new structure to the plays, and not place first the perfection of the work. There is a nearly incredible passage in the *Fatzer*—I cannot quote by heart, it is very important—where it says more or less: now look to the story, we have set up everything—"Ihr aber seht jetzt das Ganze. Wir haben es aufgestellt/ In der Zeit nach genauer Folge"—and with the exact words, so that *you*, the audience, by speaking the chorus, and by listening to the words, you decide "was eigentlich los war"—you decide what really happened, or what did not fit together, because we were divided. We didn't know: "denn/ Wir waren uneinig." So there is the point, in the context of *Fatzer*, where it happens only in the moment, let's say, of discussion, of filling in new material in a structure, or in a field of words and sentences, of gestures, where the theater begins and the meaning comes. And this is something which I want to relate very closely to the movement in the Beckett texts, following the meaning slowly, very slowly, which, as you reach for it, is still retreating to a point where the human beings, the audience and the actors, the performers, meet in the common need to produce the ephemeral, momentary meaning, and not to receive any meaning whatsoever constructed by an author or director. This is why I refer to these recent philosophical notions of the political, because this is what I find important. We did not talk much about it, except for what you said, Walter Asmus, about the two worlds. And since then we have lost something of the political, the *polis*-dimension of the theater. I think the only thing we should have to reflect upon in talking about Beckett and Brecht is how to gain back this polis-dimension of theatrical practice in a media situation, with and against the media. There I would see a starting point.

Carl Weber: I would like to pick up on one thing, since you mentioned it in an interview you gave, Walter, where you said Beckett said, maybe you paraphrased: "The way it is written is the meaning. There is no meaning beyond that." Again that could be a quote by Brecht, absolutely literally. He said quite similar things quite often in rehearsals, when actors began to ask about subtexts, and motivations, and psychology, in the same way that Beckett always refused to talk about psychology.

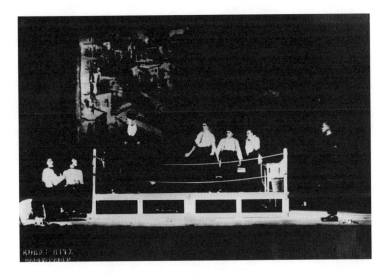

Das kleine Mahagonny, Baden-Baden, 1927. Probenfoto mit Bertolt
Brecht und Lotte Lenya. Brecht-Archiv.

Unter den sich verdunkelnden Schatten: das Beckettsche Moment(um) und die Brechtsche Verzögerung

Despite the dramaturgical gap between a critical arrest in the service of "Verfremdung" and somatic immersion in the "science of affliction," there are affinities between Brecht and Beckett, in the act of perception itself, or in the subject of thought. As for the efficacy of the A-effect, aiming to dispel illusion by turning the theater against itself, what we encounter in Brecht as in Beckett, all the texts for nothing, the nothing to be done, is that it may only be an illusion but—"this...this...thing," the unnamable thing itself—there appears no end to that.

Trotz der dramaturgischen Distanz zwischen einer kritischen Verzögerung im Dienste der "Verfremdung" und somatischer Versenkung in der "Wissenschaft des Schmerzens" gibt es Affinitäten zwischen Brecht und Beckett, im Akt der Wahrnehmung selbst bzw. im Objekt des Denkens. Was die Wirksamkeit des V-Effekts anbelangt, das die Illusion verscheuchen will, indem es das Theater gegen sich selbst wendet, begegnet uns sowohl bei Brecht als auch bei Beckett, alle Texte für nichts, das Nichts, das gemacht werden kann, und zwar mag es nur eine Illusion sein, aber—"dieses...dieses...Ding," das unnennbare Ding selbst—davon gibt es anscheinend kein Ende.

Among the Deepening Shades: The Beckettian Moment(um) and the Brechtian Arrest

Herbert Blau

I t may not be, as Nietzsche said in *The Birth of Tragedy*, that illusion as the "reflection of eternal contradiction, begetter of all things," will lead to "a radiant vision of pure delight, a rapt seeing through wide-open eyes."[1] But if, as Freud thought, illusion has a future, with civilization and its discontents, it must surely include certain illusions about illusion and the means by which it is produced—what Brecht called the "apparatus," through which society absorbs "whatever it needs to reproduce itself," and which imposes its "views as it were incognito."[2] If one may speak not only of the illusion of reality but the reality of illusion, what shadows Brecht's critique is the question that prompted Nietzsche and has always haunted the theater—synoptically there in Beckett's *Breath*, or in the "Mere eye. No mind" of the "[*Repeat play*]" of *Play*[3]—as to whether the illusion produced is a doubled over redundancy, now you see it now you don't, mere eye insufficient, whether dazzled or baffled, distracted by the gaze, in a world made out of illusion.

The canonical drama dwells on that, and despite the deconstruction that was—after the Berliner Ensemble came to Paris in 1954, shortly after the appearance of *Waiting for Godot*—a partial outgrowth of Brechtian alienation, there is a residue in our thought of the resonance of illusion: all the world's a stage, life is a dream, the insubstantial pageant fading . . . into the "precession of simulacra," as Jean Baudrillard would say, when he announced the end of the real,[4] or into the Society of the Spectacle, which, as Guy Debord had said in the wake of the sixties, "is *capital* to such a degree of accumulation that it

---

1   Friedrich Nietzsche, *The Birth of Tragedy* (and *The Genealogy of Morals*), trans. Francis Golffing (New York: Anchor/Doubleday, 1956) 33.

2   Bertolt Brecht, "The Modern Theater Is the Epic Theater," in *Brecht on Theater: The Development of an Aesthetic*, ed. and trans. John Willett (New York: Hill and Wang, 1964) 34; will be abbreviated as *BT*.

3   Samuel Beckett, *Play*, in *Collected Shorter Plays* (New York: Grove, 1984) 157, 160; will be abbreviated as *SP*.

4   Jean Baudrillard, *Simulations*, trans. Paul Foss, Paul Patton and Philip Betichman (New York: Semiotext[e], 1983) 1-79.

Where Extremes Meet: Rereading Brecht and Beckett / Begegnung der Extreme. Brecht und Beckett: Eine Re-interpretation
Stephen Brockmann et al., eds., *The Brecht Yearbook / Das Brecht-Jahrbuch*
Volume 27 (Pittsburgh: The International Brecht Society, 2002)

becomes an image."[5] Nor is that any the less illusory for being thought of as commodification in a factitious economy of invisible power. In a notorious passage of his *Short Organum* Brecht wrote scathingly of the capitulation to such power in tragic drama: to the gods who, beyond criticism, punished Oedipus, and of "Shakespeare's great solitary figures bearing on their breast the star of their fate," life becoming obscene as they collapse, "those dreamlike figures up on the stage," while the representation of their fate remains, through the "irresistible force of their futile and deadly outbursts" (*BT* 189), also beyond criticism. Despite the force of Brecht's remarks, irresistibly absorbed into an almost relentless critique of tragedy in poststructuralism, feminism, the new historicism, those dreamlike figures persist in thought, sometimes so vividly if distressingly that what we took to be illusion seems more like reality principle, with demystification itself drawn into its service.

So it was with Derrida, at the end of an essay in which he virtually identified with the ideas of Artaud, whose theater of cruelty, as the beginning of the essay insisted, "is not a *representation*. It is life itself, in the extent to which life is unrepresentable."[6] Whatever life may be or, if all the world is not a stage, however theater emerges from whatever it is it is *not*—reality? what's left of the real? what is presumably *not theater*—Derrida had to concede that "to think the closure of representation is to think the tragic: not as the representation of fate, but as the fate of representation. Its gratuitous and baseless necessity" (250). As for thinking the tragic in Beckett, or its leftover symptoms there, his solitary figures may not be great, in their futile and deadly outbursts, whether Pozzo, Hamm, or the Mouth, or without any figures at all the "recorded vagitus" of *Breath*, the two identical cries (211), but he would certainly understand the gratuitousness and the baselessness, with the declension of necessity into "Something is taking its course,"[7] instead of a star on the breast, inside the breast "a big sore" (*Endgame* 32), or something dripping in the head—"A heart, a heart in my head" (18)—or, even more alarmingly, a vagrant flea in the crotch.

If such, with painful laughter, is the Beckettian fate of representation, let us go back for a moment to commodification: while

---

[5]   Guy Debord, "Separation Perfected," in *Society of the Spectacle* (Detroit: Red and Black, 1983) item 34, n. pag.

[6]   Jacques Derrida, "The Theater of Cruelty and the Closure of Representation," in *Writing and Difference*, trans. and intro. Alan Bass (Chicago: Univ. of Chicago Press, 1978) 234.

[7]   Beckett, *Endgame* (New York: Grove, 1958) 13.

the markets are described by distinguished economists as being in an essentially unstable state of "dynamic disequilibrium," controlled if at all by an "invisible hand," the spectacle is still being rehearsed in critical theory, along with the apparatus of representation, as an "economy of death," as if, Hamletically, it were ghosting itself. Preempting the ghost was, of course, the initiating prospect of Brechtian method, by strategic repetition or quotation refiguring representation, breaking down the apparatus by turning it against itself, thus producing a dynamic disequilibrium for subversive purposes, supplanting the invisible hand with a signifying body or an acutely visible sign, the *gestus*, or what Frederic Jameson calls "a properly Brechtian materialism."[8] In a curious turn of his own, Jameson sees the source of that materialism now in the Taoism of the Chinese Brecht, and he seems to be invoking another kind of ghostliness when he says of the secular and skeptical, disruptively cynical Brecht that a "hermeneutics of suspicion" is suspended "for the metaphysics that have become impossible" (12)—by which Jameson means, in his own disappointment with the future of an illusion, the metaphysics in the teleology of Marxist utopianism. It is, to be sure, the metaphysics that have become impossible which, with a dynamic of attrition in the disequilibrium, accounts for the repetitiveness in Beckett, like a pulse of dispossession or momentum of deferral that, in the permutations of absence, seems not at all strategic, or if so, vain, ill seen ill said, which is itself a kind of ghosting, of what, not sure: "No longer anywhere to be seen. Nor by the eye of flesh nor by the other. Then as suddenly there again. Long after. So on"[9]—approaching in the warped teleology of its compulsive vanity, aphasic, unutterable, nohow on, the asymptotic mirage of whatever it is, or was, "that time you went back that last time to look,"[10] even if it wasn't, "no better than shades, no worse if it wasn't" (*That Time* 231), the impossible thing itself.

As to what you went back to look for, Brecht would agree with his friend Walter Benjamin that "nothing that has ever happened should be regarded as lost for history," but Benjamin would seem to encompass Beckett as well as Brecht when he says, in his "Theses on the Philosophy of History," that "the past can be seized only as an image which flashes up at the instant when it can be recognized and is never seen again." This is not a matter of recognizing, as in an older

---

8   Frederic Jameson, *Brecht and Method* (London/New York: Verso, 1998) 8.

9   Beckett, *Ill Seen Ill Said*, in *Nohow On: Three Novels*, intro. S. E. Gontarski (New York: Grove, 1996) 56.

10   Beckett, *That Time*, in *SP* 229.

misguided historicism, "the way it really was," but rather of taking hold of "a memory as it flashes up at a moment of danger."[11] But the danger for Beckett is that whatever flashes up is in "no time gone in no time" which recurs again and again in *That Time* (235), "from the first and last that time curled up worm in slime when they lugged you out and wiped you off" (230), without anything like the "temporal index by which," as Benjamin says in the "Theses," the past "is referred to redemption" (256). As for history, if it is not there in the "old style," as Winnie might say of the Portrait Gallery, "when was that," in *That Time*, "there before your eyes when they opened a vast oil black with age and dirt someone famous in his time," or "there in whatever thoughts you might be having whatever scenes perhaps way back in childhood or the womb worst of all or that old Chinaman long before Christ born with long white hair," then it is "just one of those things you kept making up to keep the void out just another of those old tales to keep the void from pouring in on top of you the shroud" (*That Time* 229-230). It may be that the tales, the old tales, belong to "the whore called 'Once upon a time' in historicism's bordello," as Benjamin says ("Theses" 264), but the relay of voices in *That Time*, "without solution of continuity" (227), the void pouring in, the shroud, would seem to do what he wants, and what Jameson quoting Benjamin attributes to Brecht, that is, "to blast open the continuum of history" (264). As it turns out, in a peculiar twist upon the void, nobody does that better than the shrouded Hamm—making metaphysics impossible too—when the shroud is taken off: "But what in God's name do you imagine? That the earth will awake in spring? That the rivers and seas will run with fish again? That there's manna in heaven still for imbeciles like you?" (*Endgame* 53).

We are endowed, Benjamin says, with "a *weak* Messianic power," in a "secret agreement" with the past ("Theses" 256), through which we come to the present "as the 'time of the now' . . . shot through with chips of Messianic time" (265). If there is the dying fall in Beckett that suffuses the time of the now, the vehemence, when it erupts, seems something more than weak, as when Hamm assures Clov, "*with prophetic relish,*" that he will one day go blind too: "Infinite emptiness will be all around you, all the resurrected dead of all the ages wouldn't fill it, and there you'll be like a little bit of grit in the middle of the steppe" (*Endgame* 36), which may lack the luster of a Messianic chip but has its history too. And if memory flashes up, it is

---

[11] Walter Benjamin, "Theses on the Philosophy of History," in *Iluminations*, ed. and intro. Hannah Arendt, trans. Harry Zohn (New York: Harcourt, Brace and World, 1955) 256-57.

out of the bottomless pit of an incapacity to forget, if not history, the illusory promise of myth, and so it is in the gray chamber when Clov stares at the wall. "The wall!" rages Hamm, as if he had conflated the Book of Daniel with the Platonic Cave, the archetypal site of illusion: "And what do you see on your wall? Mene, mene? Naked bodies." Clov: "I see my light dying" (12).

But speaking of danger and redemption in the light of that dying light, as if the secret agreement were being made, and made again, by those dreamlike figures on stage with what, recurrently, is a ghost of the past: "What, has this thing appeared again tonight?" What was asked on the ramparts of *Hamlet* (1.1.21)–and what I've written about before, the illusive substance of theater, which does not exist if it does not appear—became in the hollow of *Endgame*, "This . . . this . . . thing" (45), while the nothing that came of nothing in pursuit of the thing itself became the Beckettian premise: "Nothing to be done."[12] As for this too, too solid flesh—for all the talk of the body as discourse, words, words, words, the words flying up, the body remaining below, naked body, libidinal body, all the bodies that matter or, with *its* repetitive acts, the body of "performativity"[13]—if it resolves into a dew, adieu, adieu, it is born astride of a grave, the light gleaming an instant, then gone, with maybe a forlorn sense, as always in Beckett, that it might have been once or never—even when parodied, all the more poignant for that—a visionary gleam: "Look! There! All that rising corn! And there! Look! The sails of the herring fleet! All that loveliness!" (*Endgame* 44). Or so it was in Yeats, recalled in . . . *but the clouds . . .* , " when the horizon fades . . . or a bird's sleepy cry . . . among the deepening shades . . . ." Even in the measured countdown, there on the video screen—"*5 seconds. Dissolve to M. 5 seconds. Fade out on M. Dark. 5 seconds*" (*SP* 262)—we are still the stuff of dreams, rounded to a sleep, though if dreams are wish fulfillment they may not feel as we wish, no more than the begged appearance, "a begging of the mind, to her, to appear, to me," by the voice in the "little sanctum" of the figure with "robe and skull," and the sleep may be dubious too, begging there in vain, "deep down into the dead of night," alienated in being, whether awake or asleep, and—even with "break of day, to issue forth again" (260-01), voiding the little sanctum—can we be sure of that?

---

12   Beckett, Waiting for Godot (New York: Grove, 1954) 7.

13   See Judith Butler, *Bodies That Matter: On the Discursive Limits of "Sex"* (New York/London: Routledge, 1993) 9, 12.

Meanwhile, the question of vision persists through the eternal contradiction which is—even with eyes wide open in the dispensation of the gaze—more like a failure of the begetting in some perversion of sight. Thus it is with the woman in *Rockaby*, "famished eyes / like hers / to see / be seen" (*SP* 279), among the "successive fades" which have replaced the deepening shades—"jet sequins to glitter when rocking" and pale wood "polished to gleam"(273)—saying to herself when being rocked, or in that othered, recorded voice, "time she stopped / *time she stopped*" (277) till "the day came / in the end came" (278) and "dead one night / in the rocker" and the rocker "rocking away" (280)—like O rocks in *Film*, cringing "away from perceivedness" (*SP* 168) but not immune to the gaze—"fuck life / stop her eyes / rock her off / rock her off," but even through the ending echo "coming to rest of rock" (*Rockaby* 282), something is stirring still, what, or what where, not sure, since it seems to escape perceivedness—and in all the texts for nothing, by whatever number or name, it may only be an illusion but there appears no end to that.

Nor to the various ways we think about it.   If illusion commingles with faith and, to all appearances, may be thought of as fantasy too, it may also be, as in Brecht's *Galileo*, with history taking its time, "consciousness impatient for truth," as Althusser said in an essay on the Piccolo Teatro and Brecht.   Or it may be "the image of a consciousness of a self living the totality of its world in the transparency of its own myths."[14] As a function or necessity of the political, illusion may be social construction or what, without knowing it, in the ether of ideology, we have somehow come to believe. And while it is this, of course, that would seem most germane to Brecht—whose "principal aim," as stated by Althusser, "is to produce a critique of the spontaneous ideology in which men live" (144)—it is not quite where we will see certain affinities with Beckett. That is more likely to occur with various degrees of subjectivity in the act of perception itself, despite the dramaturgical gap between a critical arrest in the service of *Verfremdung* and somatic immersion in the "science of affliction," where—as Beckett said in his essay on Proust, a proleptic definition of what infected his own thought—"the poisonous ingenuity of Time" subjects the individual to a "constant process of decantation,"which leaves it "innocuous, amorphous, without character."[15]

---

[14]   Louis Althusser, *For Marx*, trans. Ben Brewster (London: Verso/NLB, 1982) 144.

[15]   Beckett, *Proust* (New York: Grove, n.d.) 4-5.

Yet, while Brecht moved from the deobjectified characters of his early plays to those in a more gestic solid state, we have to deal in his work, as we do more egregiously in Beckett, with the perceptual status or analytics of the performative body, from Galy Gay as a human fighting machine to Dumb Kattrin's blinded eye, eye of flesh, eye of prey, to the predatory presence of the Inquisitor, alone, silent, stately, incising an empty stage, bringing to Galileo the liabilities of perceivedness, as with the swiveling light on the bodiless heads in the funeral urns of *Play*.

There are characters in Brecht who, like Anna Fierling, never miss a trick but fail to see, though we are likely to find little in Brecht that, like Beckett's body parts or absent bodies, severely abstracting or disfiguring space, not only direct but demoralize, even stigmatize perception, in the stigma directing it even more: Winnie, up to her diddies in the mound; a back, a bare foot, an arm, or even the "trace of a face";[16] or, with "head bowed, grey hair," the dreamer of *Nacht und Träume* and, with the dreamt self, dreamt hands, palm upward, joined, gentle, those dreamt commiserable hands, not like those in *Catastrophe,* with "fibrous degeneration" (298), crippled to begin with and, speaking of a Brechtian *gestus*, made to look like claws. If that suggests, affect aside, or because of it, that there's a chastening semiology in Beckett, it is not quite, even in *Catastrophe* (dedicated to the imprisoned Havel), like Brecht's pointing toward the action not-done through the action that *is*, deciphering and exposing social cause. Yet it is possible to see in *Catastrophe*—its exposure of the production apparatus, the director's tyranny and the assistant's servility, what is pernicious and vitiating in the constructed mise-en-scène—a more virulent critique of the theater itself than almost anything staged in Brecht.

Meanwhile, if there is the "agony of perceivedness" (*Film* 165) there is the wanting to be seen, or in the inquisitional light of *Play* something equivocal about that: "Am I as much as . . . being seen?" With a slightest shift of accent (being *seen, being* seen) the issue of recognition passes into the notion that, however unnerving it may be, "mere eye," just the gaze, to be looked at—"Just looking. At my face. On and off" (157)—there is no being at all, nothing like identity, without being seen. Which is what Didi conveys when he advances on the Boy from Godot and says, "(*With sudden violence.*) You're sure you saw me, you won't come and tell me tomorrow that you never saw me!" (59). Here, through the stasis of the waiting, dispossession, desperate, is speaking for itself, as P in *Catastrophe* does at the end,

---

16   Beckett, *Catastrophe,* in *SP 299.*

however minimally, when he raises his head and confronts the audience with more than a trace of a face. Which is something else again than the willing anonymity of the agitators in Brecht's *The Measures Taken,* who "must not be seen," blotting out their faces on behalf of the oppressed workers of Mukden, "To win the victory / But conceal the victor. . . ."[17] This is the problematic context in which the Young Comrade, who puts "his feelings above his understanding" (87) and, taking the revolution upon himself, tears off his mask, revealing his "naked face, human, open, guileless" (102), before capitulating to the will of the Party, accepting the measures to be taken, extreme as they are, letting himself be shot and thrown into the lime pit.

The play has been attacked as an anticipatory defense of Stalin's purge trials and, despite the animus of Brecht's critique, defended as tragic drama, and its dialectic is such that, were it to be rethought today in rehearsal, as the *Lehrstücke* were in theory meant to be, we might theorize alternatives to the Young Comrade's chilling sacrifice. This is, of course, an extremity to which Brecht himself was never quite submitted, in his more agile and cryptic dissidence in East Berlin, nor in his cautious debates with Lukács about the proprieties of socialist realism. Yet he considered the play absolutely central to what he was attempting in the theater, and it remains a temporal index of a question persisting through his work, as to how much subjectivity not only the revolution can allow, but also the epic theater, as it sublimated, say, the unappeasable appetites and narcissism of Baal, the utterly carnal version of the Canaanite fertility god, seen in cosmic scale in the opening Grand Chorale, as if he were the eroticized avatar of illusion itself. Grown in "his mother's womb so white"—and so primal, ecstatic, synesthetic, he seemed like the sky itself, "Naked, young and hugely marvelous"—Baal comes into being as something more than a subject, or less, with the voracious innocence and assurance of the modernist criminal/saint: "Baal will drag his whole sky down below,"[18] as if, incestuously, the Great Mother imaged there, he would seduce the universe itself.

When he does seduce a young woman, who drowns herself in shame, he sings a song—with another sort of detachment, not yet of the A-effect—about her slow descent: "The opal sky shone most magnificent," but as the song continues we get the nether side of Baal,

---

[17]   Brecht, *The Measures Taken,* in *The Jewish Wife and Other Short Plays,* trans. Eric Bentley (New York: Grove, 1965) 81, 83.

[18]   Brecht, *Baal,* trans. William E. Smith and Ralph Manheim, *Collected Plays, Volume 1,* ed. Manheim and John Willett (New York: Vintage, 1971) 3; these editions will be abbreviated as *CP,* with volume number.

who could be embraced by beauty itself, all that loveliness! and, as if longing for desecration, never leave it at that. As she floats downstream like Ophelia, there are no transfiguring garlands, no willows askant the brook, only "wrack and seaweed" clinging, with creatures and other growths, to the forlorn body that rots—as Baal's does eventually too—and he seems to relish that: "I see the world in a gentle light; it's the good Lord's excrement" (*CP 1*: 46). If that, for Yeats, is where love has pitched his mansion, it is also not far from Beckett, nor is Gougou far from Gogo, but with "a cold in the lungs," in the scene at the abysmal bar, the mordancy takes over in a tone resembling Hamm's. "A slight inflammation. Nothing serious." And when Baal says of the past that it seems a strange word, Gougou ignores the notion of any secret agreement, of which, according to Benjamin, the historical materialist is aware. "Best of all is nothingness. . . . Yes, that's paradise. No more unfulfilled desires. All gone. You get over all your habits. Even the habits of desire." And when the beggar woman Maja—with a child in a crate, about as promising as the boy out the window in *Endgame*—asks, "And what happens at the end?" Gougou says, grinning, "Nothing. Nothing at all. The end never comes. Nothing lasts forever. . . . " It is here, momentarily, that Baal seems to take a position like that of the later Brecht, or a parody of him, as he rises in drunken indignation, or a mockery of it: "The worms are swelling. Crawling decomposition. The worms are glorifying themselves. . . . Bag-of-Worms, that's your name," he says to Gougou (43-44).

As it happens, "crawling decomposition"—like the disjunct narrative of the man crawling on his belly in *Endgame*, and not only him, but "the place was crawling with them!" (68)—would seem to be a fair description of the momentum of Beckett's aesthetic, though the crawling accelerates from the muck in the waiting or the mud of *How It Is* to the "lifelong mess" of *That Time* (230), with its curled up worm in slime, or the vertiginous "out" of *Not I*, not merely decomposition, "but the brain— . . . what?" (217) and the body with it, never mind desire, "whole body like gone . . . just the mouth . . . lips . . . cheeks . . . jaws . . . never– . . . what? . . . tongue?" (*SP* 220), torn between screaming and silence, "crawl back in," and then through all the buzzing, "godforsaken hole . . . no love . . . spared that" (222), until the wished-for end, "God is love . . . tender mercies," bag of worms aside, "back in the field . . .April morning . . . face in the grass . . . nothing but the larks . . . pick it up—" (222-23). If the larks are not exactly, though "God is love," singing hymns at heaven's gate, the entreaty to pick it up may suggest the final scene of *The Good Person of Szechwan* when Shui Ta/Shen Te, who has been washed in gutter water and also known the muck, entreats the Enlightened Ones to stay, though the gods—having had enough of how it is, which is how it is going to be—fly homeward to their own nothingness, leaving the tender mercies to the audience, to whom the epilogue is addressed: "That you yourselves should ponder till you find / The ways and means and measures tending / To help good people to a happy ending" (*CP* 6: 104). Which—lips, cheeks, jaw . . . never— . . . what?—sounds like tongue in cheek.

It would certainly make Gougou laugh, or Garga of *In the Jungle of Cities*, who says, "We thought the planet would change course on our account. But what happened? Three times it rained, and one night the wind blew."[19] As for Baal, who is at the end the stinking image of crawling decomposition, Brecht apparently did not entirely realize that almost everything about him, when the play was first done, would be seen as politically incorrect. But some years later, reviewing his early work, he took note of the criticism: "*Baal* is a play which could present all kinds of difficulties to those who have not learned to think dialectically. No doubt they will see it as a glorification of unrelieved egotism and nothing more."[20] If the dialectic seems a little devious, given the antisocial nature of Baal, he remains through Brecht's reassessment a virtual prototype of the lifestyle social protest, not unideological but at the extremity of it all, that we encountered in the sixties, when the apparently apolitical waiting for Godot could be taken as a model of passive resistance—as it was in San Francisco when I first directed the play, in 1957, the same year I staged the first American production of Brecht's *Mother Courage*. As I have pointed out before, it was *Waiting for Godot* that turned out to be, against the grain of the political left, or—to use Benjamin's phrase from the "Theses"—"brush[ing] history against the grain" (259), the most influential play, politically, of that period,[21] taken up then by the left, which was ready to dismiss it as avant-garde indulgence. We did not do *Baal*, but we should have, because—despite its apparent misogyny—it opened up ideas of sexuality that, as Sue-Ellen Case pointed out in the eighties,[22] we are still coming to terms with now. If the Young Comrade is his dialectical opposite, Baal remains a model of a polymorphous perverse spirit taking the pleasure principle to the

---

[19] Brecht, *In the Jungle of Cities*, trans. Gerhard Nellhaus, in *CP* 1: 158.

[20] Brecht, "On Looking Through My First Plays [ii]," in *CP* 1: 345.

[21] See, for instance, the preface to my *Sails of the Herring Fleet: Essays on Beckett* (Ann Arbor: Univ. of Michigan Press, 2000) 4-5.

[22] Sue-Ellen Case, "Brecht and Women: Homosexuality and the Mother," *The Brecht Yearbook* 12 (1983): 65-74.

threshold of exhaustion, where reality kicks in like the woodcutters going out, suggesting as they go a little *Verfremdung*: "Try to look at things more objectively. Tell yourself that a rat is dying. See? Just don't make a fuss. You have no teeth left." And then, as one man leans down to spit in Baal's face, another gives an additional piece of advice: "Try to schedule your stinking tomorrow" (*CP 1*: 55-56).

Yet, if Baal is omnivorous about his living he is about dying as well. And if the anarchic nature of his corporeally indulgent body had to be curbed to the ideological policy of the later plays, it is not entirely extruded, for as even one of the woodcutters had to concede: "He drank like a sponge, but there's something about that pale lump of fat that makes a man think" (56). Which is about as good as you're going to get in defining the materiality of the A-effect, its arresting substance (which is what Joseph Beuys understood when he picked up the fat and used it, conceptually, in his estranging installations). One may ask: where does Baal, however surreptitiously, make his appearance in this or that play, as with the Priapic figure in the garden in Galileo's meeting with the Little Monk, and when does he disappear, as Azdak does (rather like Falstaff in *Henry IV, Part II*) when a more rational order needs stabilizing toward the end of *The Caucasian Chalk Circle*? To the degree that his science is self-indulgence, an appetite, insatiable, Galileo is eventually excoriated. It is as if Baal represents, too, at another level the murky intuitive process which, as Brecht says in his essay on Chinese acting, commenting on Stanislavski, "takes place in the subconscious." This may be where it should be in what we call Method acting, but the subconscious, Brecht adds, "is not at all responsive to guidance; it has as it were a bad memory" (*BT* 94).

In a sense, then, Brecht struggled throughout his career with techniques for managing or disposing of Baal, though killing him off was itself a dangerous project: "Sometimes Baal plays dead. The vultures swoop. / Baal, without a word, will dine on vulture soup" (*CP 1*: 4). If there is nothing so cunningly lethal in Beckett, his plays and short prose, as if with a failure of memory, appear to be taking place at some level of the psyche below the subconscious, though we may have to remember that the forgetting as it turns up in the *un*conscious is, as Freud remarked, the deepest form of memory. As for Brecht in the period of *Baal*, and *In the Jungle of Cities*, it may be the wrong word, but a sort of faith accompanied his cynicism, or to use President George W. Bush's phrase, a "faith-based initiative," as when Shlink urges Garga not to quit because, speaking of things below, "the forests have been cut down, the vultures are glutted, and the golden answer will be buried deep in the ground" (*Jungle* 160). But then he may be speaking, too, in the Chicago setting of that play, of environmental depredations, corporate profits, and like President Bush today, reserves of oil in the ground.

In what would seem another definition of the Brechtian *gestus*, "a configuration pregnant with tensions" (or what Roland Barthes, writing of Brecht, calls "the pregnant moment"), Benjamin remarks that "thinking involves not only the flow of thoughts, but their arrest as well," giving the "configuration a shock, by which it crystallizes into a monad" ("Theses" 264-65). That figure is, however, in the allure of its crystallization, better suited, perhaps, to the Imagism of H. D. and Ezra Pound or, epiphanically, certain ideographic moments in the poems of T. S. Eliot. But if, as Eliot once said, as a virtual preface to the writing of Beckett (who was not at all indifferent to Eliot), words slip, slide, decay with imprecision, will not hold still, the monad is always threatened, which Brecht (whose early work, we forget, emerged into modernism with Eliot's) certainly understood. The trouble with thinking, always—to cite that dreamlike figure again, who is if anything pregnant with tensions—is that there is nothing either good or bad but thinking makes it so. If, then, the complex pedagogy of *The Measures Taken*, its painful dialectic or unbearable lesson, is characterized by the oxymoron of an ambiguous didacticism, the apparent nihilism of *Baal*, its sheer perversity, is eventually relinquished in the desire for a supportable pedagogy, which is not so much what Brecht wants us to think but rather the method by which he causes us to think.

Speaking of a certain calculated unreality, like a dead man singing, in the manifestation of a *gestus*, Brecht remarks in a footnote what we have come to expect, that this does not preclude an element of instruction, though the irrationality or even seeming lack of seriousness contributes to the gestic content which registers and defines the theatrical moment as meaning, though with the metaphysics at bay the meaning may be provisional. In Beckett, of course, with a seeming lack of seriousness the impossible and the provisional are maneuvered into a laugh: "We're not beginning to . . . to . . . mean something?" But before Hamm says "(*Vehemently*.) To think perhaps it won't all have been for nothing!" he pauses to wonder, "Imagine if a rational being came back to earth, wouldn't he be liable to get ideas into his head if he observed us long enough" (*Endgame* 32-33). And whatever he says to mock it, if you did not get ideas, a myriad of ideas—as in the circuitous, self-cancelling, tortuous thinking of thought that Beckett calls the *pensum*—you must be out of your head. And the ideas, moreover, if you observed them long enough, that is, as they occur in performance, whatever the nothing done, arise from a certain ordering of perception that corresponds to an issue further defined by Brecht, still resisting illusion in the apparatus of representation. Yet, though he might put it another way, it is as if he agreed with Eliot's remark that, confronted as we are by the indeterminacies of the modern and a culture of disbelief, what we need to do is improve the quality of our illusions.   Among which is the possibility entertained by Beckett, despite and by means of the derision of Clov, that we do "Mean something! You and I, mean something!" (33). As for the theater, what makes it mean something is, if by nothing more than intelligence (which was at a premium in the American theater when they first came on the scene), shared by Beckett and Brecht.

If in the culinary theater, as Brecht describes it in the *Short Organum*, the eyes wide open may signify a trance, as with the sleepers of the house who stare but do not see, the eye which observes long enough, "which looks for the *gest* in everything is the moral sense."[23] Yet, if what Brecht is seeking is a moral tableau, as Diderot might have defined it (what Barthes later admired), it is not without an element of subjectivity, as when, suspended in the gaze, Galileo studies the moons of Jupiter or when, with voracious appetite and inarguable passion, he says he believes in the brain. If Beckett had any affectation it was the habit of denying its importance, but he also had quite a brain, and considerable erudition. Yet if in the elemental substance of his obsessive subjectivity—the subject seeking its subject in the regressive desperation of a never-ending quest—there is the *risus purus*, the laugh laughing at the laugh at anything like a moral sense, he is by no means without that either. And while there would seem to be a world of difference, though the actions in each instance are similarly unmomentous, between Mother Courage closing her pocketbook on the life of her son and Gogo pulling at his boot or Didi's buttoning his fly or Gogo later leaving his boots neatly at the edge of the stage, for another who may come, "just as . . . as . . . as me, but with smaller feet," he gives to that *gestus* or tableau the perhaps pathetic irony of a not unmoral sense, even through what may seem to be the burlesqued jaundice of the following exchange, about the boots being left behind:

VLADIMIR.	But you can't go barefoot.
ESTRAGON.	Christ did.
VLADIMIR.	Christ! What has Christ got to do with it? You're not going to compare yourself to Christ!
ESTRAGON.	All my life I've compared myself to him.
VLADIMIR.	But where he lived it was warm, it was dry!
ESTRAGON.	Yes. And they crucified quick.

---

[23]   Brecht, "The Modern Theater is Epic Theater," *BT* 36n.

Didi, after a silence, says there's nothing more to do there of the nothing already done, and Gogo quickly replies, "Nor anywhere else" (*Godot* 34), which is not exactly promising for social change. But what could be seen in the whole sequence about the boots is the sort of sly paradox or cunning reversal you can also find in the capricious jurisprudence of Azdak in *The Caucasian Chalk Circle* or in the waterseller Wang's opening remarks, while waiting to welcome the gods, in *The Good Person of Szechwan*. As he sizes up passersby, he says of two gentlemen, they "don't strike me as gods, they have a brutal look, as if they were in the habit of beating people, and gods have no need of that."[24]

One might make the case that the moral sense, in subtle and nuanced ways, suffuses the plays of Beckett, as it does through all the apparent caprice, hyperbole, and gratuitous cruelty of Hamm when he says, at one point in his narrative about the man who crawled toward him on his belly and wanted bread for his brat, "In the end he asked me would I consent to take in the child as well—if he were still alive. (*Pause.*) It was the moment I was waiting for. (*Pause.*) Would I consent to take in the child . . ." (*Endgame* 53). And the moment is suspended, with the moral issue, as Hamm breaks off the narrative, until the end of the play, before he puts on the stancher, when he comes back to the child, if, whoever he is, "he could have his child with him . . . ":

> It was the moment I was waiting for.
> (*Pause.*)
> You don't want to abandon him? You want him to bloom while you are withering? Be there to solace your last million last moments?
> (*Pause.*)
> He doesn't realize, all he knows is hunger, and cold, and death to crown it all. But you! You ought to know what the earth is like, nowadays. Oh I put him before his responsibilities!

If that is not a moral distinction, at the sticking point of thought, I do not know what is, though it is a disturbing moral. And there is nothing here like what we might see elsewhere in the almost demonic eloquence of Hamm, there at the nerve-ends, going to the quick, an extraordinary passion deflated by irony. As for the moral sense in epic theater, it may be hard to work out the proportions of detachment and subjectivity, through an always strategic irony, but in any case, as with

---

[24] Brecht, *The Good Person of Szechwan: A Parable Play*, trans. Ralph Manheim, in *Collected Plays, Volume 6*, ed. Manheim and John Willett (New York: Vintage, 1976) 3-4.

the three cases distinguished by the voice of . . . *but the clouds . . .* , or
the "fourth case, or case nought" (*SP* 261), Brecht might have been
making a case for Beckett when he said, "out of mistrust of the theater"
which, whatever the case, "theaters it all down, . . . [s]ome exercise in
complex seeing is needed." When he adds, however, that "it is
perhaps more important to be able to think above the stream than to
think in the stream,"[25] it might be hard for Beckett to imagine anything
like that, for imagination dead imagine the stream is all there is. And if
you can not step into the same river twice, as Heraclitus said, that is
because you are always in it, even in *Come and Go.* "May we not
speak of the old days? [*Silence.*] Of what came after?" But the after is
more of the same and—"Holding hands . . . that way. /Dreaming of . . .
love" (*SP* 195)—you can somehow never get out.

If the complex seeing occurs in other ways, Brecht
nevertheless also shares with Beckett, despite the rap about
Verfremdung subduing emotion by detachment, a "sensitivity to
subjective differences," while there is a similar compulsion to
differentiation that, as Adorno remarks about Beckett, "glides into
ideology" too. Which does not, as Adorno also says, in countering
Lukács' charge that Beckett reduces humans to animality, qualify
Beckett to "testify as a key political witness . . . in the struggle against
atomic death. . . ."[26] For in Beckett's writing the terror of such death
seems to be as it always was—the dreadful thing has already happened,
"a heap, a little heap, the impossible heap" (*Endgame* 1)—inseparable
from the ordeal of being human. If Beckett is not guilty, as Lukács also
charged, of "an abstract, subjectivist ontology" (Adorno 15), his view of
the subject—or at least the subject of modernity—might have been
defined by Brecht when, in his earliest definition of epic theater, he
said in no uncertain terms, "The continuity of the ego is a myth. A man
is an atom that perpetually breaks up and forms anew. We have to
show things as they are."[27] The new purpose, for Brecht, in the era of
"the petroleum complex" may have been "paedagogics," as he says in
an essay on "Form and Subject-Matter," but the fact of the matter for
the subject, in things being shown as they are, is that it can no longer
appear in the drama with the old features of character, nor with the sort
of motives imputed by Hebbel, Ibsen, or even Chekov. In a world

---

[25]   Brecht, "The Literarization of Theater (Notes to *The Threepenny Opera*),"
BT 43-44.

[26]   Theodor W. Adorno, "Trying to Understand *Endgame*," *New German
Critique* 26 (1982): 15.

[27]   Brecht, in an interview, "Conversation with Bert Brecht,"*BT* 15.

where "fate is no longer a single coherent power," but dispersed into "fields of force" radiating in all directions, actions must be shown as "pure phenomena" (*BT* 29-30), as they are with a motiveless specificity in *Baal* and in *In the Jungle of Cities*, more devastatingly so there than in the more rationalized epic of *Galileo* or in *Mother Courage*.

Yet, Courage pulling her wagon, after the death of Dumb Kattrin, aimlessly at the end—"infinite emptiness" all around her, as Hamm says apocalyptically in his warning to Clov, and imagination dead imagine the resurrected dead of all the ages combining with those of the ceaseless war—is an even bleaker image of a pure phenomenon than the dying Shlink asking for a cloth over his face, like Hamm, because "he doesn't want anyone to look at him" (*Jungle, CP 1:* 161), or Garga in the office of the late Shlink, saying in the final lines, "It's a good thing to be alone. The chaos is used up" (163). Or even the dying Baal, that pale lump of fat, with no teeth left, crawling on all fours like an animal to the door, for one last look at the stars. With the used-up chaos as the datum of thought, or the fields of force more entropic, this is all the more so in Beckett as he encapsulates the gratuitous and baseless necessity of the utterly negated subject, with its excruciating consciousness, or disjunctures of it, from the hollow in the wall of *Endgame* or the seeds which will never sprout to the diminishing returns or spastic brevity of the aphasic later plays.

Moreover, what we appear to encounter in Beckett—even in the plays with a more explicit political content, such as *Catastrophe,* and the clownish cycle of torture ("give him the works until he confesses") that followed in *What Where* (*SP* 315)—is not merely "the nausea of satiation" or "the tedium of spirit with itself," which Adorno invoked in his essay on *Endgame* (11), out of his own aversion to the politics of Lukács. Never mind the abstract, subjectivist ontology that Lukács charged Beckett with and Adorno rejected. Lukács may even be right, and there may be something like that there, though abstractions live in Beckett, like the pauses and silences extruded from Chekovian realism, in the lymph nodes and bloodstream of thought, where alienation is a reflex with illimitable affect that elides in the pure phenomena certain figures and gestures resembling the A-effect, as if the Brechtian arrest were in the Beckettian moment(um) the subject of thought itself. As for the subjectivist ontology, what may be most compelling or unnerving in Beckett is his response to a certain harrowing stillness in the barest rumor of being which is, all told, and told again, till the telling is intolerable, thus further dispersed in thought, as with the ceaseless stirrings of the equivocal word *still* (is it motion? or time? as endurance? or all of it under duress?), the ontological ground, if ground there be, of the subtlest, most seductive, imperceptible form of illusion, what in the living end dying can never be seen, or seen as being, and therefore never told.

Still: "Something is taking its course." Estrange it as we will, it still seems passing strange, only the passing certain, as in the stasis of the momentum and the plaintively quizzical moment of the waiting for Godot, when Didi wonders, with Gogo falling asleep, and he not sure he is awake, whether in the nothing that happened twice anything happened at all, "That Pozzo passed, with his carrier, and that he spoke with us? Probably. But in all that what truth will there be?" (58). It was precisely that, the apparently impotent subjectivity of a ubiquitous indeterminacy, all the more alluring for its teasing out of illusion—"They make a noise like wings. / Like leaves. / Like sand. / Like leaves" (40)—which Brecht thought he might change when he considered revising the play, linking its oddities and incapacities to material interests and the past that is disremembered ("a million years ago, in the nineties"[7]), or not remembered at all ("What were you saying when?"), surely not the beginning ("The very beginning of WHAT?" [42]), bringing it in line with a more progressive sense of history. Yet, for all the ideological pressure of recent years to historicize! historicize! one is occasionally tempted to say with Gogo—who either forgets immediately or never forgets, who knows only that "Everything oozes" and that "It's never the same pus from one second to the next" (39)—"I'm not a historian" (42). And for the moment, arrested, still in the time of the now: the boots, the carrot, the tree, from one second to the next, no time that time, and the waiting consigned to illusion.

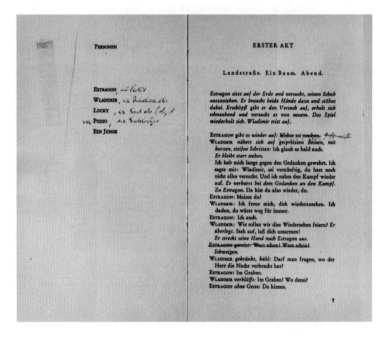

Samuel Beckett: *Warten auf Godot.*   Berlin: Suhrkamp, 1955. Nachlaßbibliothek Bertolt Brecht.

Discussion of Herbert Blau's "Among the Deepening Shades"

Herbert Blau

Q*uestion (Q)*: This is as much a comment as a question. You quoted the essay on the closure of representation.

Herbert Blau (HB): That's the Derrida essay.

Q: Right. I find it fascinating that a generation ago we used to speak about the dichotomy of Artaud and Brecht, and here we seem to have slipped Beckett in, where Artaud used to be. It is as though Beckett has come to substitute for this closure of representation. I wonder if you want to say a few words about how you see that.

HB: I didn't necesarily see Beckett as displacing Artaud. You remember in that essay Derrida says virtually nothing about Beckett. He does talk about Brecht. He points out in relationship to Artaud that Brecht, or people who are doing Brechtian kinds of theater, are not doing at all what Artaud was talking about, because Artaud was after the unrepresentable. Artaud, however, resembles Beckett in this regard, you may recall that in that essay, or never mind the essay, in Artaud, there is a sense in which Artaud is trying to create theater which is not theater. Since he was dealing with the impossible task, that is the abrogation or abolition of representation, he wanted theater that would never repeat itself. But Artaud was hip enough to realize that at some sort of end of this utterly impossible desire, he would have to have theater, so to speak, with microscopic or minimal repetition. And the minimal repetition would be of such a nature that it would disguise itself, it could just virtually rotate on its own axis. In a certain sense Beckett does that in the later pieces. It is utterly aphasic, what is going on in these later pieces of Beckett. But it is only in that sense that I might talk about Beckett sneaking in. In the Derrida essay itself he is not a factor.

Q: Could we have an exchange? I think there might be more in what you said and what you suggest than you are seeing right now. The essay talks about the theological stage. It's just before the passage that you quoted, the theological stage which has this author, residing like a God with the text. You talk about a play with gods, *The Good Person of Szechwan*, where you have a theological stage. In Brecht, even if you don't believe in the book of rules, you have a Brecht who is trying to say: it's sad that you don't believe in the book of rules. And

Where Extremes Meet: Rereading Brecht and Beckett / Begegnung der Extreme. Brecht und Beckett: Eine Re-interpretation
Stephen Brockmann et al., eds., *The Brecht Yearbook / Das Brecht-Jahrbuch*
Volume 27 (Pittsburgh: The International Brecht Society, 2002)

you talk about the *Massnahme*, which is Brecht on the cusp of closure of the theological stage. It is an interesting point you are making, and I just wondered if Beckett then becomes the practical man of the theater Artaud could not be that comes to the edge of this theological stage, the end of the theological stage.

HB: I would simply put it differently. I see what you're saying, and maybe I do not see what I'm saying, which is half the issue. But look, the line in Beckett that I have quoted more than any other in the book on Beckett I just published, and therefore have scrupulously kept out of this essay, was: "Use your head, can't you, use your head, you're on earth, there's no cure for that!" There is no cure for that. As long as you've got that, you're going to have a theological stage.

Q: Your talk was lyrical, but so dense. I'd like to try and pick up on what I think I followed, especially after the last panel that also seemed to be a kind of treatment of Brecht, which I wouldn't have heard ten or fifteen years ago, more Brecht as the parable that retreats from the referent of history than the other Brecht. I could see that you were doing this very canny reading together of Brecht and Beckett through the construction of the subject in his thinking, and particularly going to *Baal* for that, whereas maybe ten years ago people would have talked a little bit more about the object of the plot as being the place that would distinguish Brecht from Beckett. So I am wondering where you would place that sort of *Neue Sachlichkeit* mode, the sort of thing that for *Galileo*, even though I understand him, and agree with the momentum, with the thinking that is the mark of the subject, was still the notion that there was something that he was looking *at*, that he could *know*.

HB: I tried to deal with that to some extent, when I talked about the brain. It is also what I meant in the prefatory remarks, when I said, if you deal with the issue of politics, eventually, and I'm not talking about people in general, just in my experience in the theater, somehow or other it came back again to a distinction between Brecht and Beckett. It turned out, adventitiously, none of us anticipated this, when we did *Mother Courage* and *Waiting for Godot*, in 1957 in San Francisco, when the Sixties were beginning to ferment in that environment, it suddenly turned out, though *Mother Courage* was quite a controversial production and got a lot of attention, that in fact it was *Waiting for Godot* that turned out to be the production with political efficacy, though it has no political intention that we can normally see, certainly not in the Brechtian sense. So while the object of its dramaturgy was presumably not political, in some ways it seemed to merge with sentiments, instincts, developing cultural reflexes that eventually came out in the Sixties.

You can see it now in retrospect, and I've written about it elsewhere. In a way the waiting characterized the first phase of the Civil Rights movement, which was passive resistance, sit-down. I was involved in the San Francisco sit-down early on. That was the same period, by the way, in which young people were coming back from Korea. You remember, that was the time when we fought wars, we didn't call them wars, we called them "bandit actions" and things of that kind. These guys, who had just been over to Korea, used to come back and see both *Waiting for Godot* and *Endgame*, when we did a second production of *Godot*, and they'd come back as if to a kind of ritual event. They'd say, I was just over there, it looked like that: the tree. They were there in that bleak landscape of Korea. I don't know if that addresses exactly your point.

But when I say, as I will often say, I'll even say it occasionally in a seminar in a certain kind of fit of impatience, something like: "Look, I believe in the brain. That's what we're doing here, we're thinking." Sometimes somebody says in a reflex from old method acting: "Gee, Herb, I'm not sure I can do this, I don't feel..."—"I don't give a shit what you feel. I only care what you think. All we're doing here is thinking. It doesn't mean I don't care about your feelings." It has nothing to do with that, but feeling was cheap under the circumstances. The question is how we can think about this. That's harder. So I may believe in the brain under certain circumstances, and I'll say it with that intensity. Under other circumstances, I'll say we're thinking a little too much, let's move over here. It only works up to some threshold moment to say anything as if in fact that were the valid way of looking at things, and that's the only way you could look at things.

Q: I guess my question was: that which the brain knows *about*. So when Brecht says we need a new play about the conditions of petroleum, this is a new theater. For *St. Joan of the Stockyards*, we need to know about meat prices and how they are manipulated in Chicago. Particularly now, with Bush wanting to drill in the Arctic, we need to know about petroleum. It's not so much about the *knowing* sometimes, so much as what you're knowing *about*.

HB: I'm sorry, you're perfectly right in making that point. I just moved to Seattle, and when I was there they asked me to serve on a committee. They have a drama group which apparently with some efficacy has moved around the campus, and gone into classrooms and done improvised events that people seem to like. They were talking about what they were doing, and the guy who headed it, a graduate student, though he's gotten a lot of support from the administration to do this, was describing something that happened in a class, an anthropology class. It sounded like a kind of nifty improvisational event. I raised a question, which was a question of knowledge. I'm certain, as he described it, that students who were there and observed the event were excited by it. You've done enough theater work, and I've done enough theater work. You know excitement is often factitious excitement. You can excite people easily in the theater. But the issue that I raised then was, if they're going to go from class to class, to what degree are they prepared to talk in a substantive way about what it is that's being presumably learned in that class? To create excitement in the class, that's easy. To be able in fact to *know* something at the same time, that's quite another matter, and there Brecht certainly did have in mind a substantive content to the dramaturgy. But, I think, so did Beckett. He didn't make a big issue of it in the same way, though I would never make the case that it existed to the same extent as Brecht. I would never make that case.

Q: I was asking myself something in relation to that last question. We could not say that the theater is about only knowing, but knowing *if* we know, knowing *that* we know, or knowing that we signify something or that we didn't do something. I think that's a big difference between Brecht and Beckett. Brecht was always looking for a different way of confirming this knowing that we have the knowledge, by transforming it into a matter of social practice. Beckett was in a different situation, which is difficult to explain, of knowing if one knows something that is not illusion, of knowing that I do something by *performing* something. There remains a more radical way out of any possible state of insecurity. It would be perhaps interesting to ask both theater practices this question: what forms are there in which they are looking for the possibility of knowing that they know?

HB: That too for me is circumstantial. In specific contexts I wouldn't hestitate for two minutes to say: look, shut your mouth, you don't know the first thing about this. I know a lot about this, and I know that I know it. I don't even have to think twice about that. There are critical moments which are very different. For example, take the business of oil reserves, or the environment, or any of those issues. Those of us who are more or less on the left know that we have a kind of indisposition to certain things that the Bush administration, say in the United States, is tempted to do. But there are certain areas having to do with everything from terrorism, through the missile shield, to environmental control, to the holes in the ozone layer, in which we are all *vastly* uninformed. Most of us don't know how to make decisions about these things. We have sentiments. I cannot claim to know. I would know to some extent how I might know more, if I were privileged to know more. But that's about all I could claim. And even those who appear to know, scientists and others, are divided on a lot of these issues. So it's very hard to make judgments in a lot of these areas in which we tend to make reflexive judgments, which I often distrust, even though I have my sentiments too. I know what my position is on the environment, vaguely.

Q: Sir, the common man, who happens to be...

HB: Like me.

Q: ...No, who happens to be the most powerful man in the world, President Bush. Could President Bush relate to anything that either Brecht or Beckett wrote? If he could not, do you find that it might be your privilege to endeavor to interpret?

HB: No, I don't think he could. I'd be myopic, if I felt that. Not only President Bush, most of the members of our Congress would be relatively indifferent to what we're talking about here. But that doesn't strike me as strange. That seems to be normative. I was talking to a seminar here yesterday. They were speaking about the impeccability of both Brecht and Beckett. The work, for better or worse, was utterly impeccable and was designed for certain contexts, and usually for no more than say a hundred to two hundred people. We go and do these works, and maybe have some discussions afterwards, and somebody says, well what kind of audience do you intend for this? I would love to have 18,000 people in a stadium adore the work I was doing, but I'd be utterly naive if I thought that this is the kind of work that's going to circulate in a large public forum. It's just not. It may, by some sort of trickledown economy of the aesthetic, eventually get to where you don't expect it. For example, I won't simply attribute it to him, but there's a sense in which you wouldn't have nine tenths, you wouldn't even *have* what you have on mtv, were it not for people like Beckett. Or even things far more way out than Beckett. It's one of the reasons I wrote a book on fashion. What you've got in fashion are extremely hip people doing it. People like Karl Lagerfeld are nine times smarter than most of the people who are theorizing issues today. He's a very smart guy. And before things are thought of here in the classroom, he's got it going already in fashion.

So it gets around in other ways. But I certainly can't expect Bush to go to a production of *Endgame*. [*Laughter*] He ought to.

Q: When *Waiting for Godot* was done in San Quentin, was there a feeling then that that was the reason it was so successful, or was it just that the audience could empathize with the form, the content, or the waiting, the pattern of the repetitions?

HB: Let me tell you what actually happened there. People don't realize this. That was the first time that a production of any kind was performed in any maximum security prison anywhere in the world. When we were invited to San Quentin, which came about through the head of our Board, who was a judge, we first proposed doing a play of mine, not realizing then that you couldn't take women into the prison. So we couldn't take that play. Now you could do a play with women in the prison, but you couldn't then. We happened to have just done *Waiting for Godot*, and I proposed *Waiting for Godot*. They didn't have big therapeutic services at San Quentin at that time. They had a single psychiatrist. Imagine that! He objected strenuously. He read the play and he objected to our doing it, because he felt it would be too traumatic for the inmates. Now I had never been in a prison before then, though about twelve years after that we spent quite a lot of time in prisons. But there was a debate between the psychiatrist, myself, and Warden Duffy. Just the three of us were there. Warden Duffy struck me as something of a southern redneck, as we say, but he listened to the debate between me and the psychiatrist. Then he tapped me on the chest at one point and said: he seems like a nice guy, let him do it. He may have had some intuitions about my wisdom and judiciousness, but he said: let's do it. So we did it.

There were 1800 men in the mess hall and we had no idea how this would turn out. There was a jazz band playing in the front of the stage, before we went on. It was quite surreal because they had a rule that prisoners who smoke—they let them smoke on this occasion— for some reason could not douse their matches below the table. So all during peformance they would throw lit matches up in the air, which was really quite beautiful. During the whole production you saw these matches flying. But the jazz band was playing, and I gave a talk to the inmates before the production. Since I was aware—it was certainly true—that many of them had never been to the theater at all, any kind, I said: this is not like most of the movies you've seen or if you have gone to the theater, theater events that you've seen, it doesn't quite have a story in that sense. I said: in a way it's like this crazy jazz band—they were playing some really hot stuff—and as soon as I said that, the drummer hit the cymbal. He said: Yeah! Then we opened.

We had no idea what it would do. But it had an immense impact in the prison. I did have some sense that it corresponded in some ways to the nature of their experience. That would seem almost self-evident. But there was still no way of anticipating that it would have the reception that it in fact had. As some of you may know, because it was so well received, the newspapers for two days on end were just full of articles about it, we then helped them to form a drama group. Over a period of eight years we got each year one person paroled, including Rick Cluchey. Some of you have probably heard of Rick Cluchey. Has he been here? He has written a play called *The Cage*. It was written in prison. It has been performed now around the world. He was in for armed robbery and attempted murder. He was in for life. He was paroled. A couple of years later Ruby Cohn and I introduced him to Beckett. He named a child after Beckett. And Beckett then directed him in a couple of plays in Berlin. Then they formed the San Quentin drama group that was in Chicago.

Recently I was in Berlin, I guess it must have been six or seven months ago. They had a big festival of prison drama with inmates from all over Europe, and performances in the prisons, which would never have happened without a certain impetus which came from that production. I'm not saying from that alone. Again, it was adventitious, which is to say that production happened, but somehow or other Western culture was ready to do certain kinds of things in prisons. What was interesting was exactly what happened. I talked to some of the inmates at Tegel prison. They were actually rehearsing *Endgame*. They wanted to hear about the San Quentin thing, so I talked briefly about that. Then they asked for comments on *Endgame*. I made some comments. I was talking to about forty inmates. They prided themselves on the German prisons. They said our prisons are better than your prisons, because we have TV sets in each cell and showers every two cells. And they wanted to know about American prisons. I don't know as much about prisons as I used to. I haven't been in prisons for years. But I did say, there is this difference. As I talked to these forty men, there was opposite me one young man who was black. I said: when we did the performance in San Quentin, there were 1800 men there, and maybe there were 40% of them at that time who were black. If you went to an American prison today, it would probably be 85 or 90% who are black. Here you have only one. That's a major difference between the prisons. So there are different things you would encounter, if you were rethinking what you would do in a prison today.

Q: I would like to ask if you have any views about translations of Beckett into other media, like film?

HB: What can I say? Most of the time it has nothing to do with translations into other media, it has to do with the fact that the media are not able to engage sufficiently with Beckett. Let me address that issue, because it was addressed earlier on, and I have written about this in the book that I've recently published on Beckett. I think there's an interview I gave there, which makes reference to this. It has to do with the JoAnne Akalaitis performance, but with much beyond that. JoAnne Akalaitis grew up in our theater in San Franscisco. I've known her since she was very young. I did not see the production that was stopped by Beckett. I happened to be in Paris. I had heard that he had stopped the production, and I knew he had been doing that for a while. I always felt that it was unbecoming of him, because he never saw the productions. There were certain people who would tip him off every now and then for various reasons, all of which I found repugnant. Nonetheless that was happening.

I was meeting with him at that seedy hotel he liked near the Boulevard Saint Jaques. After we sat down, I said: Sam, I heard you stopped the production. He and I had debated things over the years. We even disagreed on various things and would have interesting intellectual conversations, but we never had an argument of any kind. And he got almost instantly, you'll have to take my word for it, he *did*, he was immediately, I felt, oversensitive to the issue. I said: look, why did you stop the production? That led him to say some things. And I said, you know JoAnne. He knew the Mabu Mines people. She grew up on your plays, she was virtually weaned on your plays. So she's putting it in a subway. I don't know what she's doing, whether it's good, bad, or indifferent, but she knows the plays so well, maybe she's trying to do something a little differently.

By the way, each time I would go to see him, the one thing he and Ruby kept pestering me about was why I stopped doing theater work. Every time I'd see him, that was almost the first question. When are you going to start doing theater again? This was in the background, and I kept pressing the issue. I said: look, she knows your work well, she maybe just wants to see something else. And he got more intemperate. So much so that I said to him at one point: maybe after all Alan Schneider is your most appropriate director. Alan would very conscientiously, when he was directing Beckett, write him letters, fly over to see him and, I don't mean to say this with any condescension, would get the words from the master's voice and try to do what Beckett wanted. Authorial intention was the big issue in his productions, in so far as you can translate that way in the age of the death of the author. As a matter of fact, this is what really upset him. I said: here we are in Paris, everyone's talking about the death of the author. Normally he would have laughed, but he got furious when I said that. That's when I brought up the business of Schneider, and again we had some sort of exchange. I said: Sam, you've asked me many times why I'm not doing theater again. One thing I would say, given what you feel about this, is that if I were to do theater again, I would promise you that as long as you're still living, I could never do one of your plays. In fact, I don't see any reason particularly, given all of what's available to us, and how we can do things today, the multifariousness of what is available to us to see and hear and so on, why, when you do plays that are reasonably well known, you wouldn't want in some way to rethink them, or think through them, which might induce you to do something else with them. Not because you disrespect them, but because you can say: yes, I know people who can see this, but this is kind of interesting, I'd like to really make an issue of this. I tend in general to be quite bored, I'm only speaking for myself, when I go to see theater, Shakespeare plays, whatever, if they're reasonably dutiful productions, whatever that means.

Q: Did he give you any answer?

HB: No, he kind of tapered off at that point. It was an uncomfortable session. We went on to something else. He may have quoted William Butler Yeats, which he was in the habit of doing.

Q: You spoke about Beckett's inability to share the work, to renew the work, to address new relationships with the work. I think in many ways that response to improvisation of the work contradicts the spirit of that work, it doesn't make sense, it doesn't add up.

HB: In *Sails for the Herring Fleet*, the book I just published, there's an essay called "The Bloody Show and the Eye of Prey." I was asked by the Beckett Society—this is when theory first began to make its way into theater studies—to talk about Beckett and deconstruction. One of the things I'm certain I demonstrate there is that Beckett gave us the grounds for thinking about dematerializing texts, bracketing the author. He gave us the conceptual, and more than the conceptual and ideational, he gave us the *visual* grounds for doing that: to rethink, to think it over, to turn it over. I've got it, and then I don't have it. He gave us the very basis for that.

Q: I saw Beckett at what must have been just about the same time, and asked him almost the same question. He did joke about it with me. He said, I've heard somewhere that people prefer to work with dead authors, but I'm not dead yet. I'm a dying author, certainly, but not a dead one.

> *HB*: Yes, he said that too.

> *Q*: I said, why is it less important to respect the author's text after he's dead? And he said, well only because then you can't really feel it.

> *HB*: Yes but, by the way, let me say this: I myself saw only two productions that Beckett himself directed, and I thought they were boring. I honestly did. I'm not being condescending.

> *Q*: Which ones did you see?

> *HB*: I saw *Endgame*, and I saw *Krapp's Last Tape*, which Rick Cluchey played in.

> *Q*: It can sometimes go the other way. I walked out of a production of Brecht in Berlin where these chaps in spacesuits were jumping around on styrofoam. The words were there, but I found it offensive. I would say, go and write your own play if you want to....

> *HB*: Look we've seen all kinds of productions with obtuse updating. I've seen them too. I know what you're talking about. Very early on, when I first went to Europe, I met for the first time, because we felt we had a lot in common, we thought we were doing similar things, I met people like Giorgio Strehler, and Roger Planchon. These are not dopes. Roger Planchon, who was at that time a virulent communist, did a production, which he called *Falstaff*, of *Henry IV*, Part One and Part Two. Almost its entire animus was in fact to expose the omnipresence of the Roman Catholic Church in France. And even to me—I've nothing to do with the Roman Catholic Church where I am—it was extremely powerful. It ignored a lot of stuff, it misrepresented other kinds of things, but it was really important and it was intelligently thought. That's very different from the sort of thing you're talking about. We've seen all kinds of shit, but we've also seen such productions when they're done dutifully, and we've seen them when they're done radically.

- 140 -

Brecht las, und er machte Pläne fürs Theater. Inszenieren
wollte er nach "Galilei" nicht mehr, das könnten jetzt die
Schüler tun, war seine Meinung. Er wollte seine Theorie
weiter ausarbeiten. Auf seine Bitte brachte ich ihm
Becketts "Warten auf Godot" ins Krankenhaus. Er stellte sich
eine Aufführung vor, bei der - während Estragon und Wladimir
auf Godot warten - im Hintergrund Filme über Revolutionen
in aller Welt laufen.

Von einem Freund hatte ich mir die unveröffentlichte
Chrustschow-Rede von XX. Parteitag, der im Februar statt-
gefunden hatte, besorgt, d.h. er hatte sie mir übersetzt
und ich stenografiert. Jetzt schrieb ich jeden Tag 5-6
Seiten auf der Maschine, die ich Brecht ins Krankenhaus
brachte. Er war tief getroffen.

Nachdem Brecht das Krankenhaus verlassen hatte, machte er einige
einige Notizen dazu:
"Die geschichtliche Würdigung Stalins bedarf der Arbeit der
Geschichtsschreiber. Die Liquidierung des Stalinismus kann
nur durch eine gigantische Mobilisierung der Massen
Weisheit der Massen durch die Partei gelingen. Sie liegt
auf der geraden Linie des Kommunismus..."

Nach seiner Entlassung aus dem Krankenhaus lag Brecht
zu Hause meist im Lehnstuhl, mit einer Decke zugedeckt.
Aber er schonte sich auch jetzt nicht. Er beriet die Vorbe-
reitung der Tournee, die das Berliner Ensemble im Juni 1956
nach München mit "Pauken und Trompeten" unternahm, er

Käthe Rülicke: Notiz, ca. 1990.

Durch die Linse Heiner Müllers: Brecht und Beckett—Drei Punkte möglicher Konvergenz für die Zukunft

This article discusses three points of historical convergence between Brecht and Beckett, focusing on the Euro-American theater during the past twenty years and speculating briefly on the future. The subjects are: Heiner Müller, particularly the texts written or assembled late in his career which aim at "the zero point" of theater (*Description of a Picture* and *Quartet*, for instance); intertextuality and copyright law, particularly the legal battle over Müller's last play, *Germania 3*, and other cases in which performance rights have been subject to controlling restrictions; and American solo performance, particularly the way its technique of self-characterization by opposition and contrast has introduced a revivified, individualistic form of "Verfremdung."

Dieser Artikel bespricht drei Schwerpunkte geschichtlicher Konvergenz zwischen Brecht und Beckett, indem er das europäisch-amerikanische Theater der letzten zwanzig Jahre ins Auge nimmt und kurz über die Zukunft spekuliert. Die Themen sind: Heiner Müller, besonders die Texte, die am Ende seiner Karriere zusammengestellt worden sind, und die einen "Nullpunkt" des Theaters anvisieren (*Bildbeschreibung* und *Quartett*, z.B.); Intertextualität und Urheberrechte, besonders in Bezug auf Müllers letztes Theaterstück *Germania 3*, und auch andere Fälle, in denen Aufführungsrechte einer verengenden Kontrolle unterstellt worden sind; und amerikanische Performance-Kunst, besonders ihre Technik der Selbstcharakterisierung durch Opposition und Kontrast und die daraus resultierende wieder belebte, individualistische Form der "Verfremdung."

Through the Lens of Heiner Müller: Brecht and Beckett—Three Points of Plausible Convergence for the Future

Jonathan Kalb

In his penetrating 1968 essay comparing theater and film, Peter Handke declared that among mankind's basic miseries was "his belief that he must, *in general*, compare."[1] One can, after all, compare anything with anything else and walk away convinced that the resulting friction amounts to illumination. At first glance, the idea of comparing Samuel Beckett to the late East German author Heiner Müller would seem to be a prime illustration of this "misery." The very prospect of hunting for analogies between Beckett and this most prominent and significant of Brecht's spiritual heirs reminds me of the opening of Werner Hecht's groundbreaking 1966 article on Brecht's plans to adapt *Waiting for Godot*. Hecht called his article "Brecht 'and' Beckett: an absurd comparison," and he began his text with the following snide remark: "Of course, one can compare virtually everything: the banana with the rhinoceros, the egg-shell with the urn, the recording tape with the palm tree. One can, of course, also compare Brecht with Beckett."[2]

In a volume appropriately titled *Where Extremes Meet*, one needs to proceed with a certain humility in the face of this patent absurdity and misery. The other contributors to the volume have all laid out many important, perceptive, and penetrating ideas. I am conscious, however, that there is (to borrow Shaw's formulation from *Major Barbara*) also a certain amount of tosh about the purported affinities between Brecht and Beckett. These really are two extremes, and one accomplishes little by scotch-taping them together with, say, quick applications of the concept of *Verfremdung*, as many critics have done. My purpose today is to suggest what seem to me three points of truly plausible and important historical convergence between them. All three of my points, or subjects, relate to the Euro-American theater of the last decade or two, up to the present day, and all of them contain hints of speculation about the future, seen through the lens of Heiner

---

[1] Peter Handke, "*Theater und Film*: Das Elend des Vergleichens," in *Prosa Gedichte Theaterstücke Aufsätze* (Frankfurt/Main: Suhrkamp, 1969), 314. All translations in this essay are by Jonathan Kalb unless otherwise noted.

[2] Werner Hecht, "Brecht 'und' Beckett: ein absurder Vergleich," *Theater der Zeit* 14, Aug. 1-15, 1966, 28.

Where Extremes Meet: Rereading Brecht and Beckett / Begegnung der Extreme. Brecht und Beckett: Eine Re-interpretation
Stephen Brockmann et al., eds., *The Brecht Yearbook / Das Brecht-Jahrbuch*
Volume 27 (Pittsburgh: The International Brecht Society, 2002)

Müller. They are, in order: Müller himself, intertextuality and copyright law, and American solo performance.

I. Heiner Müller

Strangely enough, Beckett was one of Müller's chief influences during the latter's period of astonishing dominance over the German theater (from the early 1980s to his death in 1995, at age 66). Beckett figured importantly among the dozens of authors (ranging from the ancients to Müller's younger contemporaries) whose style and artistic paradigms Müller adopted and adapted to his purposes in the course of constructing his sometimes maddeningly accumulative work. With Müller, however, who eventually became a virtuoso self-contradictor and public manipulator in the spirit of Andy Warhol, it was seldom certain whether any of his influences, other than Brecht, could aptly be considered fundamental. As it happens, Müller respected Beckett more than many other East German theater people did (those who knew about him, that is). One official's sneering reference to Müller as "a Beckett of the East" at the 1961 hearing expelling him from the GDR Writer's Union was typical orthodoxy.[3] Whatever the truth of this charge, Müller's public statements about Beckett always downplayed the connection, and most of Müller's critics have downplayed it as well,[4] taking the following 1988 remarks on the matter more or less at face value: "Beckett's texts come out of the experience of a history-less world. For his characters there was no history and there won't be any. And I, for biographical or geographical reasons, have always been interested in history, or had to be interested in it. That's where I see the big difference."[5]

As I explained in my recent book on Müller, I do not think this connection is at all superficial. It was of crucial importance not only to Müller's basic rethinking of Brecht's theatrical principles and

---

[3]   Heiner Müller, *Krieg ohne Schlacht: Leben in Zwei Diktaturen* (Cologne: Kiepenheuer & Witsch, expanded edition, 1994), 173.

[4]   See, for example: Joachim Fiebach, *Inseln der Unordnung: Fünf Versuche zu Heiner Müllers Theatertexten* (Berlin: Henschelverlag, 1990), 19; Thomas Eckardt, *Der Herold der Toten: Geschichte und Politik bei Heiner Müller* (Frankfurt/Main: Peter Lang, 1992), 114-16; Norbert Otto Eke, *Heiner Müller: Apokalypse und Utopie* (Paderborn: Ferdinand Schöningh, 1989), 38-9; and Ernst Wendt, "Das letzte Band und das Brot der Revolution. Über die Dramatiker Samuel Beckett und Heiner Müller," in *Moderne Dramaturgie* (Frankfurt/Main: Suhrkamp, 1974), 41-64.

[5]   Heiner Müller, *Gesammelte Irrtümer 2* (Frankfurt/Main: Verlag der Autoren, 1990), 131.

Jonathan Kalb

techniques in the 1960s and 70s but also to his still more radical conception in the 1980s and early 90s of a theater in need of renewal through "reduction and concentration," which he thought would clear space for new modes of perception. "Theater must find its minimum once again, its zero point, from which outward steps can be taken again," he said in 1994.[6] The texts Müller wrote or assembled late in his career attempting to find this minimum—primarily *Bildbeschreibung* (*Description of a Picture*, 1984), but also, to a lesser extent, *Verkommenes Ufer Medeamaterial Landschaft mit Argonauten* (*Despoiled Shore Medeamaterial Landscape with Argonauts*, 1982) and *Quartet* (*Quartett*, 1980)—point to fundamental connections not only with Beckett but more generally with the decentered dramatic landscapes he preeminently defined and bequeathed to a younger generation of theater artists.

Müller was, of course, a much more explicitly political author than Beckett, and there is no point in trying to smooth over the obvious important differences between their temperaments and worldly ambitions. The fact that fundamental affinities existed at all, however, is remarkable considering the foreignness of Beckett in the GDR cultural context. In the tradition of Georg Lukács (who dismissed him as decadent), Beckett was mistrusted by many GDR artists and almost all cultural apparatchiks for the entire forty-one years of the country's history. Beckett and Brecht were usually perceived as mutually exclusive artistic paradigms, with the latter an object of institutionalization from the 1960s on, and Beckett was not produced in East Germany until Ekkehard Schall's 1986 *Krapp's Last Tape*, which was deliberately conceived to belittle Beckett.[7] (Happily, the national premiere of *Waiting for Godot* in Dresden the following year was done in a much more fair-minded spirit, as was *Godot*'s East Berlin premiere in 1988—thirty five years after its world premiere.)

Müller was a mischievously independent spirit who never endorsed any orthodoxy for its own sake, but he was also a deeply committed if idiosyncratic Marxist who was loyal to the GDR in his way. Hence the irony that his sustained and calculated embrace of modernist Western ideas and artistic models such as Beckett, Genet, Artaud and T.S. Eliot was really an indirect result of his treatment by the GDR regime. Banned from production and publication in 1961 (the

---

[6] Holger Teschke, interview with Müller, "Theater muss wieder seinen Nullpunkt finden," *Theater der Zeit* (May/June 1994), 7.

[7] See my discussion of the production and my interview with Schall in Jonathan Kalb, *Beckett in Performance* (Cambridge: Cambridge Univ. Press, 1989), 73-5, 212-19.

year the Berlin Wall was built) because of a socialist realist play that depicted the land reforms of the previous decade in too realistic a light, he turned at first to classical adaptation (as a vehicle for political critique that cultural bureaucrats wouldn't understand—a strategy also used by the writers of "inner emigration" during the Nazi period) and then to critique of the Brechtian *Lehrstück* (learning play) that would prove the undoing of all received notions of drama, including the entire tradition of the Brechtian *Fabel*.

From the ground of this regenerative Brecht-critique—involving a radical expansion and elaboration of *Lehrstück* ideas, such as the use of non-professional performers, the priority of process over product, and the questioning of individual identity through choral staging and the exchanging of roles—Müller went on to develop an aesthetic of assemblage and collage that he called "the synthetic fragment." Synthetic fragments, such as *Die Schlacht* (*The Battle*, 1951/74) and *Germania Tod in Berlin* (*Germania Death in Berlin*, 1956/71), were piecemeal constructions in which disparate scenes, often with unconnected plots, were juxtaposed in sequences that aimed not at unity but at clashes of images and subjects, usually from German history and myth.

Several of these featured prominent Beckett allusions. In *Leben Gundlings Friedrich von Preussen Lessings Schlaf Traum Schrei* (*Gundling's Life Frederick of Prussia Lessing's Sleep Dream Scream*, 1976), for instance, the character called Lessing Actor speaks of "yearning for silence" and is left in the end burrowing around in a sand pile understood as a junk heap for humanist culture.[8] In *Germania Death in Berlin*, two clowns replay Hamm and Clov's game of centering the chair, one of Hitler's guards offers a decidedly Clov-like report on conditions outside the bunker ("a dog walked by"), and one entire scene, entitled *"Nachtstück"* ("Night Play"), is conceived as a *Gegenstück* (counterplay) to *Act Without Words I*, depicting a "man who may be a puppet" suicidally frustrated by invisibly controlled props.[9]

The truth is, though, that the uses of Beckett in a work like *Germania Death in Berlin* are cosmetic, even narrow. Isolated in his own country for years and permitted to travel to the West from the mid-1970s on, Müller wielded such allusions as part of an increasingly aggressive oppositional stance, keeping one foot at all times on each side of the Berlin Wall and insisting that GDR politics and culture had

[8]   Heiner Müller, *Herzstück* (Berlin: Rotbuch, 1983), 35.

[9]   Heiner Müller, *Germania Tod in Berlin* (Berlin: Rotbuch, 1977), 43-4, 59, 74-5.

reached a point of frozen standstill that Western-style avant-gardism was necessary to disturb. His purpose, as always, was "to look history in the whites of the eyes,"[10] but by that time that gesture had become frustratingly difficult. Western artists were perpetually distracted by consumerist trivialization, he thought, and Eastern ones were intellectually hamstrung by ignorant and arbitrary autocratic control. Müller's obsessive fragmentation was consequently part of an effort to do an "end run" around all the confusion and frustration. He sought a democratically "open" dramatic form for the "disassembled subject" of the *Lehrstück* without resorting to the patriarchally "closed" form of the parable, and Beckett was a convenient trope for the socio-political conditions that made that effort necessary—a figure for frozen standstill and the historical impasse of revolution.

This sort of troping is extremely reductive, and it is fortunate for Müller's work that the attitude eventually deepened. The change really began with *Gundling's Life...* and *Hamletmachine* (1977), a work that ends with a character being wrapped histrionically in gauze, as Hamm is ultimately re-covered with his "old stancher," in preparation for a period of indomitable waiting through what Müller calls "the ice age" (read: capitalism).[11] In *Quartet*, the figures complain in precisely the same tones as Didi and Gogo about feeling trapped in roles they do not quite believe in, on an incompletely metaphorical stage.

In these works, Müller does not merely utilize, minimize or reductively circumscribe Beckettian tropes but rather suggests, through a grave tone of closure, a real entrapment within and inescapable fascination with them. These works mark a crucial transitional period in which his fame was exploding abroad, transforming him by default into a national hero at home, and he was beginning to feel artistically defanged by the barrage of distorting attention. One consequence was a loss of faith in his longstanding preference for fragmentation in itself. He now considered this tactic too susceptible to "fetishization" and the "police identification" efforts of journalists and critics,[12] and his defense was to shift his strategies around in every new text in a variegated search for a more enduring frame for indeterminacy. (The same obsessive shifting also characterized his more and more frequent directing projects at the time.)

---

[10] Heiner Müller, *Rotwelsch* (Berlin: Merve, 1982), 141.

[11] Heiner Müller, *Mauser* (Berlin: Rotbuch, 1978), 97.

[12] Heiner Müller, *Gesammelte Irrtümer* (Frankfurt/Main: Verlag der Autoren, 1982), 56.

The culmination of this effort was *Description of a Picture*, a work as clearly influenced by Müller's collaboration with Robert Wilson as it is by the model of Beckett. Müller himself once described this work as "an endpoint or zero point" in his career.[13] Consisting of seven pages of dense prose broken only by commas and an occasional colon, it contains no stage directions or character indications and describes a nearly still, dreamlike, Wilsonesque picture that becomes the site and occasion of a theater event based primarily on the "movement" of the imagination. It begins:

> A landscape between steppe and savanna, the sky Prussian blue, two huge clouds swim in, held together as if by wire skeletons . . . on a tree bough sits a bird, the foliage concealing its identity, it could be a vulture or a peacock or a vulture with a peacock's head, gaze and beak directed at a woman who dominates the right half of the picture, her head divides the line of mountains, her face is gentle, very young, her nose too long, with a swelling at the base, perhaps from a punch . . .[14]

A man who may or may not be the woman's murderer is introduced next, holding a bird in a death grip, the murder having possibly occurred during violent sex on a chair that is now broken. And about two-thirds through, the narrator, without having resolved any of the myriad uncertainties about content, turns to hypotheses about the picture's meaning and about the future.

> . . . is the woman with the furtive look and the mouth like a suction cup a MATA HARI of the underworld . . . or is the angel hollow under the dress because the shrinking meat counter under the ground won't give up any more bodies, a BAD FINGER that's held up by the dead in the wind against the police of heaven . . .[15]

This wind strongly recalls the one that blows Walter Benjamin's angel of history. In the end, the narrator announces a search for "the possibly redemptive error" in the picture—a visual distraction of the killer, say, or laughter by the woman before the violent act. And then, unlike Beckett's Mouth in *Not I*, the voice resolves itself into an "I," or rather several of them.

---

[13]   Ibid, 184.

[14]   Heiner Müller, *Shakespeare Factory 1* (Berlin: Rotbuch, 1985), 7.

[15]   Ibid, 12.

the MURDER is an exchange of sexes, FOREIGN IN ONE'S OWN
BODY, the knife is the wound, the neck the axe, the fallible
surveillance belongs to the plan, on which device is the lens attached
that sucks the color out of the view, in which eye socket is the retina
stretched, who OR WHAT asks about the picture, LIVING IN THE
MIRROR, is the man with the dance step I, my grave his face, I the
woman with the wound on the neck, right and left in hands the
divided bird, blood on the mouth, I the bird, which shows the
murderer the way into the night with the writing of its beak, I the
frozen storm.[16]

To anyone familiar with Beckett's later oeuvre, certain features
of this text should be obvious at this point. Like so much of Beckett's
late prose, dramatic and nondramatic, *Description of a Picture* presents
a fragmentary, possibly post-death body "amputated by the picture's
border" and a willfully indeterminate picture that the reader/spectator
must mentally "construct" in the course of listening. The largely mental
action consists of the collision between that construction process and
the speaker's creative journey. That is why reading the words can feel
in itself like a dramatic experience, even though Müller insisted that
this is a theatrical work and not merely a text for reading. In either
case, the mental construction of the timeless picture necessarily occurs
in time, so the mind, whether reading or listening, cannot help
repeatedly stopping to ponder what it has been told (a "Prussian blue"
sky?), momentarily regarding incomplete interim pictures as complete,
like theatrical scenes or film frames, despite the continual addition of
new information. The listener/onlooker tends to be pulled into the
process of fragmentation that (in a final irony) binds the narrative
together ("who OR WHAT asks about the picture")—just as in *Play*, *Not
I*, *That Time* and other Beckett works. The knife *becomes* the wound,
the neck *becomes* the axe, and the victim *becomes* the perpetrator
precisely because the "surveillance" of the author/speaker (or
reader/spectator) is "fallible." Or, as Beckett once put it succinctly: "to
be an artist is to fail, as no other dare fail."[17]

As already mentioned, it is remarkable in itself that Müller, an
artist who, in his own words, "started where Brecht left off,"[18] in
essence ended his career where Beckett left off (and where Robert
Wilson and others were still working)—that the culmination of his forty-

---

[16]   Ibid, 14.

[17]   Samuel Beckett, "Three Dialogues," in Disjecta: Miscellaneous Writings
and a Dramatic Fragment (NY: Grove Press, 1984), 145.

[18]   Heiner Müller, Gesammelte Irrtümer, 129.

year quest to redeem Brecht's dream of a truly "democratic" theater "for the scientific age" took the form (again in his words) of "a landscape beyond death . . . the explosion of a memory in a dead dramatic structure."[19] Even if this were not an odd biographical twist, though, the Beckett-Müller connection would stand as an important paradigm for the impasse or closure-point many critics have observed in traditionally defined playwriting during our media-dominated era.

Nearly every study of recent innovative and experimental theater touches in some way on Müller and the shift he popularized toward decentered characters and stages conceived as quasi-"conscious" or "intelligent" landscapes. The most comprehensive study of this kind that I know of is Hans-Thies Lehmann's *Postdramatisches Theater*, which analyzes dozens of artists and groups throughout the Euro-American field and consistently views Müller as a weathervane and harbinger of the future. Lehmann coins the controversial term "postdramatic theater" for a huge phenomenon he would no doubt claim subsumes all the tendencies described by other recent studies, such as Elinor Fuchs' *The Death of Character* and Jeanette Malkin's *Memory-Theater and Postmodern Drama*. Fuchs views Beckett (and by extension, Lee Breuer and Mabou Mines) as the true pioneers of Müller's diffused spectatorship. For her, the most advanced theater presumes a "post-Beckett spectator" as witness to "an endgame for the Cartesian dramatic subject"—the prime insight of Breuer and Mabou Mines having been that Beckett's "'I's' were not so much concrete, individual characters as the great drone of the 'universal bagpipe' inside everybody's head."[20] Malkin examines the "rupture" in our era "between memory and history" as "paradigms for a vision of the world" in dramas written after the early 1970s. She finds Beckett both attached to and separated from the sort of exploded-memory theater Müller represents.

Lehmann traces the roots of "postdramatic theater" to Brecht's vision (primarily in his *Fatzer* material) of "theater with a minimum of dramaturgy, that is, almost no dramaturgy" (the words are Müller's).[21] The linking formal features of this theater are too numerous to list (Lehmann's examples run from Robert Wilson, Jan Fabre, Heiner Goebbels, Einar Schleef and Robert Lepage to Hans-Jürgen Syberberg,

---

[19]   Heiner Müller, *Shakespeare Factory 1*, 7-8.

[20]   Elinor Fuchs, *The Death of Character: Perspectives on Theater after Modernism* (Bloomington: Indiana Univ. Press, 1996), 173.

[21]   Hans-Thies Lehmann, *Postdramatisches Theater* (Frankfurt/Main: Verlag der Autoren, 1999), 30.

Tadeusz Kantor, John Jesurun, Eugenio Barba, Theater Angelus Novus, La Fura dels Baus and Théâtre de Complicité), but Lehmann is careful to stipulate that "postdramatic theater is a post-Brechtian theater." It flourishes in "a time after the authoritative validity of Brecht's concept of theater," with its patriarchally directive emphasis on *Fabel.*[22] In our time, he says, "one can speak of a post-Brechtian theater that has nothing to do with Brecht, that rather knows itself to be affected by the sedimented claims and questions in Brecht's work but can't accept Brecht's answers anymore."[23] Hence, today, "Robert Wilson can be understood as no less legitimate a Brecht-heir than Heiner Müller,"[24] and so can Beckett, particularly in his later plays. *That Time*—a crucially self-conscious work that Lehmann sees as "parodying" the classical unities of place and time, not just subtly subverting them as in Beckett's previous drama—receives one of the most sustained analyses in the book.

Müller, unlike Beckett, was the willing subject of frequent interviews, and during his last decade he told several interlocutors that he was having trouble formulating his thoughts in dramatic form. Always deeply political in spirit, he had nevertheless tired of perpetually searching for new ways around the parabolic wholeness, healthiness and patriarchalism of Brecht's guilt- and history-based political forms. The basic insight behind his impasse, or block, however, was Beckettian: that the future of theater that resists the norms and assumptions of a materially glutted age lay not in new material or information but rather in changed modes of perception, in fresh means of questioning what is and is not "I."

II. Intertextuality and Copyright Law

Between 1996 and 2000, a dispute concerning Heiner Müller's posthumously published and produced last play, *Germania 3: Gespenster am Toten Mann (Germania 3: Ghosts at the Dead Man)*, developed into an important legal case whose ironies and overtones provided a fitting coda to what was already known about Müller's extremely liberal attitude toward originality and intellectual property. This liberality, of course, echoed Brecht's. The case began when the heirs of Bertolt Brecht (Barbara Brecht-Schall, Stefan Brecht and Hanne Hiob—with Brecht-Schall as the principal agent) took legal action to prevent the play's publisher, Kiepenheuer & Witsch (Cologne), from

---

[22]   Ibid, 48.

[23]   Ibid, 31.

[24]   Ibid, 48.

selling or distributing it, because it contained passages from two Brecht plays (*Galileo* and *Coriolanus*) and a paraphrase from a Brecht poem ("Ich benötige keinen Grabstein" ["I need no gravestone"]) for which the heirs had not given publication-permission. A temporary injunction against Kiepenheuer & Witsch was granted in May, 1996, which was then lifted by the Oberlandesgericht (Court of Appeal) in Brandenburg. During the next several years, the heirs pursued the matter, won a favorable ruling from the Oberlandesgericht in Munich, and the case ended up before Germany's highest court, the Bundesverfassungsgericht (BvG), which adjudicates constitutional questions. In July, 2000, the BvG ruled in favor of Müller and, in a strongly worded reversal, ordered the Brecht heirs to pay all legal costs. In order to understand the implications of this decision, one must first understand a bit about the play and the outlines of the case.

Germania 3 belongs to the class of collage works about German history and myth that, as mentioned before, Müller generally called "synthetic fragments." It is the most rigorously disjunctive and least tonally unified among them, consisting of nine scenes, each of which introduces an entirely new setting and story line. The work is a veritable treasury of exploded clichés about the Teutonic, its astonishing variety of episodes complemented by a bewildering diversity of ironies. It is also among Müller's most densely allusive writings—a point that seems to have given him pause, since the text proper (81 pages) is followed by 34 pages of excerpted encyclopedia articles about the places, people, institutions and concepts cited in the action.

Only occasionally realistic, the play's scenes use sizeable quotations from German literature (1-3 pages, usually set off with italics, and with the sources acknowledged in a "Text Inventory" at the end) to help establish a tension between craven individual interest and blinkered group interest as the Ur-conflict in Germany. Thus, for instance, the "Now, O immortality, you are wholly mine!" speech from Kleist's *Prince of Homburg* is inserted after two starving German officers come upon a rations cannister at Stalingrad, eat its contents rather than sharing them with their company, and then shoot each other, apparently as a point of honor.

The main linking theme of *Germania 3* has to do with rationalizations for killing and other barbarity in the name of various seductive ideals: *Deutschland über alles*, the Deutsche Mark, party unity, revolutionary solidarity. In one scene, the socialist heroes Ernst Thälmann and Walter Ulbricht patrol as guards along the Berlin Wall when a would-be fugitive is shot at and arrested. Stalin and Hitler both make appearances, delivering long, self-justifying monologues that establish their mutual dependency and similarity. At one point, three widows of Nazi officers in 1945 beg a fleeing Croatian SS-officer to kill them so they won't be raped by "Asiatic" Russian soldiers.

The Brecht material appears in a scene set at the Berliner Ensemble shortly after Brecht's death and provocatively titled "Massnahme [The Measures Taken] 1956." The scene actually conflates historical events that happened at different times during that year. "Three Brecht Widows," identified as Helene Weigel, Elisabeth Hauptmann, and Isot Kilian (all three were Brecht's lovers, but Weigel was his legal widow and Kilian was actually the former wife of the philosopher Wolfgang Harich), trade regrets and recriminations in the head office while listening to a radio news report about Harich's arrest. They then listen in on a rehearsal for *Coriolanus*, via a loudspeaker, where the Brecht protégés Peter Palitzsch and Manfred Wekwerth argue over whether the production ought to include an explicit critique of current events.

The recent Soviet invasion of Hungary looms in the background and Kilian, referring to the suppressed workers' uprising in East Berlin three years earlier, remarks at one point that Brecht "raised his cap to the tanks in fifty three." The *Galileo* quotation, the so-called "Parable of the Little Monk"—about the threat that Galileo's sort of new knowledge poses to the contented ignorance and innocent piety of the Monk's farm family—follows a remark by Palitzsch to the effect that he sometimes thinks, "mostly at night, or half asleep," that "the Little Monk is right, not Galileo." The dialog from *Coriolanus* is spoken by the rehearsing actors and highlights the title character's contemptuously anti-democratic nature while also echoing the subtler despotic politics of Wekwerth and the spying widows. The paraphrase from the "Gravestone" poem ends the scene, inverting Brecht's famous line "He made suggestions. We carried them out." Müller's version: "He made suggestions We didn't carry them out Why should we."[25]

According to Helge Malchow, Editor-in-Chief of Kiepenheuer & Witsch, permission was requested to use the Brecht material before *Germania 3* appeared, but Brecht-Schall's representatives responded by demanding several unacceptable conditions. The *Coriolanus* scene had to be replaced by another Shakespeare adaptation of the publisher's choice, not by Brecht. The *Galileo* parable could be used as long as the proper names of the Brecht Widows were cut from the text. And the "Grabstein" text had to be replaced by Brecht's original poem, the argument here being that Müller's text "distorted" Brecht's "biographical portrait." Malchow said that Brecht-Schall, the daughter

---

[25]   Heiner Müller, *Germania 3: Gespenster am Toten Mann* (Cologne: Kiepenheuer & Witsch, 1996), 64.

of Brecht and Helene Weigel, felt that Müller had made "Brecht appear to be a 'pessimist,' and Papa was never a pessimist." "But that's exactly the point," continued Malchow, "The gravestone text, which just about everyone knows, becomes a new thought in the poetic fracture."[26]

In remarks quoted around this time in the *Berliner Zeitung*, Brecht-Schall admitted that the real problem was that she felt insulted. She also claimed that Müller had agreed to cut the names of the widows in his manuscript before he died, and had even considered cutting the entire scene. Furthermore, Müller's widow, Brigitte Mayer, knew this and was therefore party to what Brecht-Schall took to be a betrayal. "I think it's a low-down dirty trick," Brecht-Schall said. "It's just out of order, and I told him that very bluntly. We were on a footing where we could be totally blunt with one another. I'm very devoted to Mama and I won't let anybody make a fool of her [*lasse sie . . . zur Minna machen*]." The whole matter could be handled with a few supplementary footnotes, she insisted: "All they'd have to do is print four or five pages anew."[27]

The temporary injunction was issued as *Germania 3* was receiving its world premiere at the Bochum Schauspielhaus in May 1996, directed by Leander Haussmann. Another production, directed by Martin Wuttke, opened at the Berliner Ensemble in June. Oddly enough, Brecht-Schall allowed these productions to go forward on the sole condition that the names of the Brecht Widows be omitted from the scripts and the programs. Both theaters reportedly agreed. Carl Hegemann, Head Dramaturg at the Berliner Ensemble—the theater that Brecht founded, it should be remembered, and that Müller led until his death six months before these events—said at the time: "I find Müller's play so important that I don't want to endanger a production due to such a formality."[28] The program for Wuttke's production identified the women only as "Brecht Widow 1," "Brecht Widow 2" and "Brecht Widow 3."

In the Bochum production, however, the program carried the designation "Brecht Widow*" beside all three actresses' names, with the asterisk denoting a note at the bottom of the page: "Due to an agreement made by Henschel Verlag [the publisher in charge of performance rights] with the Brecht heirs, we were asked not to

---

[26] Hans-Dieter Schütt, interview with Helge Malchow, "'Pessimist' war der Papa nie," *Neues Deutschland*, June 4, 1996, 10.

[27] "Mama nicht zur Minna machen!", *Berliner Zeitung*, June 5, 1996.

[28] Peter Laudenbach, "Trotz Buchverbot auf die Bühne," *Berliner Zeitung*, June 4, 1996.

mention the names 'Weigel,' 'Hauptmann' and 'Kilian' in the cast list."
The proper names were also announced from the forestage by a
grinning jester as the scene began, after which the women appeared in
sexless black dresses, sensible shoes, and long beards, planted like
monuments on a plush couch, with one of them literally sitting on the
"master's" works. This lampoon attracted ample national publicity,
which Kiepenheuer & Witsch was unable to take advantage of due to
the injunction.

In Carl Weber's English translation of *Germania 3*, published
in 2001 by Johns Hopkins University Press but typeset before the BvG
decision was announced, the disputed play quotations and the widows'
names were omitted due to Hopkins' fear of a lawsuit. In lieu of the
quotations are italicized editorial notes that blend in with Müller's stage
directions: "*He quotes from the speech of the Little Monk, who defends
the wisdom of the Catholic Church; Galileo, Scene 8*"; "*Rehearsal
through the intercom. Marcus refuses the plebeians' demands for
affordable corn; Coriolanus, Act 1, Scene 1.*"[29] Given the implication
here that readers are free to look up the omitted passages, one might
bear in mind that, while Eric Bentley's English translation of *Galileo* is
easily available in the United States, Ralph Manheim's 1973 translation
of Brecht's *Coriolanus* has long been out of print.

In all likelihood, a frustrating and troubling book will be
written some day about the obstructionist practices of the Brecht heirs
in administering rights to their father's works. I will not attempt any
nutshell analysis here. It is important to understand, however, that the
Germania 3 affair fits into a pattern of behavior dating back to the early
1960s, with its roots in Cold-War politics. In 1970, for instance,
Helene Weigel reneged on an agreement already finalized between the
Berlin Schiller Theater and Suhrkamp Verlag for a production of *The
Threepenny Opera*, because the Schiller had produced Günter Grass's
The Plebeians Rehearse the Uprising in 1966, which Weigel felt
"distorted" Brecht's position on the 1953 East German workers'
uprising. In 1981, Dario Fo broke off rehearsals and left East Berlin in
reaction to Barbara Brecht-Schall's intrusions on his Berliner Ensemble
production of *Threepenny Opera*; this production starred her husband,
Ekkehard Schall, who reported regularly to her about Fo's artistic
choices. In 1993, Brecht-Schall took legal action to prevent the
director Einar Schleef from using Brecht's hymn "In praise of
Communism" in Schleef's production of Rolf Hochhuth's *Wessis in*

[29]   Heiner Müller, *A Heiner Müller Reader*, trans. Carl Weber (Baltimore and
London: Johns Hopkins Univ. Press, 2001), 206.

Weimar. There is no need to multiply the examples.[30] The point is that this stringent vigilance has had a false ring to it from the beginning, in light of Brecht's self-confessed "fundamental laxity in" and "reprehensible indifference to" questions of literary property—a laxity from which the heirs have earned a considerable sum over the years.[31]

Once one understands this, however, it is even more important to understand that both Brecht's and Müller's works raise fascinating questions regarding multiple authorship—questions whose complexity is belied by the petty simplifications of these proprietary squabbles. The sticky issue of collective creation in the name of a communal ideal, for instance, and the voluntary self-sacrifice and self-effacement that accompany it, is unavoidable with Brecht's ouevre, as it is with Müller's collaborations with his second wife, the poet Inge Müller, in the late 1950s. As is well known, a minor conflagration occurred in scholarly circles when John Fuegi's book *Brecht & Co.* (the object of yet another lawsuit by the Brecht heirs) appeared in 1994 and took an intemperately conspiratorial view of this activity, suggesting that Brecht had cheated and exploited his most trusting and loving collaborators. My own view of this matter is that the flaws in Fuegi's book should urge others to do a better job, not to drop the inquiry, and that questions of due credit are in any case merely the tip of this iceberg.

In Müller's works, with their shameless plunderings and brilliant amalgamations of new and received creativity, the broader subject of intertextuality asserts itself more immediately and urgently than in any other late 20th-century drama. Pride in his own bricolage-handicraft was the closest Müller ever came to endorsing a coherent moral platform: honesty defined as candor about what Mikhail Bakhtin called "the dialogic imagination," the admission that one is a mere link in a historical chain, uncertain what, if anything, is purely one's own. Müller's work is a veritable laboratory for experimentation with the new "postindustrial" creative paradigm that Michel Foucault described in his famous essay "What is an Author?" (1977, reworked from a 1969 lecture). The world would soon redefine "the author function," Foucault predicted, replacing such traditional critical questions as "Who really spoke? Is it really he and not someone else? With what authenticity or originality? And what part of his deepest self did he express in his discourse?" with other questions more attuned to the

---

[30] A useful chronicle of such incidents was published in *Der Tagesspiegel*, "Die Heiligen Witwen der Gerichtshöfe," June 19, 1996.

[31] These are Brecht's words from two widely quoted 1929 newspaper interviews. See Klaus Völker, *Brecht: A Biography*, trans. John Nowell (NY: Seabury, 1978), 132-3.

slippages in meaning that accrue from historical contradictions and collisions. For instance: "What are the modes of existence of this discourse? Where has it been used, how can it circulate, and who can appropriate it for himself? What are the places in it where there is room for possible subjects? Who can assume these various subject functions? And behind all these questions . . . What difference does it make who is speaking?"[32]

Foucault died in 1984, too early to witness the flowering of the information age, when digital music sampling, data networks, chat-rooms, on-line reference materials and other electronic library resources would pose challenges to received notions of private, individual authorship on a more massive and popular scale than he ever envisioned. Müller, however, lived until the end of 1995 and clearly understood both the open nature of the new age and the battles that would be waged in it to preserve the traditional boundaries of private property in the form of copyright. Recent controversies surrounding such works as Alice Randall's *The Wind Done Gone* (a retelling of *Gone With the Wind* from a slave's perspective, blocked from publication by Margaret Mitchell's heirs), Pia Pera's *Lo's Diary* (a "spinoff" of Vladimir Nabokov's "Lolita" told from the nymphet's point of view, whose English-language publication was initially blocked by Nabokov's son Dmitri) and Susan Sontag's *In America* (a novel about the actress Helena Modjeska, challenged for its uncredited use of historical sources) are cases in point. As many critics have observed, Western copyright laws are rooted in a two-century-old Romantic model of authorship whose assumptions about the sanctity of individual creation are ill-fitted to many current circumstances.[33] The BvG decision involving *Germania 3* is part of a growing body of case law in the West that is mapping out boundaries for the new era.

This legal decision—excerpts from which I have translated and included in the revised paperback edition of *The Theater of Heiner*

---

[32] Michel Foucault, "What is an Author?" in Josué V. Harari, ed., *Textual Strategies: Perspectives in Post-Structuralist Criticism* (Ithaca: Cornell Univ. Press, 1979), 160.

[33] This is the main subject of Martha Woodmansee and Peter Jaszi's essay collection, *The Construction of Authorship: Textual Appropriation in Law and Literature* (Durham and London: Duke Univ. Press, 1994). The closest American parallel to the *Germania 3* case is probably "Campbell v. Acuff-Rose Music," the 1994 ruling by the Supreme Court concerning the rap group 2 Live Crew's use of lyrics and a bass riff by Roy Orbison in the song "Pretty Woman." The Court found that this use of copyrighted material constituted legitimate parody.

Müller[34]—does not propose any bold new definition of authorship. Nor is it written with any unusual sensitivity either to intertextuality per se or to Müller's East German political disposition; the judges' Western Cold-War orientation is evident. The decision does, however, offer an interesting argument for weighing concrete claims of ownership against much more abstract and nebulous claims of historical consciousness. The gist of the reasoning is that although Müller's use of the Brecht material "clearly oversteps" the established legal bounds of "fair use," it should nevertheless be permitted because it constitutes a serious critical argument (*Auseinandersetzung*) with an important literary and historical figure.

Several American legal scholars I have consulted have assured me that the framework does exist in United States law to protect an American publisher faced with a similar challenge. An American court, however, would most likely have to base its decision primarily on the principle of "fair use," which has been stretched and adjusted over the years to accommodate the conflicting rights of copyright and the First Amendment in the United States; the BvG, by contrast, had recourse to an explicit guarantee of artistic freedom in the German constitution, or *Grundgesetz* ("Basic Law," Article 5).[35]

What is the tie to Beckett in all this? It is the fact that he and his heirs have also had famously strong opinions regarding intellectual property and exerted strict control over certain questions of rights over the years—particularly concerning permissions for stage adaptation. It seems to me inevitable that maintaining this strictness during the current historical moment and throughout the coming era will be terribly destructive of Beckett's cultural stature.

As everyone knows, Beckett was one of the twentieth century's most erudite authors. He was as much the master allusionist as Borges, Eliot or Müller, only his attitude toward the enormous cultural baggage

---

[34] Jonathan Kalb, *The Theater of Heiner Müller*, expanded edition (NY: Limelight Editions, 2001), Appendix A.

[35] Special thanks to Professor Alfred C. Yen of Boston College Law School for discussing this decision with me. Article 5 of the German *Grundgesetz*, or "Basic Law," reads in part: "(1) Every person shall have the right freely to express and disseminate his opinions in speech, writing, and pictures and to inform himself without hindrance from generally accessible sources. Freedom of the press and freedom of reporting by means of broadcasts and films shall be guaranteed. There shall be no censorship. . . (3) Art and scholarship, research, and teaching shall be free." *Basic Law for Federal Republic of Germany*, trans. Christian Tomuschat and David P. Curry (Bonn: Press and Information Office of the [German] Federal Government, 1998), 41.

in his work differed from theirs. For Beckett, the borrowings were grains of sand from the great humanist heap whose futility as a redemptive or humanizing influence he took for granted—*tactically*. The subject is futility but, biography notwithstanding, we are speaking of rhetorical futility: the three certainties—"I was born, I must die and for reasons unknown and unknowable, I cannot keep silent." For Borges, by contrast, the true subject is always the cyclical nature of time and the artist's sense that all literature is essentially the work of the same creative spirit, the gloriously self-abnegating self consumed in the lifelong toil of revealing the absurdity of Self. And for Brecht and Müller, borrowing is an aggressive act of remembrance, a polemical stone thrown in the teeth of pervasive forgetfulness and the unbearable lightness of being. Brecht's work has been occasionally dismissed as the last gasp of dialectical hopefulness, a nineteenth-century delusion, but Müller captivated the serious Euro-American theater public through two decades of late twentieth-century consumerism with a more cryptic and subjectively exploded version of the same delusion.

Humanism—as he showed with his signature brand of cynicism—is just not so easy to kill, and neither is the theater, even in Borges, Brecht, Müller and Beckett. As Ortega y Gasset wrote in *The Revolt of the Masses*: "The cynic, a parasite of civilization, lives by denying it, for the very reason that he is convinced that it will not fail."[36] Müller believed—with all the earnestness of which he was capable—that civilization needs such parasites. In our time, we call them artists.

To return to the main theme, my point here is that Beckett occupies an important and legitimate point on the scale of intertextuality. He is not off the scale or beside the point simply because of his modernist stance on authorial control or because he wrote more beautifully and persuasively about futility and the sense of cultural-historical ending than any other author of his time. He is, like all great authors, a mine of intertextual richness, and as the world's attitude toward such richness begins to change, so too must his work be allowed to breathe the air of the new era. In practical terms, people in the theater ought to be allowed to try new ideas, even if they are patently stupid ones. As I have written many times, it almost always proves true that Beckett's theatrical conceptions turn out to be more interesting and enduringly provocative than other people's improvements. Most cross-genre adaptations and spinoffs of Beckett are plainly misguided: he is nowhere near as easily malleable as Brecht

---

[36] José Ortega y Gasset, *The Revolt of the Masses*, trans. anonymous (NY: W.W. Norton, 1932), Ch. 11.

or Müller. Posterity, however, is a better judge of this than we are, and it should be left to do its work of judgement. If these projects are not allowed, if Beckett is kept protected as some sacred object in a legally sealed, romantically copyrighted vitrine, then imaginative people everywhere will soon start to lose interest in him—and this will happen very fast. The promise and terror of the coming age is that the heap, grain upon grain, is generally seen to belong to everyone, and everyone wants the sense of using *and* discarding it in his or her own way.

III. American Solo Performance

This last topic is as much a product of my experience as a New York theater critic and theatergoer over the past decade as it is of scholarly reading, and I should also concede that it has more to do with Brecht than with Beckett. Here too, though, I see a point of important convergence, and again I make my approach through the lens of Heiner Müller.

In mid-1995, shortly after the final disintegration of the five-member, post-Wall directorate of the Berlin Ensemble that left Heiner Müller sole leader, I asked him whether Brecht would continue to be central to that theater's repertory. "Absolutely," he said. The German critics who were then loudly insisting (along with some former members of the directorate) that Brecht was an outdated paradigm were "idiots," and Müller had half a dozen exciting Brecht projects in mind that he hoped to begin in the near future (pending approval by the recalcitrant Brecht heirs) in order to maintain his theater's provocative political profile. I felt compelled to justify my question, explaining that, in my country, Brecht was not only currently out of fashion but had never been properly in fashion, even during his lifetime, even among the theatrical intelligentsia. Puffing on his cigar, Müller said quietly, "That's because Americans are all innocents." The most difficult audiences in the world, and "the most dangerous people," are "those who feel innocent of everything."

The whiff of intellectual bigotry in these remarks aside, they contain a truth that reaches beyond Brecht to the challenges of political theater generally in the United States. It has been thirty-three years since Guy Debord coined the term "society of the spectacle" for the conditions of sweeping, media-driven trivialization and perpetual public distraction that began to emanate from America to the rest of the consumerist world after the Second World War.[37] By now these

---

[37]   Guy Debord, *The Society of the Spectacle*, trans. Donald Nicholson-Smith (NY: Zone, 1995).

conditions are familiar on every continent, making the primary preoccupations of political theater in many countries the restitution of elided memory and history, and the canny yet tentative re-introduction of critical thinking as a species of fun. Müller pinpoints one of the biggest enduring hurdles in America: for much of its history, American culture's congratulatory self-image as the world's benefactor, as well as its deeply ingrained myths of optimism, possibility, and self-reliance, have made it doggedly resistant to any theater based on guilt.

A particular group of contemporary American solo performers—some of whom do and some of whom do not acknowledge their ties to the idea of documentary—have offered a powerful response to this and other challenges. These artists seem to me to fuse a psychological and political appeal, linking compassion and identification with objective scrutiny in a way that, though Brecht might not have approved of it, amounts to a new, peculiarly American form of individualistic *Verfremdung*.

The artists I have primarily in mind are Anna Deavere Smith, Marc Wolf, Danny Hoch, and Sarah Jones: not an immediately harmonious grouping, perhaps, for those who know their work. My linkage of them depends on steering the discussion of solo performance away from its usual emphasis on identity politics and toward a more elementary debate about the public's receptivity to politics and critical thinking per se. It also depends on loosening the definition of "documentary" to a point where it could apply as well to John Leguizamo, Eric Bogosian, Eve Ensler, David Cale, Lisa Kron, Spalding Gray, Dael Orlandersmith, Whoopi Goldberg and dozens of other soloists whose work may not be a product of field research—i.e. it may not qualify as documentary per se—but is unthinkable apart from their experiences in some degree of first-hand witnessing.

The essence of my point here has to do with the exhaustion of a huge number of theatrical strategies that once qualified as effective *Verfremdung*. Solo performance is partly a reaction to what has not worked in larger-scale theater, the past quarter century or so having been a conspicuously dismal period for political theater in America. Happily, we have now emerged from the era of "splinter theater," when many of the country's most politically vital groups voluntarily ghettoized their creative and political energies by playing only to select communities defined by ethnicity, party, gender or geography. In fact, though, the basic complacency and unreflectiveness of the commodity-obsessed public have remained largely unaffected by the gradual "mainstreaming" of race- and gender-bending practices, as is also true of the continued use of dated and impotent agit-prop techniques by expressly "Brechtian" companies such as The San Francisco Mime Troupe and Irondale Ensemble.

The show that the Mime Troupe toured in 2000 about urban development and gentrification, *City for Sale*, co-written by Joan Holden and Kate Chumley and directed by Keiko Shimosato, was to me a perfect example of an application of the 1950s and 60s "nuts-and-bolts" approach to *Verfremdung* that seems irredeemably naive today. Holden and Chumley were very good at clarifying the complexity of the housing issues they raised, but precisely because of that clarity, the cartoonish characterizations and broad clowning in the piece were irritating. The technique seemed to apologize for the material's complexity, like a set of children's theater blatancies arbitrarily imposed on a subtle, adult tale.

If today's general American theatergoing public thinks of political theater at all, it most likely thinks of innocuous, media-friendly sketch comedy in the vein of Capital Steps (a Washington group founded by former Congressional staff members), or of moralistic parables like *City for Sale*, or the plays of Odets, Hellman and Miller. (The 1960s and 70s "social protest drama" of such authors as Imamu Amiri Baraka and Miguel Piñero has dropped off the popular radar.) The sentimental parable tradition of Odets, Hellman and Miller, also sometimes known as American "social protest drama," has long been popular and is likely to remain so because, as Brecht pointed out, it allows spectators to congratulate themselves on their sympathetic feelings without seriously questioning their behavior or beliefs. But the sad truth is that the ostensibly anti-sentimental tradition of Brecht is scarcely more effective in our savvy and self-satisfied era, because his parables come off much more as didactic exercises in oversimplification than as fervent efforts to make the world appear changeable (the theoretical basis of *Verfremdung*). *City for Sale* is all too typical. Almost every new play written in this tradition leaves me broken-hearted; it invariably starts out as a passionately told story about specific people, then ends up as an underwhelming cliché about, say, the fact that Chicanos exist (as in the California group Culture Clash's 1998 piece *Culture Clash in Border Town*), or the fact that a powerless woman grasping for sexual independence will be exploited (as in Suzan-Lori Parks' 1999 play *In the Blood*).

These are the outlines of the general impasse out of which a few clever forms of guerilla theater, documentary theater, and solo performance have shown possible paths in the information age. "The question is," as the guerilla preacher Reverend Billy put it succinctly when I interviewed him in the winter of 2000, "how do you tell an 'original' story in 2000?" That is, how do you tell a truly personal tale "that will not be immediately folded into some big meta-story that politicians or the media manufacture?" How can the artist "be heard, and heard politically" by people who do not tolerate being compared with any fictionally drawn category of exploiters and who prefer not to think politically in any case? Effective political art in Clinton-Bush America must be cunning—much more so than in previous ages when institutional targets had less complex cosmetics and were less proficient at seeming nebulous—and the documentary impulse is a form of cunning even if its practitioners do not always see it that way. Nearly half a century of media saturation has made us stupider in many ways, but one way it has made us smarter is in our unprecedented familiarity with stories. Among its many other motives, documentary solo performance is a search for a freshness and unpredictability that carries the force of gossip, for powerful topical narratives that are not easily dismissed or second-guessed, and for performance circumstances in which *Verfremdung* becomes a living concept again because the reality of the performer-researcher has been made an active part of the art.

It's crucial to remember, in considering this work, that no previous society has ever placed the sort of burden of self-invention on its citizens that contemporary America does: that of constructing a fully satisfying self from scratch with little more than the trivializing idiocies of consumer- and pop-culture as guidance. As the social philosopher Zygmunt Bauman recently wrote: "The way individual people define individually their individual problems and try to tackle them deploying individual skills and resources is the sole remaining 'public issue' and the sole object of 'public interest.'"[38] However little we may really be interested in anyone else, we do seem willing to listen to people's *individual* stories as possible keys to our own *individual* development—and that is the narrow political opportunity the solo performers exploit. The fact of their authentic *individuality* (or that of their stories) seems to me far more important in explaining their popularity than any ostensible authenticity in their research, if they even do real research.

Anna Deavere Smith, as is well known, based her two most prominent productions on the same technique of interviewing large numbers of people about selected tumultuous events (the 1991 riots in Crown Heights, Brooklyn, and the 1992 riots in Los Angeles) and then impersonating some of them onstage using their exact words and mannerisms. Marc Wolf applied precisely the same method to the subject of the American military's "Don't ask, don't tell" policy on homosexuality, basing his 1999 show *Another American: Asking & Telling* on impersonations from about 200 interviews. With both these performers, the process of impersonation was at all times more compelling than the facts and information conveyed, and the fact that

---

[38]   Zygmunt Bauman, *Liquid Modernity* (Cambridge: Polity, 2000), 72.

both actors were always visible beneath their intensely studied character surfaces was crucial to the pieces' strangely persuasive textures.

Danny Hoch and Sarah Jones, in contrast, perform fictional character sketches drawn from their experiences as young New Yorkers moving in social circles not commonly represented on American stages. What complicates their enacted portraits politically is their precise yet fearless mimicry across borders of race and class. Hoch, a white, 30-year-old from Queens, plays black and white rappers and wannabe rappers as sympathetically and persuasively as he does, say, a Puerto Rican woman preparing for a date with her bisexual boyfriend and a Cuban father whose son has been killed by the police. And 25-year-old Jones, a dark-skinned woman of mixed race, plays a predatory Italian cop and a bigoted old Jewish woman with the same meticulousness and polemical insight she brings to dueling, male and female hip-hop poets.[39]

The greatest political strength of these solo performers, and others like them, is that they are themselves caught in the social maelstroms they invite us to probe and understand. They are meticulous mimics but also courageous explorers of both the flattering and unflattering sides of the Others they choose as alter egos. Like all political theater in America, solo performers must negotiate the terrain of guilt, mined though it is, but they have an important edge in accomplishing that: the transparency of their self-reference. That is why I call their risky project of self-characterization by opposition and contrast an all-American version of *Verfremdung*. This notion is paradoxical in basic ways. Brecht's very reason for proposing "estrangement" was to show that supposedly "natural" and "inevitable" events and behaviors were part of human-controlled historical processes, and were thus changeable through volitional action, and he avoided Naturalism because its positivist ethos seemed inconsistent with that aim. The idea that being swept up in any socio-political maelstrom might be politically useful to an artist would have been entirely foreign to him.

Nearly half a century after his death, however, in the land whose HUAC investigations sped his return to Europe, Americans sympathetic to his goals necessarily pursue them based on a more

---

[39] For a more in-depth discussion of this subject and these artists, see my article "Documentary Solo Performance: The Politics of the Mirrored Self," *Theater*, Vol. 31, No. 3, Fall 2001. Jo Bonney has also documented much important work in her collection *Extreme Exposure: An Anthology of Solo Performance Texts from the Twentieth Century* (NY: TCG, 2000).

particularized view of American society than he ever applied. The grip of psychological realism on the American imagination, for instance, has outlasted decades of avant-gardist efforts to permanently dislodge it, and the style is now divorced from its positivist heritage and available to the Left, the Right, and the apolitical alike. Today, a generation after feminists insisted that "the personal is political," the personal dominates politics as much as it does drama in theater, film, and television. (Furthermore, according to Sue-Ellen Case, the detached attitude of the smoker that Brecht proposed is now a figure for patriarchal remoteness.[40]) For politically minded, info-age Americans, estrangement lives primarily as a means of seeing ourselves voyeuristically seeing ourselves, as a non-mediated form of self-actualization based on critiques of self-actualization. Ours is an era obsessed with witnessing, and an effective *Verfremdung* is nothing less than a reason to consider one sort of witnessing more persuasive than another.

And the link to Beckett? As mentioned before, there is only an indirect one. It would be silly and facile to start theorizing about, say, the underlying loneliness of monodrama merely in order to force such extremely topical and world-conscious work into congruence with Beckett. The indirect point seems to me significant, though. The cultural-political atmosphere in which these solo figures have risen so quickly to prominence is suffused with a Beckettian aura. What I mean is that Beckett was extremely prescient about the cultural impasse we have arrived at in which our only meaningful politics involves the struggle to define and justify the Self, and the very basic act of reaching out beyond the isolated confines of the atomized self qualifies as bold risk-taking. Everyone who rises to fame in the field of live performance nowadays does so in a context of media glut, seizing a moment of direct apprehension, as it were, from a world of hyperactualized individuals generally desperate, most of the time, to return to their mediated ground state (i.e. the cast of mind primarily determined by tranquilizing and titillating experiences with various flickering screens).

Many have long admired *Krapp's Last Tape*, a play Beckett wrote in 1958 about a man isolated in a room with an electronic device whose company he finds more comforting, arousing and self-actualizing than that of any human being. I wonder, though, how many of us really imagined forty-three, or even twenty-five years ago, watching this play, that we were encountering a new paradigm for the

---

[40]   Sue-Ellen Case, "'Wer raucht, sieht kaltblütig aus': Brecht, Müller, and Cigars," *drive b: brecht 100 (Theater der Zeit Arbeitsbuch/The Brecht Yearbook 23)*, 1998, 163-9.

average Joe.   Not just for a writer, an artist, or any other special or extreme case, but for the average Joe, or Jane.   Beckett remained preoccupied with this subject for the rest of his creative life, touching on it in all the ghostly, isolated figures peopling his later stage and media plays, from Joe in *Eh Joe* to F in *Ghost Trio* to Bam in *What Where*. The final link between him and Brecht, in other words, has to do with "imagining [we] have got hold of an apparatus which in fact has got hold of [us]" (to paraphrase Brecht's famous notes to *Mahagonny*).[41]   Or as Krapp says, "in the future," on a 30-year-old tape: "We lay there without moving. But under us all moved, and moved us, gently, up and down, and from side to side.   Past midnight.   Never knew such silence. The earth might be uninhabited."[42]

---

[41]   Bertolt Brecht, *Brecht on Theatre*, trans. John Willet (NY: Hill and Wang, 1964), 34.

[42]   Samuel Beckett, *The Collected Shorter Plays* (NY: Grove Press, 1984), 63.

Beckett, Samuel: *Waiting for Godot*. Tragicomedy in 2 acts. Translated from his original French. New York: Grove Press, 1954. Nachlaßbibliothek Bertolt Brecht.

SAMUEL BECKETT

WARTEN AUF GODOT

SUHRKAMP

Samuel Beckett: *Warten auf Godot.*   Berlin: Suhrkamp, 1955. Nachlaßbibliothek Bertolt Brecht.

Brecht and Beckett in the Theater II

Everett Frost, Moray McGowan, Fiona Shaw, and Michael Colgan

Chair: Dennis Kennedy

***

Everett C. Frost
Brecht and Beckett on the Radio

I

A fragile voice travels through the air over long distances and materializes in intimate and intelligible form out of the hiss and crackle of the background static. In Samuel Beckett's *Rough for Radio I*, the main character clings desperately to such a voice as it fades—an analogy of the voice in the head; the discourse we carry on silently and ceaselessly with ourselves:

> Voice: [*Faint*]...
> He: [*With voice, shrill*] Come on! Come on!
> Voice: [*Faint*]...
> [*Silence.*]
> He: [*Low*] What'll I do?[1]

Such a voice is also an archetype of how gods communicate with mortals, like Jehovah with Ezekiel, Jonah, or Saul—an analogy parodied by Bertolt Brecht and Elisabeth Hauptmann in their melodrama *Happy End*:

> Lillian: Lots of people today think it's fashionable to laugh when God is mentioned, and say, "Yes, but have you ever seen Him? You can't believe in something you can't see." There's even a famous French astronomer who said, in print, "I searched with my telescope from one end of the universe to the other, and I couldn't find God."
>
> Mary: (rehearsing): "I searched with my telescope...."
>
> Lillian: Well, of course he couldn't find God. He was using the wrong instrument. You don't see God with a telescope. And here I thought we'd bring in the miracle of radio.

---

[1]   Samuel Beckett, *Rough for Radio I*, in *The Collected Shorter Plays of Samuel Beckett* (New York: Grove Press, 1984), p. 110.

Where Extremes Meet: Rereading Brecht and Beckett / Begegnung der Extreme. Brecht und Beckett: Eine Re-interpretation
Stephen Brockmann et al., eds., *The Brecht Yearbook / Das Brecht-Jahrbuch*
Volume 27 (Pittsburgh: The International Brecht Society, 2002)

Mary: The radio? What does the radio have to do with it?

Jane: Did he turn the radio on?

Lillian: (very fast) It's like this: One day suddenly, you're told that there are waves in the air that carry sound. And you can't see them. And you don't believe they exist. Then one day you set up a crystal set, and put on the earphones—and all at once you hear music! And then you believe!

Mary: (utterly confused) The radio? We, I suppose.

...

Lillian: God is always broadcasting. His music is always on the air. It's just a question of using the right tool, the right part of you, to hear Him with. We can all see God in our hearts, and hear His music in our souls: It's just a matter of tuning in on His wavelength.—Now, you think you can follow that?[2]

Amid the Babel of cell phones, pagers, walkmans, cable, AM, FM, short wave, portable radios, MP3, and Napster, it is perhaps impossible to imagine, now, how the fragile ventriloquism of the radio once seemed such an awesome, magical, means of communication— one that would revolutionize human civilization, transform the nature of human consciousness itself (as perhaps it has), and provide heretofore unimagined opportunities for writers and composers. The claims made on its behalf in this regard bear an amusing similarity to claims now made for the internet and the world wide web.

It was with some thought of reclaiming a bit of that original excitement for contemporary audiences that, in the Fall of 1991, I led off the Voices International *SoundPlay Radio Drama* series with a new, English language, production of the Brecht/Weill radio cantata *The Oceanflight* (in English) and concluded it a year later with a rebroadcast of our American productions of Samuel Beckett's radio plays. Brecht and Beckett were packaged together in a benighted attempt to jump start a(nother) revival of radio drama on the public radio system in the United States, but with little thought of what they might have to do with each other besides having done some notable work for radio and

---

[2]   Bertolt Brecht (and Elisabeth Hauptmann), *Happy End: A Melodrama with Songs* [from an original German play by Dorothy Lane] (New York: Samuel French, 1972), pp. 42-43.

being famous enough that the stations might actually broadcast the productions.[3]

Prompted a decade later by the occasion of the Beckett and Brecht conference at Trinity College, Dublin to reflect on Brecht's and Beckett's approach to the radio, it again seems that they don't, in fact, have a great deal to do with each other. Their sensibilities were very different and they had radically different artistic goals—Beckett's tending towards the private and the hermetic; Brecht's toward the public and the polemical. But exploring them together provides insights into each, and into radio theory, that might not be otherwise so readily apparent. I shall focus on the Brecht text for a radio work that I shall refer to as *The Oceanflight*—there are titling complications that I'll address in a moment—and Samuel Beckett's *Words and Music* because each of them was written specifically for the radio and problematized by having to be completed by the composer/collaborator who writes the music.

From its earliest beginnings, radio was understood to have had a unique and extraordinary power to conjure imaginary somewheres out of a mouthful of air, to take listeners—each one individually in the private interiority of his or her own skull—out of their everyday mundane circumstances into places intimate and spectacular, into realms exotic and familiar, into vicarious participation in (or recreation of) the actual events of history as they occur (thereby forever altering what "counts" as history being made). Brecht was interested in radio's potential for reviving a theater that had become, in his view, a decadent, moribund confection of mere entertainment. Radio, as opposed to theater, would make its contribution to drama by actively engaging the audience instead of sedating it, educating it instead of amusing it, and motivating it politically by challenging it to become an active part of the broadcast:

> For a generation whose passion consists in writing plays it is no joy to be confronted with bad theatres. ...

---

[3] *SoundPlay* was produced by Voices International (Everett Frost and Faith Wilding) in association with BARD: Bay Area Radio Drama (Erik Bauersfeld), and the Studio Akustische Kunst of WDR: Westdeutscher Rundfunk (Klaus Schöning), and distributed to the public radio system in North America, beginning October 1991, by the Pacifica Program Service (PPS). In hopes of forestalling the inevitable inquiries: Distribution rights to all our productions have expired, and it is impossible for me to make copies of them available. The WDR, Köln productions (in German) of both the Brecht-Weill and the Brecht-Hindemith-Weill versions is on a Capriccio compact disc #60012-1.

> Therefore the radio—a technical invention that still must create for itself a mass need rather than subordinating itself to an antiquated, exhausted need—is a grand productive opportunity for our plays.
>
> ...
>
> It is said that our works are only meant for the few or at least they are only suitable for a few. The first is untrue, the second unproven. Our plays are meant for many people, but not for that small elite of snobs who have already "seen everything" and who claim on every street corner that they are the ones intended. The theatre has too long been the property of a small elite that claims to be the nation. It is no accident that today, when this elite clearly no longer represents the nation, the theatre is in decline and that an invention like the radio, which in a manner of speaking has a long way to go, is simply attending to the art that was previously the theatre's obligation.[4]

Though the contexts were different, Brecht and Beckett were each given an opportunity to use the radio as a result of a view of it that has always been on the defensive and is largely gone now. Until devastated by market research and audience measurements in the 1980's, and as Jonathan Bignell has shown in a remarkable essay[5], one firm persuasion in publicly subsidized broadcast centers throughout the world argued that it was a significant part of the responsibility of this extraordinary medium to disseminate the work of the important writers and artists of the time, who would be encouraged to create work written or adapted specifically for the new medium. In return the artists would explore the as-yet-untested possibilities of the new medium, in the process contributing works of lasting value. Without some such view as this, the BBC would not have bothered to approach Samuel Beckett (an Irishman living in France, writing in French, with a reputation for being "en sauvage" about the use of his work), nor would he have responded with a half dozen rather innovative and perplexing plays. Though Brecht's communist ideology made him suspicious of the bourgeois capitalist celebration of the reputation of an artist in order to turn it into a marketable commodity, neither was he immune to exploiting the possibility. As part of his "Suggestions to Directors of Radio Broadcasting" he could not help remarking:

---

[4]   Brecht, "Young Drama and the Radio", *Bertolt Brecht on Film and Radio*, ed. Marc Silberman (London: Methuen, 2000), p. 33.

[5]   Jonathan Bignell, "Beckett in Television Studies," *Journal of Beckett Studies*, forthcoming in 2002.

Production should not be the main thing, but it should be much more intensely practiced . . . so far as radio drama goes there have been really interesting experiments by Alfred Braun. The acoustic novel which Arnolt Bronnen is trying must be tested, and these experiments must be continued by other people as well. For this only the best people should be hired. The great epic writer Alfred Döblin lives in Frankfurt Allee 244, Berlin . . . You'll also have to build up a kind of repertory, and repeat plays at certain intervals—say once a year.[6]

A year or two later, Radio Berlin began a serialized dramatization of *Berlin Alexanderplatz*.

Beckett, consistent with his more reclusive nature, was less voluble about his objectives but insisted (sigh, inconsistently) throughout his life that the radio plays were meant to be performed on the radio and were not meant to be staged or filmed. Writing to his American publisher, Barney Rosset, about efforts to stage his first radio play, *All That Fall*, in an often-cited letter, Beckett declares firmly:

> *All That Fall* is a specifically radio play, or rather radio text, for voices, not bodies. I have already refused to have it 'staged' and I cannot think of it in such terms. . . . It is no more theatre than *Endgame* is radio and to 'act' it is to kill it. Even the reduced visual dimension it will receive from the simplest and most static of readings. . .will be destructive of whatever quality it may have and which depends on the whole thing's coming out of the dark. . . .[7]

But despite the substantial differences in outlook and approach between the two men, Beckett is actually doing something very Brechtian. He is resisting the commodification of his work—its (mis)appropriation from its intended place in exchange for exposure and money earned by satisfying the need for amusement of a bigger audience; thereby alienating the author from the fruits of his labors.

As a Music Editor of Radio Berlin [the pre-Nazi predecessor to the present Sender Freies Berlin (SFB)], Kurt Weill was able to create opportunities on the air for many artists and critics, Brecht among them—the two avant garde entrepreneurs having become celebrities as a result their collaboration on the *Dreigroschenoper*; and Bertolt Brecht's primary involvement with the radio dates from the period between the 1927 broadcast of *Mann ist Mann* to his precipitous flight

---

[6]   Brecht, "Advice to Program Directors", pp. 33-34.

[7]   Clas Zilliacus, *Beckett and Broadcasting* (Abo Akademi: Abo, 1976). Unnumbered frontispiece.

from the Nazis in 1933—a period in which radio was still a very new phenomenon.

Samuel Beckett's involvement in radio dates from the mid 1950s and the BBC's abortive effort to broadcast the author's English translation of *En Attendant Godot*—which, after some meanderings, resulted in *All That Fall* and four or five other plays written specifically for the radio medium—depending on whether you count *Rough for Radio I* as an independent play or, as Beckett did, an early draft of *Cascando*. Over the next twenty-five years British, Irish, French, and German radio would create productions of the major stage plays, readings from the prose—all with varying degrees of assistance from the author. By the time Beckett came to radio it had been around long enough to have become an important component of European history and culture. However, his initial work at the BBC occurred at the moment when the implications of the technological innovations of the tape recorder as both storage and retrieval system and itself an instrument in composition were just beginning to be exploited — causing what amounted to another birth and transformation of the medium roughly equivalent to the digital and web revolution rebirthing and retransforming it now. As it had been with Brecht in the pre-war period, now again in the postwar period of the 1950s, there was time, interest, and money for innovation and experiment. I shall take up Brecht and Beckett in chronological order.

In 1929 Brecht and Weill collaborated on a broadcast of the *Berliner Requiem*, and that summer German radio decided to broadcast the arts festival that had been taking place annually in the resort town of Baden-Baden. Radio technology was massively more cumbersome and less portable then than it is now, and making the broadcast was a rather formidable labor for radio at that time. In response, participants in the Festival agreed to create works specifically designed for radio; and Bertolt Brecht and Kurt Weill invited Paul Hindemith (the Baden-Baden Festival Director) to collaborate on their already begun work-in-progress for the air waves about Charles Lindbergh's historic triumph over the sea waves two years before. For the same Festival Brecht wrote, and Hindemith scored, the *Badener Lehrstück vom Einverstandnis (Baden-Baden Cantata of Acquiesence*—hereafter *Badener Lehrstück*) in which Brecht extended the political implications of *The Oceanflight* in the light of his increasing absorption into communist ideology. Both were subtitled "Lehrstücke"—plays more intended to prompt an audience to confront rather than escape from their economic circumstances. The work, at least initially, seemed a fulfillment of Brecht's theoretical thinking that radio should be used for educational purposes.

The subsequent history of the work and even of the name of the play is complicated. The collaboration, which premiered at Baden-Baden under the title *Lindbergh, A Play for the Baden-Baden Music Festival*, satisfied none of the participants—Hindemith withdrew his music and Weill re-scored Brecht's text. Meanwhile, Brecht was altering his view of the text in the light of his evolving politics as expressed in the sequel—the *Baden-Baden Cantata of Acquiesence*. At the premiere performance the part of Lindbergh was sung by a tenor pointedly identified by a sign not as Lindbergh or the flier but as "The Listener":

> On the left side of the platform was the radio orchestra with its apparatus and singers; on the right side with the score in front of him was the listener, who performed Lindbergh's role, i.e. the pedagogical part. He sang his part to the instrumental accompaniment supplied by the radio. He read the speaking sections without identifying his own feeling with that contained in the text, pausing at the end of each line of verse; in other words, in the spirit of an exercise. On the back wall of the platform was the theory being demonstrated in this way.[8]

The idea seems to have been that the audience at home would be invited to sing along from music which would be circulated in advance (but which wasn't, as far as I've been able to determine).

Yet Brecht's idea was not as eccentric as it may now appear. German radio at the time was undertaking a number of experiments to relieve the generally perceived educational mission of the radio from the tedium of the lecture (which last was proving a disaster). Brecht's and Weill's close friend, Walter Benjamin, for example, was writing short dramaticules (as Beckett might have called them) in which, say, a husband and wife were having a dispute about household finances which would be left for the radio audience to complete at home, and then the various anticipated roles would be critiqued. Also at this time, in a kind of forecast of Karaoke, music ensembles broadcast works over the radio, leaving out solo parts or certain instruments. The sheet music was available to the audience, and musicians were intended to fill in the missing parts on their trumpets or pianos at home.

Additionally, by 1930, Brecht wanted to insert into the Lindbergh play the long poem "Ideology" from the sequel (the *Baden-Baden Cantata of Acquiesence*), and insisted that it was more politically correct to understand the trans-Atlantic triumph as not the solo flight of the hero, Lindbergh, but as the *Der Flug der Lindberghs*

---

[8]   Brecht, "Explanations (about *The Flight of Lindbergh*)," in Silberman, ed., *Brecht on Film and Radio*, p. 39.

[*Flight of the Lindberghs* (plural emphasized)], because Brecht wanted to stress that Lindbergh was not alone when he flew. Invisibly with him there flew the workers from the Ryan factory in San Diego who had put together his plane "The Spirit of St. Louis", and Brecht wanted Lindbergh to say, "I am not alone; there are eight of us flying." History, in other words, was not to be seen as in the days of "culinary" opera as made (or unmade) by heroes such as Parsival or Siegfried or Faust but by the collective will of the workers; though he seems to have been less forthright in applying the implications of this political ideology to his occasional reliance on Elisabeth Hauptmann as his co-author during this period. Be that as it may, however, to further emphasize the point, he now wanted the part of Lindbergh to be sung not by a tenor soloist but by a chorus; preferably of amateurs being instructed, not in music but in ideology, or of schoolchildren (and somewhere along the way the work picked up the subtitle of *Ein Lehrstuck für Knaben und Mädchen*—a didactic play for little boys and girls).[9]

As Brecht would later write:

> In a concert performance (which is absolutely wrong-headed), at least the part of the aviator must be sung by a chorus so that the spirit of the work will not be completely destroyed. Only through group singing of the "I" role—"I am so-and-so; I am setting out; I am not tired, etc.—can a little of its didactic effect be salvaged.[10]

Kurt Weill was predictably, and not unreasonably, adverse to Brecht's retroactively imposed conditions when these made hash of the much-labored-for and rather remarkable musical integrity of the piece. How progressive composers maintained musical standards while incorporating the kinds of popular musics not confined to the approval of an educated elite was a matter richly debated in both Europe and America at the time. Weill's use of jazz, blues, the "boogie woogie" idiom that was a craze of the time, in a cantata setting, was itself a gesture in the educational direction Brecht was pointing, and both courageous and innovative.[11] The fault lines that would soon divide the two men are perhaps first in evidence here.

---

[9] I owe a debt of gratitude to Reinhold Grimm, a consultant to the broadcast, for his help in interpreting this history in the documentary that accompanies our broadcast.

[10] "Explanations", p. 40.

[11] I am grateful to broadcast consultant Kim Kowalke and our conductor Stephen Gross for assistance with understanding Weill's score.

But history would wrench this magnificent work yet further. Both Brecht and Weill were marked for elimination by the Nazis and had to flee Germany for their lives. Their *Threepenny Opera* was held up for ridicule in an exhibition of "degenerate art" (and when it had exactly the opposite effect on the public, the Nazis withdrew it from the show!).

During their exile, Charles Lindbergh became a spokesman for "America Firsters"—Americans who believed that the Nazis were, if not right about everything, certainly not on the whole such a bad thing as degenerate socialists and communists made them out to be and, anyway, an(other) European problem which Americans ought to stay out of. In 1938 he accepted the German Cross from Hermann Goering; and, in September 1941 made a speech in Des Moines, Iowa to the effect that the Americans could not win against German air power and that the Western world was infected by people of "inferior blood" from Asia and Africa—a danger to the entire Caucasian race.

Consequently, in 1950, when Süd-Deutscher Rundfunk (SDR) sought to broadcast a revival of the *Lindberghflight* as part of a historical survey of the pre-Nazi origins of German radio, Brecht wrote them that:

> If you wish to insert the Lindbergh flight into a historical survey, I must ask you to append a Prologue to the piece and to undertake a few small changes in the Text. It is now known that Lindbergh maintained close ties to the Nazis. In those days his enthusiastic report about the invincible Nazi air force had an enervating effect on several countries. Lindbergh also played a sinister role as a fascist in the USA. In my radio play therefore the title has to be changed to "The Oceanflight" and one is required to insert this prologue and Lindbergh's name must be eliminated.

Prologue to the broadcast of the *Oceanflight*:

You will hear
a report about the first oceanflight
in May 1927.
A young man achieved it.
He triumphed over storm, ice and greedy waters. Nevertheless may his name be expunged,
because though he found his way
over uncharted waters
he lost himself in the swamps of our cities.
Storm and ice did not overcome him,
but his fellow man overcame him.
One decade later misguided by fame and fortune
He showed Hitler's slaughterers how to fly

with deadly bombs.
Therefore may his name be expunged.
Take warning:
neither courage nor knowledge
of motors and navigational charts
will earn for the antisocial
a hero's song.[12]

Since the required changes were made within weeks of Kurt Weill's death, there was no opportunity for Weill to respond. John Willett's editorial note to the English (Methuen) edition of 1997—five years after our production—indicates that:

> In the view of the Brecht Estate they (Brecht's changes) remain mandatory for performance; in that of the Kurt Weill Foundation "Kurt Weill's music may only be performed in the original version without any alterations or cuts" (p. 210).

Things are a little better than that. The production I directed uses text (translated by Lyse Symonette) and score as provided by Weill's publisher, Universal Editions—in a form jointly agreed upon by the Brecht and Weill estates. The name "Lindbergh" remains in the libretto, but we were allowed to preface the performance with Brecht's 1950 letter and poem, and to broadcast the work under the title, *The Oceanflight*. The translation presented a number of infelicities having nothing to do with the presence or absence of Lindbergh's name ["Phantom" for "Nebel" (fog), for example], some of which we were allowed to improve. It is, so far as I know, the only attempt at a nationwide broadcast of the work in the United States in English.[13]

II

Both Beckett and Brecht were informed by the modernist persuasion—derived, as Antony Tatlow has demonstrated, from Schopenhauer—that music was supreme among the arts because it spoke directly to the emotions without the intervention of cognitive thought processes and was not language-dependent and hence didn't have to be translated. Which, as Tatlow remarks, may "explain why

---

[12] Brecht, *Collected Plays*, v. 3, part 2 (London: Methuen, 1997), pp. 208-209.

[13] The Philadelphia Orchestra conducted by Leopold Stokowski premiered the work in the USA, 4 April 1931, in an English translation by George Antheil.

music takes over in Beckett where language cannot go, for example, in *Ghost Trio* or *Nacht und Träume*."[14]

Of Beckett's five radio plays, two are written in collaboration with composers, a third is, in effect, "scored" for the *musique concrète* of ocean waves beating against the strand, and a fourth engages music heavily. Only *Rough for Radio II* is immune.

Words and Music was written at the invitation of the British Broadcasting Corporation. The play was originally broadcast as part of the BBC's 40th Anniversary Jubilee in the autumn of 1962, with music by the author's cousin, John Beckett. This music was withdrawn soon after the original productions had been aired, and replaced in my production, at Beckett's suggestion, with music composed by the late Morton Feldman, from whom we commissioned an original score.

If Brecht would find in radio an ideal opportunity to develop the "Lehrstück" or teaching play as a vehicle for politically educating and enfranchising the masses, Beckett was interested in using the conjuring power of the medium that is heard but not seen to invoke interior landscapes, the mental processes of the mind itself coming into consciousness through the process of verbalization—the Cartesian *cogito ergo sum*. Brecht would need to engage and motivate an audience in order to succeed—the larger the better. Beckett's success or failure wouldn't depend on whether anyone tuned in or not. Or stayed tuned in. And yet, at least initially, in *The Oceanflight* Brecht, like Beckett in *Words and Music*, was interested in using interior monologue augmented by music to develop a dramatic portrait of the mind at work struggling to achieve something.

In *Words and Music* two characters, Bob and Joe (Words and Music) struggle in "real time" reluctantly to create a poem under the duress of a club-wielding third character, Croak. The action of the play requires that Words and Music, Bob and Joe, achieve a genuine cooperation that is emotionally powerful enough to affect Croak—and, necessarily, therefore, genuinely effective enough to move the audience also, so that, dramatically speaking, the audience is satisfied that Croak is appropriately and not sentimentally motivated. This dramatic necessity required Samuel Beckett either to create or to insert some of the most exquisite lyric lines he had ever written. He was very fond of them and could recite them from memory:

> Age is when to a man
> Huddled o'er the ingle
> Shivering for the hag

---

[14]   Antony Tatlow, "Saying Yes and Saying No: Schopenhauer and Nietzsche as Educators," in this volume.

> To put the pan in the bed
> And bring the toddy
> She comes in the ashes
> Who loved could not be won
> Or won not loved
> Or some other trouble
> Comes in the ashes
> Like in that old light
> The face in the ashes
> That old starlight
> On the earth again.
> ...
> Then down a little way
> Through the trash
> Towards where...
> All dark no begging
> No giving no words
> No sense no need...
> Through the scum
> Down a little way
> To where one glimpse
> Of that wellhead.[15]

In *The Oceanflight* words and music achieve a victory of a different kind. It follows and celebrates Lindbergh's journey over the Atlantic in a frame of "real time", as it occurs and is reported over the radio, preserving the Aristotelian unities in abbreviated form. The alternating choral and solo dimensions of the work make it at once celebratory and personal. As an example of the latter, Lindbergh sings a duet with his motor in which, in very Beckettian internalization, words and music, help each other along towards an end—both dramatic and formal—that neither could have achieved alone. In this passage Lindbergh's original enthusiasm for flying where no man had flown before is replaced by a recognition of his fragility in the face of the awesomeness of the task:

> Everyplace there is storm, everywhere fog is present!
> I can't go on! I can't go on!
> Everyplace there is storm, everywhere fog is present!
> Oh, why did I ever attempt this,
> Why did I ever attempt this?
> For now I'm afraid of dying.
> For now I must perish.

---

[15] *Words and Music*, in *Collected Shorter Plays* (London: Faber, 1984), pp.131-132.

I must give up! I must give up!
Four days before me two other men
Made an attempt to cross the ocean,
And the ocean holds their graves
And soon it shall hold mine.[16]

When giving these remarks in more cursory form to a live audience, I concluded by asking them to notice that what they were hearing and chiefly responding to in this context was neither Brecht nor Beckett, but Weill and Feldman—the circumstances of the live presentation privileged music over text (the reverse of reading the essay, in which text presides over music), and the end result depended as much on composer as on author. In each case, the authors had relinquished control over half their creation to someone else—and in each case run into difficulties on that account. So I left the conference with a puzzle: Suppose Morton Feldman had written the music to *The Oceanflight* and Kurt Weill had scored *Words and Music*.(?!)

Pause for imagining.

***

Moray McGowan
Waiting for Waiting for Godot: *Echoes of Beckett's Play in Brecht's Chosen Land*

In the context of the meeting of supposed extremes, this essay explores the extent to which the GDR—Brecht's chosen land on his return from exile, for all his relationship to it remained highly troubled—perhaps always was, and certainly became, a Beckettian place. The essay does not seek to reduce the ontological profundity of *Waiting for Godot* to a series of references to specific material conditions. But the play *is* also a series of references to specific material conditions. How could a play written in 1948/49, in the immediate aftermath of fascism and World War, with its references to barren landscapes, defoliated trees, slavery and arbitrary beatings, and to carrots as relative luxuries in a world of turnips, be otherwise? How could a play about continually frustrated hopes fail to resonate in an Eastern Europe characterized by restricted freedoms and arbitrary bureaucracies? Noting real worlds which resemble that of Beckett's

---

[16]   From the libretto published by Universal Editions (no. 9938, 1930) as translated by Lys Symonette with approved revisions for our production by Faith Wilding. Ch. 16: "In the Night of the Snowstorm", p. 23.

tramps does not reduce the play any more than does identifying real material sources for them. In sketching some material resonances of *Waiting for Godot* in GDR society and engagements with it in GDR culture, this essay, rather, seeks to add some flourishes to the overall picture of the reception in the German Democratic Republic of Beckett's works and the modernist crises of aesthetic and spiritual values they were taken to exemplify, which has been studied in detail elsewhere.[17]

When *Beckett in Berlin* was published in 1986, marking Beckett's eightieth birthday, it could ignore productions of Beckett in East Berlin and the GDR completely, for there had not been any.[18] Within months of the Paris premiere in 1953, *Waiting for Godot* had had its second production anywhere in the world at the West Berlin *Schloßpark* theater, and the German translation by Elmar Tophoven was published the same year. But by this time, Western modernism was anathematized in a GDR where a particularly dogmatic form of the aesthetics of György Lukács held sway. Jean-Paul Sartre's *The Flies*, for example, had been banned in 1949 and remained unperformed until 1987. The Western reception of *Waiting for Godot* as "the dramatic equivalent of the nouveau roman, of new music, of the new painting,"[19] all examples of the Western formalism (e.g. John Cage's minimalist compositions, such as *Waiting*, 1952) so disapproved of in this phase of GDR cultural politics, reinforced the play's exclusion from the GDR stage and its restricted presence in GDR theater publications. In the 1950s and 1960s, if mentioned at all, it is usually instrumentalized for polemical contrasts between Western stagnation and the dynamic development of socialism, and between what were

---

All translations by the author.

17 See especially: Frank Bechert, *Keine Versöhnung mit dem Nichts. Zur Rezeption von Samuel Beckett in der DDR* (Frankfurt/Main: Peter Lang, 1997), with comprehensive bibliography and review of further work on Beckett in the GDR. See also Werner Huber, "Godot, Gorba and Glasnost: Beckett in East Germany," in Marius Buning and Lois Oppenheim, eds., *Beckett in the 1990s* (Amsterdam: Rodopi, 1993), pp. 49-57; Andreas Roßmann, "Theaterberichte. Warten auf Beckett. Absurdes Theater in der DDR," *Deutschland-Archiv* 18 (1985), 8, pp. 803-5; and Roßmann, "Die späte Zusage für den Clown S.B. Tabu-Bruch auf Raten: Zur beginnenden Beckett-Rezeption in der DDR," *Deutschland-Archiv* 20 (1987), 12, pp. 1302-11.

18 Klaus Völker, ed., *Beckett in Berlin* (Berlin: Hentrich 1986).

19 Viennese critic Hans Weigel, quoted in Völker, ed., *Beckett in Berlin*, p. 43.

taken to be their dramaturgical equivalents, as in Werner Hecht's essay, "Brecht 'and' Beckett. An absurd comparison" (1966).[20] Only gradually do more differentiated analyses appear in the 1970s,[21] though there remain counter-voices, such as Peter Hacks' declaration in 1978 that Beckett was "more malignant than all our enemies,"[22] and only in the 1980s does a climate develop where productions of Beckett finally become possible.[23]

Yet, ironically, this selfsame volume *Beckett in Berlin* includes a facsimile page from Brecht's annotated copy of *Waiting for Godot*.[24] This adaptation remained a fragment at his death in 1956, and the shape it might finally have taken consequently unclear. As they stand, his annotations gloss the *dramatis personae* as follows: "Estragon, a proletarian, Wladimir, an intellectual, Lucky, a donkey, or policeman, von Pozzo, a landowner."[25] Ostensibly, these labels relocate Beckett's play firmly in capitalist society. But despite Werner Mittenzwei's claim that Brecht's adaptation would have "exposed the dogmatic extremism in Beckett's thought to the carefree laughter of his [socialist] audience,"[26] Brecht certainly did not believe that class conflict or master-servant mentalities had been banished from the GDR. His call in January 1956, just before he began to adapt *Waiting for Godot*, for

---

[20] "Brecht 'und' Beckett. Ein absurder Vergleich," *Theater der Zeit* 21 (1966), 14, pp. 28-30. See also Manfred Heidicke, "Die Versöhnung mit dem Nichts," *Theater der Zeit* 12 (1957), 11, pp. 24-6; Erhard Etto and Lothar Ehrlich, "Keine Versöhnung mit dem Nichts. Auseinandersetzung mit Samuel Beckett," *Theater der Zeit* 13 (1958), 3, pp. 31-4; and Werner Mittenzwei, *Gestaltung und Gestalten im modernen Drama* (Berlin and Weimar: Aufbau 1965), pp. 38 and 108.

[21] For instance Manfred Wekwerth's comments on the Stockholm Dramaten production in 1978: "Brecht-Theater heute. Stockholmer Seminar 1978," in Wekwerth, *Theater in Diskussion* (Berlin: Henschel 1982), pp. 220-43.

[22] In a discussion documented in Werner Mittenzwei, *Kampf der Richtungen. Strömungen und Tendenzen der internationalen Dramatik* (Leipzig 1978), p. 335. However, as with many apparently conformist utterances by GDR artists the possibility cannot be ruled out that Hacks is hoping to be read against the grain of his statement.

[23] See Bechert, pp. 110-76.

[24] Völker, ed., *Beckett in Berlin*, p. 49.

[25] See Hecht, "Brecht 'und' Beckett," p. 28-9.

[26] Mittenzwei, *Gestaltung*, p. 108.

more plays and productions which would "really divide our public," confirms this.[27]

However, Brecht's aesthetics, as opposed to his value as a figurehead, were by then generally unwelcome in the GDR. So his interest in Beckett, even if he had lived longer, might not have outweighed party antipathy. After Brecht's death, his instrumentalization in turn, in polarized comparisons of the kind cited, compounded the difficulties facing a GDR reception of Beckett.

Yet while *Waiting for Godot* was on the one hand literally absent from the GDR stage almost until the end—first GDR production 1987, first book edition 1988[28]—, on the other hand it was highly present, in allusion, oblique reference and explicit borrowings. Indeed, as Knut Lennartz argues, "Beckett's *Godot* lay like a spectre over the theatrical landscape of the GDR."[29] As a key work of modern European drama, *Waiting for Godot* was necessarily part of every GDR theater practitioner's, and many audience members', frame of reference. [30]

But the point goes further: *Waiting for Godot* came to exemplify an existential experience, that of waiting for a goal whose time of arrival and perhaps even whose actual identity resisted every effort at concretion, which not only came to be perceived as something GDR life shared with the capitalist West, but which was in fact very specific to Eastern bloc socialism. Between the 1950s and the 1980s, stasis and transformation, equated in GDR propaganda with capitalism and communism respectively, essentially change places in the perceived and possibly the actual reality of these societies. "Warten," "waiting" becomes an increasingly insistent motif in GDR culture as it moves towards its demise. And though this is outside the scope of the

---

[27]   Quoted in Christa Hasche, Traute Schölling, Joachim Fiebach, *Theater in der DDR* (Berlin: Henschel 1994), p. 31.

[28]   The first Beckett production in the GDR was *Krapp's Last Tape* at the Berlin Theater im Palast in July 1986, the first of *Waiting for Godot* at the Staatsschauspiel Dresden in March 1987. One minor work was published in 1978, followed by Samuel Beckett, *Spiele* (Berlin: Volk und Welt 1988).

[29]   *Vom Aufbruch zur Wende. Theater in der DDR* (Velber: Erhard Friedrich Verlag 1992), pp. 51-2.

[30]   Years before it could be performed publicly, it was staple fare for drama students.   See Bechert, pp. 152-3; Jürgen Klauß describes the intense experimental engagment with Western modernism, including *Waiting for Godot*, in the Hochschule für Filmkunst in Potsdam-Babelsberg around 1960: *Zwischen den Meistern in den Zeiten. Von Heiner Müller zu Konrad Wolf* (Frankfurt/Oder: Frankfurt-Oder-Editions 1996), pp. 46-7.

essay, this motif continues to inform attempts, in East German drama and theater since 1990, to understand the GDR before and since the "Wende," the turning point of 1989/90, in particular to find a voice for the continuities which make themselves felt within a new, post-Wende existential bewilderment.

We should at this point acknowledge the overlap with a much broader theme: Lothar Pikulik, in *Waiting, Expectation: A Form of Living in Times of Finality and Transition*, notes multiple forms of waiting in European culture: Christian millenarianism; enlightenment expectations of progress, romantic utopianism and despair at stagnation; fin-de siècle decadence; modernist boredom and the desire for cataclysm as escape from it; the enforced waiting of exile; the various ethical positions waiting may represent; waiting as the precondition for poetic creation. Exploring waiting as "a form of existence in modernity," from Franz Kafka to Botho Strauß, Pikulik explicitly examines *Waiting for Godot*; but does not refer to its relationship to GDR experience.[31]

Clearly, without teasing out fully the relationship between *Waiting for Godot* and these and other forms and motifs of waiting, we cannot claim, and it is anyway rather unlikely, that every reference to "Waiting" in GDR culture necessarily refers to Beckett. But precisely because *Waiting for Godot* exemplifies "a form of existence in modernity," it came to stand for a particular existential experience which the would-be shapers of GDR culture sought to deny as being part of their citizens' lives, but whose insistent truth as just such a part it became, eventually, impossible to suppress.

When the two German states were founded, the western Federal Republic's Basic Law formally enshrined its provisional status as a "Provisorium," in waiting until Germany should be reunited. In the GDR, Walter Ulbricht sought to strengthen GDR legitimacy by stressing that it was "not a Provisorium."[32] His successor Erich Honecker claimed in 1974 that in comparison with the Federal Republic, trapped in capitalist stagnation, "we have moved on one whole historical epoch."[33] Though socialism is not achievable

---

[31] *Warten, Erwartung. Eine Lebensform in End- und Übergangszeiten* (Göttingen: Vandenhoeck & Ruprecht 1997), p. 14.

[32] In a speech introducing the draft of the new constitution in 1968, quoted in *Ulbrichts Grundgesetz. Die sozialistische Verfassung der DDR*, with an introduction by Dietrich Müller-Römer (Cologne: Verlag Wissenschaft und Politik 1968), p. 9.

[33] Quoted in Hermann Weber, *Kurze Geschichte der DDR* (Cologne: Verlag Wissenschaft und Politik,1988), p. 156.

instantaneously, indeed requires significant deferment of gratification, the process of working towards it takes place in an atmosphere of active expectancy, not passive waiting. The needs of the working class "tolerate no standing still at the status quo," declared Ulbricht in 1965.[34] "Revolutionary impatience" is a key tenet of socialist realism. In Erik Neutsch's novel *Spur der Steine* (1967; roughly: *Track of Bricks*, referring to the worker Balla's past achievements and future destiny in the supposedly linear development of socialism), Balla's conversion to communism is marked by his declaration: "Wait? You can't wait any longer, building sites aren't waiting-rooms," or, later, "life is not a waiting-room."[35]

It is perhaps surprising, then, to find a play called *Warten auf Godeau* premiered in 1970 in the Deutsches Theater in East Berlin, under the noses of a hypersensitive cultural bureaucracy. But the full title is *Le Faiseur oder Warten auf Godeau*, and in his afterword the author Claus Hammel identifies his source as Balzac's *Mercadet, ou Le Faiseur* and insists too that Balzac's Godeau is not Beckett's "nebulous Messiah of unspecified class," but "the man with the fat wallet."[36]

And in fact Hammel practices not just "the materialistic concretisation of that Godot who is being waited for in Beckett," as a reviewer approvingly put it,[37] but also the provocation which, like a snake-dancer's trick with the rubber fangs, turns out to be no such thing. Audiences were as likely to link the title to Beckett as to Balzac, but their expectations of a daring critique were frustrated: apart from easy jokes about putting "Estragon" in the soup as "a foretaste of Godeau" the play itself avoids associations with Beckett, being instead a farce about stockmarket skullduggery in Bourbon France: capitalism as frenetic serial cheating. Clearly, the GDR audience was to be

---

[34] *Dokumente der Sozialistischen Einheitspartei Deutschlands*, Vol. IX (Berlin, 1965), pp. 209-10.

[35] *Spur der Steine* (Halle: Mitteldeutscher Verlag 1964), pp. 487 and 732. This was very possibly also an explicit distancing from the suggestion of congruence between the two German states in Erich Kuby, *Das ist des Deutschen Vaterland: Siebzig Millionen in zwei Wartesälen* (Reinbek: Rowohlt 1957).

[36] Claus Hammel, *Le Faiseur oder Warten auf Godeau. Komödie nach Balzac* (Berlin: Eulenspiegel 1972), p. 111. Future references identified by page number in the text.

[37] Brigitte Thurm, "Entschleierung verwirrender Mythen. *Le Faiseur oder Warten auf Godeau* von Claus Hammel am Deutschen Theater Berlin," *Theater der Zeit* 26 (1971), 1, pp. 28-30.

grateful they were not living in what Hammel calls "the Godeau-state Federal Republic."[38]

The banker Godeau never appears but is repeatedly invoked by stage figures as panacea for the crises of the market. Mercadet and his factotum Justin "sell Waiting" (72), sell shares in Godeau's arrival, rather than any material product, exemplifying capitalism's abandonment of the satisfaction of real human needs for the pursuit of profit. "Freedom" too is discredited by being invoked by foolish or mendacious figures: "Give us the freedom to trade shares, Mercadet!" (101), travestying Schiller's "Give us freedom of thought!" in *Don Carlos*, or "Godeau is freedom—the liberation from so much which has burdened us in the past." (85) The closing "Apotheosis," praising the "blessing of waiting" for the docile, manipulated creatures of a higher power, mocks both religion itself and its deployment to clothe naked commercial interests (108).

But as the GDR's would-be progress to communism stagnates, the identification of deferment and docile patience as the necessary virtues for survival in capitalism backfires, since precisely these qualities become implicitly demanded in the GDR itself. While Hammel's play was soon almost forgotten, the ideological position it represents, and the ironic reversal of that position, came back to haunt the GDR in its last years, when, tired of deferring gratification to a receding socialist future, its citizens rejected the SED's now implausible Godot for the—seemingly—more credible promises of Gorbachev or of the West, other Godeaus who also promised "freedom—the liberation from so much which has burdened us in the past."

For while the capitalist West, as it progressed rapidly out of post-war austerity into consumer affluence, took "the waiting out of wanting," as a famous slogan had it, in the GDR waiting became, or remained, a leitmotif of everyday life, reflecting the inefficiencies of a planned economy and the restrictiveness of a paternalist state: waiting in line, for a tradesman, a housing allocation, a car, a telephone, a passport, permission to emigrate.[39] By the 1980s these material experiences of waiting were creating extreme tensions and

---

[38]   "Nach der Premiere," *Theater der Zeit* 26 (1971), 1, p. 29.

[39]   As a *Spiegel* reporter put it in October 1989, "The year is the shortest unit of time in the GDR. You wait 5 years for your own flat, 10 years for a telephone, 15 years for a Wartburg [car], 40 years for unification." Hans Halter, "'Die Zone ist im Arsch.' Ost-Berlin in der Woche vor dem 40. Jahrestag der DDR Oktober 1989," in Rudolf Augstein, ed., *Ein deutsches Jahrzehnt. Reportagen 1985-1995* (Hamburg: Spiegel-Buchverlag 1995), pp. 177-80, here p. 178.

contradictions, exemplified by the anarchic trade in car order slips (fetching up to 40,000 marks) and second-hand cars (at several times their already inflated new price) and the fact that had the GDR not collapsed, those ordering cars in 1989 would have received them forty years later.[40]   That is, only through capitalist practices, access to Western money or physical migration could one escape this socialist form of "Waiting."

Artistic responses to the increasing centrality of "waiting" to GDR experience ranged from lyric poetry, where it forms a key motif in the work of many poets such as Stefan Döring or Hans-Eckart Wenzel in the 1980s,[41] through the cabaret performances of Karls Enkel, the clown duo Wenzel formed with Steffen Mensching,[42] or productions of the classics such as Jürgen Gosch's *Leonce and Lena* in 1978, which drew the angry accusation that it had turned Büchner into Beckett,[43] to dance pieces like Jo Fabian's *Waiting Room (Wartesaal)* of 1986.[44] Once again, it should be stressed that not all references to "waiting" are necessarily references to *Waiting for Godot*, precisely because the point at which materially specific forms of waiting become fundamental existential experiences can never be exactly fixed.   Let us therefore focus here on a number of examples amongst GDR dramatists of specific references to Beckett's play.

Heiner Müller's relationship to Beckett is as contradictory as much else in his complex artistic identity.   In 1993 he pronounced that "the Fatzer material by Brecht is better than all the plays of Beckett," but in 1994 that "the scene from Godot in which Pozzo enters with Lucky on a rope; that's the entirety of Brecht in a nutshell."[45] As early

[40]   See Jonathan R. Zatlin, "The Vehicle of Desire: The Trabant, the Wartburg and the End of the GDR," *German History* 15 (1997), 3, pp. 358-380; here p. 379.

[41]   See Karen Leeder, *Breaking Boundaries. A New Generation of Poets in the GDR* (Oxford: Oxford University Press, 1996), p. 53.

[42]   See David Robb, *Zwei Clowns im Lande des verlorenen Lachens. Das Liedertheater Wenzel und Mensching* (Berlin: Christoph Links 1998), especially p. 78.

[43]   The characteristically dogmatic critic Rainer Kerndl, quoted in Helmut Kreuzer, Karl-Wilhelm Schmidt, eds., *Dramaturgie in der DDR (1945-1990)*, vol. 2 (Heidelberg: Winter 1998), p. 332.

[44]   See Peter Reichel, "Fingerübungen," *Theater der Zeit* 41 (1986), 9, pp. 48-9.

[45]   Quoted in Jonathan Kalb, "Müller as Beckett," *The Theater of Heiner Müller* (Cambridge University Press, 1998), pp. 164-73; here p. 164.   See also

as 1958, Müller described the revolution—in his view, still not accomplished in the GDR—as a "hapless angel [...] waiting for history," a central motif of his work.[46]   However, this is a reference not to Beckett but to Walter Benjamin's reading of Paul Klee's painting *Angelus Novus,*[47] and thus to a horror-stained and tortuously dialectic but nonetheless dynamic conception of history.   Thus, there are Beckettian clowns in many of Müller's plays, and *Hamletmaschine,* for example, has frequently been compared with *Endgame* or, in its repetitive structure, with *Waiting for Godot.*[48]   But the closing line of *Hamletmaschine,* "When they pass through your bedrooms with butchers' knives, you will know the truth," certainly pronounces the bloody end of the patriarchal enlightenment's optimistic faith in progress, but hardly records stasis or the absence of history.[49]   Indeed, Müller's theatrical images are drenched in historical specificity, something Beckett believed impaired his own plays and resisted permitting in productions of them.   This may be why the waiting motif prominent in Müller's work never took the form of an explicit adaptation of Beckett's play, even though in an interview published in 1992, he retrospectively described the GDR in remarkably Beckettian terms, as a "waiting room" in "basically a state of Messianic anticipation.   There are constant announcements of the Messiah's impending arrival, and you know perfectly well that he won't be coming.   And yet, somehow, it's good to hear him announced all over again."[50]

Volker Braun's *The German Simplex. Scenes of Tutelage (Simplex Deutsch. Szenen über die Unmündigkeit,* 1980) explores the destructive consequences of blind obedience to internalized authority in a montage of scenes from the revolution of 1918/19 to the present. Brecht's Kragler from *Drums in the Night* becomes a fascist, his

---

Helmut Fuhrmann, *Warten auf "Geschichte." Der Dramatiker Heiner Müller* (Würzburg: Königshausen & Neumann 1997).

[46]   "Ein glückloser Engel [...] wartend auf Geschichte," in Müller, *Rotwelsch* (Berlin: Merve 1982), p. 87.

[47]   Benjamin, "Über den Begriff der Geschichte," in *Gesammelte Schriften,* vol. I/2 (Frankfurt/Main: Suhrkamp 1980), pp. 697-8.

[48]   For instance Fuhrmann, *Warten auf "Geschichte,"* pp. 137-40.

[49]   *Die Hamletmaschine,* in *Revolutionstücke* (Stuttgart: Reclam 1988), pp. 38-46; here p. 46.

[50]   Heiner Müller and Jan Huet, "Insights into the Process of Production—A Conversation," *Documenta IX,* Stuttgart 1992, pp. 96-7.

daughter Ulrike, disgusted at his hypocrisy in the post-1945 world, turns to terrorism. The epilogue, echoing Immanuel Kant's definition in his essay "What is Enlightenment?" of Enlightenment as the "emergence of humanity from its self-imposed tutelage," appeals to the audience to challenge their own "Unmündigkeit," tutelage or failure to take responsibility for their own fates.[51]

The middle section of the play, entitled "Hans im Glück" ('Hans in clover') is set in the contemporary world which, says Braun, has been "seen through" and "is being refused. [...] out of a surfeit of prosperous, exploitative, empty life, in which you either sell or are sold. Dropping out through alcohol, drugs, crime or the political underground."[52] "Hans im Glück" opens with the "Entry of Godot," to find "two hippies lying on the ground, probably Estragon and Vladimir" under a "Beckett-Bäumchen," the little tree from *Waiting for Godot*. Expecting a joyful response to his epiphanous appearance, for which he has been keeping them waiting under this tree since "that significant evening in the Théâtre Babylone," Godot is disconcerted by their apathy: "We're not waiting for anything." (204) Behind their slogans of refusal, from the anti-rearmament movement of the 1950s to the anti-nuclear and environmental movements of the late 1970s, lies an apolitical vacuity. They take turns with an inflatable sex doll, eat the tree's leaves as soon as they appear, reject education as a "treadmill" (207), and shit at a politician's house, a publisher's, a women's group, a bank or a factory as a form of purposeless rejection not only of capitalism but of all culturally constructive activity. When Godot drops his mask, admitting he's actually B. and that he invented them, they indifferently reject this idea, saying they escaped his determining control in May 1968 anyway.

Like Wolfgang Bauer's *Magic Afternoon* ten years earlier, the scene accurately identifies a subculture which is not waiting for anything, has abandoned even the false consolations Beckett's tramps cling to, but whose version of 'Marcuse's "Great Refusal" leaves it equally stranded. The play's view of Western youth protest, drawing on crude and by the late 1970s anachronistic stereotypes about vacuous hippies, and a discrediting of vegetarianism, peace and environmental protest and the sexual revolution, would satisfy any puritan SED ideologue, though he might balk at the manner of its presentation.

---

[51] Braun, *Stücke 2* (Frankfurt/Main: Suhrkamp1981), p. 222. Future quotations identified by page number in the text.

[52] "Arbeitsnotizen" for 1.7.1978, quoted in *Theater der Zeit*, 35 (1980), 7, p. 63.

But between the obviously Western references, from Cafe Kranzler to Hendrix, or to redeemer figures from Jesus and Buddha to Guevara, Braun's Vladimir and Estragon mock Godot by parodying socialist rhetoric too, linking the scene to the GDR's own younger generation and their indifference not only to future promises but also to actually existing socialism, the arrived socialist Godot. In *Waiting for Godot*, Beckett's tramps seem not to need to work to live, ammunition for the dogmatic critique of his play's supposedly privileged bourgeois position beneath the tramps' indigent surface. But socialist paternalism too secures basic needs at the price of a Spartan lifestyle, restricted freedoms and dependence on remote authority. From this perspective, Beckett's tramps are figures immediately recognizable from GDR experience too. Braun notes that absurdity is a real element of his GDR audience's lives: "Beckett's little tree is the world clock [Weltzeituhr] on the Alexanderplatz," a clock showing times around the world to a population forcibly prevented from visiting that world.[53]

Certainly, Braun does not show supine hippie refusal as a viable alternative to unthinking obedience, since it perpetuates "Unmündigkeit" in another guise. Braun commented in 1980 that "the worst [in the sense of most damaging] hope of the people was always that history would be made by others."[54] Braun's poetic goal, the "Training des aufrechten Gangs" ("Training to Walk Upright"), echoing another motif of Kant's essay "What is Enlightenment," is a tireless urging to the GDR working class to exercise that power in their state which they supposedly have. As the scene closes, B. accepts Wladimir's invitation to mount the sex doll, only for it to burst. This dethroning of the author by revealing his mere humanity behind the mask of authority could of course be applied to any grand narratives, including those party narratives which seek to abrogate the GDR public's capacity for initiative. The B. figure is not the historical Beckett—who certainly never claims to be remotely identical with whatever Godot represents—but the would-be guardians of historical processes of any ideological color. Thus Braun's appropriation of *Waiting for Godot* is not satisfied with the resigned recognition of the existence of *Waiting for Godot* experience in GDR society, but seeks to provoke the audience to reject their own system's proclivity to place them, existentially, in the situation of Beckett's tramps.

Heinz Drewniok's play *When Georgie comes* (*Wenn Georgie kommt*, 1983) transfers *Waiting for Godot*'s sense of aimlessness into

---

[53] "Arbeitsnotizen" for 7.1.1980, quoted in Ulrich Profitlich, *Volker Braun* (Munich: Fink 1985), p. 126.

[54] Quoted in Jay Rosselini, *Volker Braun* (Munich: Beck 1983), p. 135.

an ordinary GDR family's fruitless wait for the absent Georgie—the blank projection screen for each figure's different dreams and compensations—which degenerates into petty squabbles. Reviewers treated Drewniok's echoes of *Waiting for Godot* relatively indulgently, perhaps precisely because the flattening effects of psychological realism blunted the existential implications.[55] Christoph Hein's *The True Story of Ah Q* (*Die wahre Geschichte des Ah Q*), premiered at the Deutsches Theater in Berlin in the same year, proved much more controversial.[56] Two dropouts, Ah Q and Wang, wait for a Revolution in a crumbling temple with a leaking roof, and cope meanwhile like Vladimir and Estragon with discomfort, boredom and loneliness, are bewildered by circumstances of which they seem helpless victims, engage in surreal dialogs and aimless philosophical pondering, experience time as something which, at best, merely passes without linear order or purpose, and live in the shadow of mortality, manifest in their own bodies' decay. Hein's mysterious "gracious Overlord," like Godot, is much discussed but never appears. There are, finally, some direct quotations from *Waiting for Godot*.

But how closely, actually, does Hein's play echo Beckett's at a deeper level? Ah Q and Wang, like Beckett's tramps, complain that their activities are "meaningless" and "useless" and that this futility actually increases following the (failed) revolution.[57] This directly challenges the orthodox assertion—for example in the standard GDR handbook *Wissenschaftlicher Kommunismus*—that all aspects of life, and even death, in a socialist state are "meaningful."[58] Beckett's tramps

---

[55] For instance Peter Reichel, "Raum zwischen den Figuren. Der Dramatiker Heinz Drewniok," *Theater der Zeit* 38 (1983), 2, pp. 62-3; Volker Trauth, "Warten auf Georgie," *Theater der Zeit* 38 (1983), 3, pp. 37-8.

[56] The influential critic Ernst Schumacher complained of too much "navel-gazing" and of "existential observation, not the identification of meaningful existence," *Berliner Zeitung*, 10.1.1984. *Neues Deutschland* supposedly planned but then withdrew a bitter attack by Rainer Kerndl; however the paper's complete silence on the play itself signals disapproval. See Michael Töteberg, "Der Anarchist und der Parteisekretär. Die DDR-Theaterkritik und ihre Schwierigkeiten mit Christoph Hein," *text + kritik* 111 (1991), pp. 36-43; here p. 43.

[57] *Die wahre Geschichte des Ah Q*, in *Die Ritter der Tafelrunde und andere Stücke* (Berlin: Aufbau 1990), p. 16. Future references identified by *AhQ* plus page number in the text.

[58] Quoted in Hilary Wiesemann, *"Ohne Hoffnung können wir nicht leben": Atheist Modernism and Religion in the Works of Christoph Hein*, Ph.D.

await the sense of purpose which Godot's arrival will supposedly bring; Ah Q and Wang long for the advent of "the task [...] for which we have been born" (AhQ16). By the end of both plays, the characters cling to hopes they know are self-deceptions, giving their lives spurious meaning, but depriving themselves of the liberty that could be theirs if they rejected false consolations.

But the Beckettian references in Hein's play do not entail a claim of their universality. They are not, as a GDR reviewer rightly noted, just "a maliciously sarcastic Beckettian endgame,"[59] but a provocation, to force to the surface issues about the stagnation of progress in the GDR. Hein links the stasis and stagnation to specific political causes: his play's revolution "relates to that of 1911 in China, a revolution which changed nothing."[60] Incomplete revolution, not a universal human condition, is responsible. It is even possible that certain critics' angry attack on the Beckettian elements served to deflect attention from this point.

Ah Q complains that the backwater village with its crumbling, leaky temple is "unchanged. The same hole. The world turns, the planets orbit, here time stands still." (AhQ34) Wang agrees: "The world turns, it doesn't move from the spot [...] if you know your way around history you're safe from surprises [...] everything repeats itself. It's disgusting. It's exhausting." (AhQ53) The real provocation here is that Hein interweaves Beckettian and Sartrean pessimism—the enervating, nauseating repetition of events—with elements of the marxist reliance on historical laws, which leads to the idea that you can "know your way around history."

Moreover, Hein deploys Beckett's ideas both against attitudes which invoke these ideas to rationalize inaction, and against attitudes which reject Beckett as irrelevant to socialist experience and precisely in doing so perpetuate impotent waiting. Hein's alternative is what he calls "anarchism," by which he means, he says, the anticipatory energy of "social dreamers and catalyzers," and "destruction for the sake of a *tabula rasa*, in order to get to a new beginning, to find a new hope, to

---

dissertation, Sheffield 1998, p. 54. Wiesemann traces in detail the links between Hein's and Beckett's plays.

[59] Martin Linzer, "Rätespiel ohne Botschaft," *Theater der Zeit* 39 (1984), 3, pp. 52-4; here p. 54. Linzer's review of the second GDR production, in Zwickau in 1984, avoids mentioning Beckett at all: "Die wahre Geschichte des Ah Q," *Theater der Zeit* 39 (1984), 5, p. 4. Only one further production followed before the Wende, in Schwedt in 1987.

[60] Quoted in *Theater der Zeit* (1983), 10, p. 56.

unmask illusion as illusion."[61]   Since, for example, the GDR *Duden* defined anarchism as a "petit-bourgeois, anti-marxist ideology," this was necessarily provocative, since the anarchic energy is directed against the stasis caused by the Godot-like illusions into which, Hein believes, the GDR's leaders had allowed socialist ideals to decay.

In March 1987, after numerous abortive attempts to stage it in the 1970s and 1980s, *Waiting for Godot* was finally performed in the GDR, directed in Dresden by Wolfgang Engel. The ground had been prepared by influential revisionist readings by Christoph Trilse and others,[62] but approval still had to be sought up to Central Committee level, where Tisch, chief of the Free German Trade Union Federation, supposedly asked: "Are we giving up all our principles and allowing them to perform this decadent play?"[63]   The crush for tickets delayed the start of the premiere, and there was slow-hand-clapping by an audience impatient for the end of their 25-year wait for *Waiting for Godot*. At the start, the red plush curtains which closed off the stage were not drawn aside, but ripped down, and, struggling and choking in the clouds of decades-old dust, the actors playing Vladimir and Estragon stammered: "Waiting for—Samuel Beckett."[64]

Engel avoided any attempt to locate the production where the GDR cultural authorities would have wished: as a parable of capitalist alienation.   Pozzo was not Brecht's landowner, but the kind of authority figure one could encounter in any GDR government office. And at the point when Pozzo struggles with Godot's name—"this ... Gono ... Godot ... Gobo ..." the actor savored the moment, inching closer and closer to the Godot in every East German's mind: "Gorbo ... Gorba ...."[65]   The effect was tumultuous, but this was one of many moments in the theater of the GDR's last phase which were both electrically topical and aesthetically crude.[66]

---

[61]   Quoted in Töteberg, "Der Anarchist und der Parteisekretär," p. 40.

[62]   Trilse, "Der Clown S.B.—oder: Spiele einer großen Absage," *Sinn und Form* 38 (1986), 4, pp. 851-875.

[63]   A possibly apochryphal remark, repeated by Engel in an interview in Michael Raab, *Wolfgang Engel* (Frankfurt/Main: Fischer 1991), p. 46.

[64]   See Ingeborg Pietzsch, 'Clownsspiele', *Theater der Zeit* 42 (1987), 5, p. 3-4; here p. 3.

[65]   See "Warten auf Gotbatschow? Horst Thiemer befragt den Dresdner 'Godot'-Regisseur Wolfgang Engel," *Theater heute*, 28 (1987), 5, pp. 58-9.

[66]   Peter Dehler, who directed *Waiting for Godot* in Schwerin in 1996, commented in an interview that Engel's production had, with its direct reference to Gorbachev, made "a decisive concession to the audience [...] a

Engel's young cast—he chose actors who had spent their whole lives in the GDR—expressed the impatience of the GDR's younger generations at the hollow rhetoric of "revolutionary impatience," rendering the production too fast-paced for some critics who wanted to savor this modern classic in the rhythms of the original.[67] The draft cast list, drawn up in November 1986, shows that Engel had planned a still more radical re-vision, proposing to cast women actors in all four main roles, until warned that Beckett would almost certainly veto it.[68] Engel also looked beyond stasis. At the end, the tramps lie on the floor flailing like overturned beetles, desperately trying to stand: another reference, surely, to Kant's image of the emergence from tutelage as the struggle to walk upright, and thus an image of latent change: a problematic concession, it can be argued, to both the GDR authorities and to the GDR audience.[69]

In the last months before the explosion of Autumn 1989, the theme of waiting is ever-present in the GDR theater: Christoph Hein's *Knights of the Round Table* (*Die Ritter der Tafelrunde*, 1989), where a younger generation waits for a sclerotic leadership to vacate the positions in which they block change; Uwe Saeger's *Attempted Flight* (*Flugversuch*, 1988), with its central question: "Whom am I waiting for?"[70]; Werner Buhss' *The Fortress* (*Die Festung*, 1986), in which a border garrison in an isolated fort stare into a blank and seemingly unchanging future; Lothar Trolle's *Barrack-dwellers* (*Barackenbewohner*, 1989), a poetic meditation on "those who wait in all epochs," drawing on images of refugee camps and of the Children of Israel waiting for Moses to return from Mount Sinai[71]; and Volker Braun's *The Transitional Society* (*Die Übergangsgesellschaft*, 1981, first performed 1988), which adapts a motif from Chekhov's *Three Sisters*: the dream of a future move to Moscow as a substitute for present

---

huge mistake": *Impuls. Zeitung des Mecklenburgischen Staatstheaters Schwerin* 21 (1996), p. 13.

[67] See Pietzsch, p. 3. The second GDR production, at the Volksbühne in East Berlin in 1988, took place in a significantly less charged atmosphere and marked a more reflective engagement with Beckett's text; see Ingeborg Pietzsch, "Verdrängungen," *Theater der Zeit* 43 (1988), 12, pp. 23-4.

[68] Production documentation, archive of the Staatsschauspiel Dresden.

[69] See Bechert, pp. 324-31.

[70] *Flugversuch*, in Peter Reichel, ed., *Die Übergangsgesellschaft. Stücke der achtziger Jahre aus der DDR* (Leipzig: Reclam 1989), pp. 401-44; here p. 425.

[71] See Ingeborg Pietzsch, "Und ich...?" *Theater der Zeit* (1990), 3, p. 43.

action, a procrastination which in Braun's play no longer functions. As director Thomas Langhoff remarked: "The hopelessness, that which is comparable to Beckett's *Godot*, which is inherent in Chekhov's term 'Moscow,' is now no longer inherent in it, but has become just the opposite."[72] Braun meant his title to have a double meaning, implying that the "transitional society" GDR was no longer a society whose complacent claim to be in transition from socialism to communism explained away its stagnation, but rather one that needed to address real reforms. But as the year 1989 progressed, the "Übergangsgesellschaft" proved to have a triple meaning, for it was, with increasing speed, a society in dissolution. "The binding spell of mutual complicity in mass deceit," the collective willingness to be duped like Beckett's tramps, "began to be broken."[73]

Then suddenly the Wall was open, and Durs Grünbein's poem "12/11/89" could note: "Lamentation of waiting, boredom in Hegel's narrow country/past now like the steely silence [...] Gradually watches are gathering speed."[74] A forty-year period (or twenty-eight years, if one dates the complete stasis of the GDR from the erection of the Wall in 1961) had ended, a period in which, metaphorically and sometimes literally, GDR citizens had been either Waiting for Godot, expected and to some extent able to rationalize their existential dissatisfactions with reference to the Godot of a socialist future, or waiting for *Waiting for Godot*, for the re-connection to Western modernity.[75]

On the very day that Samuel Beckett died, 22 December 1989, Helmut Kohl, in front of the world's media, officially reopened the Brandenburg Gate, restaging the opening of the wall which had taken

---

[72]   In Helmut Kreuzer, Karl-Wilhelm Schmidt, eds., *Dramaturgie in der DDR (1945-1990)*, vol. 2 (Heidelberg: Winter 1998), p. 559.

[73]   Mary Fulbrook, *Anatomy of a Dictatorship* (Oxford University Press, 1995), p. 247.

[74]   "Wehleid des Wartens, Langeweile in Hegels Schmalland/Vorbei wie das stählerne Schweigen [...] Langsam kommen die Uhren auf Touren"; quoted from Karl Otto Conrady, ed., *Von einem Land und vom andern. Gedichte zur deutschen Wende* (Frankfurt/Main: Suhrkamp, 1993), p. 26.

[75]   One writer drew the comparison between the GDR and Sleeping Beauty, protected as the former had been from the hectic pressures of Western capitalism by the thorn hedge of the Wall. See Martin Ahrends, "The Great Waiting, or The Freedom of the East: An Obituary for Life in Sleeping Beauty's Castle," trans. Stephen Brockmann, in *New German Critique* n. 52 (Winter 1991), pp. 41-49. Originally published as 'Das große Warten', *Die Zeit*, 17 November 1989, pp. 65-6.

place in a spontaneous upsurge of popular energy six weeks earlier, ending one epoch of stasis and political powerlessness for the residents of East Germany.   Now, this opening of the wall was restaged as an official act, reasserting the primacy of the state in political action, and setting the stage for a new epoch in which Beckett's images of powerlessness and stagnation would be no less potent. But that is another story.

* * *

Fiona Shaw

think that all great plays are hidden. That is usually why theater practitioners get excited by them, because they are often barnacled with theater history or with assumptions, or politically they've been borrowed, or used, or become necessary. It's the job really of theater practitioners to try and scrape away even their own preconceptions about plays, to try and discover what they are in the moment that you are discovering them. If there was any theory to be applied to plays, we could all apply the theory and every play would come out as well every time. In a way the difficulty is trying to allow the play to chime with the moment we're in. You can't make it chime, and sometimes they don't.

I'll just talk briefly about two productions and not make any great connection between them.   I was asked in 1989 to do a production of *The Good Person of Sichuan* at the National [Michael Howard's translation of The Santa Monica version, which uses the pinyin spelling in the title, directed by Deborah Warner]. We went with some trepidation. Because it was a public play, we were being asked to perform it in the Olivier Theatre, which is a very big theater and seats 1200 people. That itself is another issue. These big theaters were built on the assumption that right to the end of the century there would be big public debate plays about the state of the nation or other nations. In fact, as is now happening, it is very clear that the private has absolutely taken over from any notion of public plays. So we went to *The Good Person of Sichuan*. I can only say that we fought for a long rehearsal period, as we always do. On the basis that if you keep on hammering at plays that have become slightly dead, due to being slightly out of fashion, no longer relevant, you can find new meanings in them. And I have to say that it defeated us.

We spent weeks trying to try it, trying to not believe that this play could have been thrown on, as it might have been by Brecht's team, because of course its context was so relevant to that time. Even though outside the National Theatre there were people lying under

London Bridge, and there was a lot of talk about that at the time. There were exhibitions of the photographs of people lying under Waterloo Bridge, lighting fires, so that the bridge was cracking due to the poverty that Thatcher's government had brought upon the city. And my big memory of it is that we could have done it very much quicker, because it doesn't respond, unlike maybe Ibsen or a Greek play, even though they seem to be as far away in their barnacledness.

It just wouldn't rise, except that we made some very interesting discoveries. We had a designer called Sue Blane who had famously designed the Rocky Horror Show, so she had really invented Punk. There was an element of trying to drag some of Brecht's aesthetic into this post-Punk period. And I do remember one of the family of ten or whoever they are, they all had earings made of teabags which were very useful and cheap to make. Also because the play is so much about the East meeting the West, Deborah Warner and Sue Blane had spent a long time in Hong Kong and were full of photographs to design the play, to try and get this thing of East meets West.

Yet I have to say that it defied categorization because it played to something like 70% in the Olivier Theatre. An enormous number of people came. There's no doubt that the audience are often ahead of the play. There is something magnificent about the size of it, about the size of territory it tries to deal with. It isn't complex in the sense that it doesn't yield after seven or eight weeks of rehearsal anything more than it yields after about three. But it has a sort of breadth and I was very pleased to have done it.

Then in 1994, I think, we did a production of Beckett's *Footfalls*. I am not neutral about the Beckett Estate, because I feel like Milton's Lucifer. Having been cast from Heaven, I can say what I like now about God. I am banned from playing Beckett by the Beckett Estate and it has colored my entire interest in Beckett.

We were allowed, an unusual development, by the mid-Nineties, to start rehearsing plays in the place you are performing them. This is something the Germans have been doing for years. At the *Schaubühne* they often used to rehearse entirely on the stage, which is something unheard of. It's very traumatic for actors, when they move from the rehearsal room. They lose an enormous amount of the three-dimensional reality of their experience of rehearsing when they are moved to another place. It's literally like moving house. Your bedroom is no longer your bedroom, the sitting room no longer feels like your sitting-room. So, imaginatively, things fall away. People adjust pre-cognitively to a place they are rehearsing in.

We were asked in the West End, in the Garrick Theatre, would we like to put on a production whilst rehearsing it? Two things interested us at the time. It wasn't solo productions but small productions which have become very popular in the last ten years, just as shorter books have become popular. It was a short play. We were hoping to present *Footfalls* just as it was, not with another play attached to it, not as an evening of Beckett plays, not as a celebration of Beckett particularly, but rather as all theater should be, as an experiment in what happens to plays that seem to have gotten outdated, unfashionable as it may sound, to see whether they could live again in a new decade.

So with our forces we turned up in the theater and rehearsed for weeks and weeks and weeks this tiny twenty-minute play. And one of the things we tried to do was to not perform. All of you will know that, in *Footfalls*, Amy or May either exists or doesn't exist, either was there or wasn't there, or is a ghost now. But certainly an audience was going to receive the presence of somebody called Amy or May. And where might this person appear? If you were to walk into a theater that was slightly desolate, she might not choose to appear on the stage. And so I performed the first section of the play. This was after much trial and error, not any intellectual decision. I can't tell you the amount of trial and error, it was beyond boring in the end. Every seat of every row we played it in. In the center of the stalls we built a platform, which I thought would be the place we would end up. We were trying to find what was the area of most heat, really, for where this person might appear, who may or may not exist. And the audience we would worry about later.

We thought it was going to be on the stalls. For a long time we were rehearsing on the stalls, and then found really perhaps the most precarious place was on the balcony. It was just a proscenium arch, 19th century West End theater. Eventually I felt it was most likely this person might appear on this balcony. So we built a platform on the front of the balcony. The audience entered through the auditorium, which had already been slightly distressed and slightly decorated, or undecorated. There were things like hangers in the bathroom. There were mops left. There were things that had been left by people that might have inhabited the building. So the audience were already in a slightly heightened theatrical state on entering the auditorium. And then they found that the seats were strapped up in the stalls since there was no point in sitting down and looking at the stage, because the character then appeared on the balcony. So I did appear on the balcony. Then half way through there was a kind of pause, and May or Amy comes down for that last speech, and I exited down the stairs and appeared on the stage.

This is not radical drama. This is just a theatrical idea. The audience came in and they stood around. They didn't know where the play was going to happen. Sure enough, when a light went on on the balcony, they all turned round and looked up. Then after a good ten or twelve minutes, however long the play is, down came the character and appeared on the stage, and that was the end of the play. There was much more written about this production than the play either deserved, the production deserved, or indeed perhaps much more than was in the play. The play was much shorter than the amount of journalistic activity it ignited. We were indeed banned, having of course caused a sensation, which guaranteed a very full house. So in that way we were a good help to Beckett.

There were very interesting reasons for our being banned. I can't remember them all now. I honestly don't like even revisiting it, as it was a most uncomfortable time. One was that the pause between my being on the balcony and getting onto the stage was longer than seven seconds, which was the pause that people believed Beckett intended it to be. This I can respect intellectually, but I just find it unspeakably hard to bow to it. I find it oppressive. Anyway, a pause should be the length of time that people can endure concentration between one thought and another, which is often less than seven seconds. But if it is seven seconds or over, good for the production, I would say.

Secondly, I wore a red dress, and I was standing against red plush seating. As some of you may know, the stage directions are very explicit and say that May or Amy must wear a grey dress. But of course it was first performed in a grey box. Now we live in a decade where dayglow exists, which really means that nearly most other colors are grey. One could argue that red against red cancels itself to become a kind of grey. Not so in the Beckett Estate. They were very keen on the grey. Also a man stood at the back of the auditorium with a stick and beat out the rhythm he believed to be the rhythm of the play. I find this one of the biggest insults I have ever received in the theater. And whether they are speaking on behalf of themselves or Beckett, I don't thank them for it. Jonathan Kalb mentioned that most productions of things are dreadful. True. Most plays are dreadful. True. I just think that the notion that wild lunatic student idiots on a rampage want to damage the reputation of Beckett, when nothing in our previous behaviour had indicated that that was our *modus vivendi*, I found that stuck in my craw. Having said that, I was delighted to have the experience. And I hope Beckett would have been. By the Saturday night when the injunction was coming in, I was being asked to perform anyway, without payment, so that we could call it a private performance. We would let the public in privately. We would go to the High Court, and even to the Court of Human Rights or something. This was all being suggested. My concentration on the play was getting challenged by the second, but it was fantastic to see outside three white limousines, and chihuahuas, and people in fur coats having flown in on the Concorde in order to see this production. I'm not sure this is in any way worthy of this conference, but that was the media *folie* of it. And that was my experience.

There are two things I discovered about Beckett and, I think, Brecht. When Dennis Kennedy asked me to come, he said speak of your experience. But I began reaching for books on Brecht, reading about his lack of desire to have any of his theatrical notions really connected to the emotionality of his poetry. But I remember the center of *The Good Person of Sichuan*, which has a speech where Shen Te says to the airman Yang Sun: "In this our country"—she sings a song—"And in these times, we should be rid of dull and gloomy evenings. Likewise high bridges over the rivers. And the hour before the dawn appears and the freezing winter time each year. All of these are fraught with danger. For man's unhappiness is so intense. A single suggestion would be sufficient cause to throw his unbearable life away." And I just realized that the writer is not necessarily his own best critic, that of course Brecht, as all great theatrical practitioners, functions from a heartbeat of emotional power, whether he admits it or not.

And in Beckett I feel not dissimilarly that the desolation of his writing belies a sort of amorous activity of writing at all. There's a wonderful speech that May has in which she says: "A little later, when she was quite forgotten, she began to—[*Pause.*] A little later, when as though she had never been, it never been, she began to walk. [*Pause.*] At nightfall. [*Pause.*] Slip out at night fall..." And in these pauses in the "began to" you see for the first and perhaps the last time the literature of the theater leaves the stage itself and jumps into the silence of the audience's mind. And they're left going: gosh, has she forgotten her lines? Or how much does this cost, God Almighty? Whatever they think has become the text in itself. There's no doubt that Beckett has become a sort of cul-de-sac which is terribly difficult, as it was for Irish poetry to shake itself from Yeats. So these giants are monsters.

Dennis Kennedy: It might be worth mentioning we may well be entering a new era with regard to Beckett copyright, in that Jérôme Lindon died four weeks ago. He was the one, as many of you will know, who was most rigorous in the application of his idea of what Beckett productions should be. So it may well be, Fiona, that you will become unbanned in the future. Perhaps you maybe ought to be more careful in what you say.

FS: I'm looking forward to the fatwa being lifted.

***

Brecht and Beckett in the Theater II: Discussion

*D*ennis Kennedy (DK): Michael, maybe you'd like to start by talking about the film project.

Michael Colgan (MC): I produced all the nineteen Beckett plays, and I produced one Brecht play. I suppose that shows there's some imbalance in my allegiance and indeed in my interest, and necessarily in my knowledge between the two of them. It isn't necessarily because I think one is greater or better or whatever than the other, it's just that when you make choices as an artistic director, you do exercise your own prejudice, no matter how else you look at it. And I've been doing that for seventeen years at The Gate. My prejudice would be towards Beckett. The reason for that prejudice is, I suppose, something to do with my own psychological shortcomings and my own psychological needs. I would have a preference for Schubert over Mozart.... But it's not just because of my sensibility necessarily, there are other factors. I have to look at things from a producer's point of view. Brecht, to his great shame, wrote plays that had 35/45 people in them. It's just very difficult for people to do that. Whereas Beckett is the most producer-friendly writer you will ever meet in your life. He never changes the set. It's fantastic. You don't have directors coming to you saying, what should I do here? You say, it's in the text, just follow that. And there's usually no more. I think the biggest cast of all is *Godot*, with five. And you don't have to pay the boy full money. So it's really only four. So he's very producer-friendly in that way....

Dennis has asked me to talk about the films. I have to be very careful, because with Lucifer [Fiona Shaw] here on my left, I may actually end up being her amanuensis, because I don't know whether, because of making these films, I am going to be vilified.... But I will say this, and let it be recorded here, and I don't know whether she will greet this with relief or indeed disappointment, but Fiona is not banned by the Estate, because when we were talking about making the films, I remember saying: what about Fiona Shaw, or is there a problem there? The Estate said, there's no problem whatsoever. So you're not banned, Fiona. But I think you might prefer to be. The problem that I have is that having made these films, I think there are a lot of people who are involved and have been involved with the Estate, who think that it was wrong, that it's a heresy to do such a thing, to put them onto film. And that is a really very big subject, whether you should or you shouldn't do it.

Question (Q): A question for Michael. Speaking of a cast of thousands, there's *Eleutheria* which is a Beckett play with a lot of people in it. Is there any hope of The Gate doing that?

MC: I have a sort of deal, well it's not a deal, it's a conversation. As you know, Sam didn't want the play to be done. You ask yourself the question, if he didn't want it to be done, why didn't he destroy it? Then at the same time you have to say, well he doesn't want the play to be done. It's a difficult question. So I said to Edward [Beckett], real producer-style, I said, if somebody wants to do the play, and is going to do it professionally, why don't you tell them that The Gate have the rights. Then we'll do it. And if that case came, I think that we would. But I'm confused, Fiona, about whether it's right or it's wrong; I can't make a judgment on *Footfalls*. I don't think red will ever become grey, and I'll say that to Fiona now. But I can't make a decision on whether staging it the way she did it was wrong, because that's nothing to do with me really. I actually think it was probably very interesting and a great idea and gave life to it. I just made the decision that knowing him, and meeting him, and talking to him, and him asking me to do productions, that I would do them as he wanted them done. But I would hate the world to be doing plays as authors wanted them done. But I think there is a place in the world for one producer or one person to try and do them as he wanted them done. But can you imagine if we all did Shakespeare as he wanted it done? Can you imagine if we decided that Shakespeare wasn't meant for film and we didn't film it, or indeed that we didn't film *Streetcar Named Desire?* Maybe one day *Eleutheria* will be done.

Q: Were there films you particularly preferred, or successes or failures?

MC: I think there were, but I'm not going to tell you. Necessarily, there are. There is no doubt that you are giving a director, whoever he or she may be, a difficult task with some of the plays. I think it's a sort of a peach, though I didn't think it at the time, to give *Act without Words II*, where Enda Hughes, who is an extraordinary talent, can take a piece like that, which is a mime piece set against what is supposed to be a frieze. This piece doesn't actually sit well in the theater. When we put it onto film, and he used film, and all those little sprockets as the frieze, he could do something in a very Chaplinesque way with these actors. I just feel very strongly that Beckett would have adored that. That moved into film very well. I actually think that Anthony Minghella's *Play*, even though the Estate are very upset with it—it is the one they are most upset with—I actually think it's the most successful in some ways, because if you go to see *Play* on stage, and there are three people in an urn, you become very suspect about why Beckett is doing this.

I've heard so many academics and people saying, as he does with Winnie, or as he does with telling May or Amy to walk nine paces up and down, he's limiting the interpretive ability of the actor by putting them into an urn. And of course that's not what he's doing. We have all talked about how he limits actors in so many ways. But you know what we do, when you see three urns here and you see a white floor like this, you're actually listening to the story of *Play* about the triangle, the affair. What you're not getting is the context. Why are they in urns? That became a joke for Beckett. That became what people put in cartoons: the rubbish can, because Nagg and Nell are in the rubbish can, because he confined the actors. But it needed, I'm not sure we did it in *Endgame*, but it needed some way—and Anthony Minghella had the courage to go forward and fight with me, and fight with the Estate, and fight with me again—to actually contextualize it. So when you look at Anthony Minghella's film *Play*, there are not only three people in an urn, they're in this sort of Dantesque bog, in some sort of Purgatory. What they're saying and this affair, the story, is a cliché. It is beautifully written, no doubt about it. Better than Graham Greene. But it's still a cliché. They could be saying anything, because what they're doing is rehearsing the trivia of their lives over and over and over again. And why are they doing that? Because they're in an urn, because they're in this limbo, because they're in this Dantesque world.

Now there is no production in the world where you're going to get these three urns touching each other on a black floor in a black box, that's going to give you the context. It will give you the story. It won't give you the context. So what you can do, and what I would like to do and want to do, when I get permission, is actually do these ninteen films again in twenty years time. When I can actually say to nineteen directors: you interpret this. You give me sense out of this. We didn't do it this time. We couldn't do it. But I want to do it more than anything, more than filming Pinter, more than Pinter Festivals. That's what I want to do, because I think Minghella made sense for me. And in *What Where*, when you can actually look at the man being interrogated, when Bam interrogates Bom and Bim and Bem, and you look at the face and the expression of fear, when Bam says: "He didn't say where?... It's a lie. [*Pause.*] He said where to you." You see this man who comes in with the information, smiling. He's pleased. And then you see his face disintegrate, collapse with fear of what this play's about. You can't do that on stage. You can't get in that close because on the stage the person's face becomes a thumbnail. In *Rockaby* you can actually cut to her hands when she dies and the grip relaxes, you can actually see this for the first time. There is no doubt there are great successes, not by me, by these directors in filming it. But there are others that I think were just very difficult to do. And in a normal world maybe you wouldn't have decided to make a film of, for example, *That Time*, unless you were going to be able to open it out. So I think there are winners and losers.

Q: A question, for Fiona, about this cul-de-sac of theater in Europe after the death of Brecht and Beckett and Heiner Müller. Most people, when they drive into a cul-de-sac, turn round and try to come out of it. What do you think?

Fiona Shaw (FS): I think what has happened is that people have started making theater out of things that are not necessarily theatrical writing. And we are not expecting the dramatist to take entire responsibility for the event. People would now climb out of those jars. That would be exciting, theatrically. So the theater has ceased to be necessarily about theatrical writing.... None of these things work necesarily. There is an element about how we would like to feel about these writers, but we can only feel what we feel. Jonathan Miller once said that when he asked his son what he was going to do with himself, he said, I'm hoping to want to be an engineer. I think we're hoping that we can go on liking these writers and turn them into classics. They will only be classical writers if they survive, and they can't survive even when Michael was saying he'd like to do a project of trying to serve these writers. The writers are only served if the audience are engaged at that moment by them. These are laws that are way beyond anything except the aesthetic of the time. We should be watching Beckett and Brecht all the time. We can't, because that's not where we are. I think that's an on-going problem for the theater. As Peter Brook says, you often don't find the plays, the plays have to find you.

DK: Fiona, now that we've learned you've been unbanned, would you be interested in doing more Beckett, and if so, what would it be?

FS: I would, the writing is fantastic, and the possibilities are enormous, which is possibly why in the generation of the writer's life, there had to be restrictions. I can understand that. Because the writing is potentially so free, it could be anywhere. And of course there has to be responsibility in that kind of freedom. But I think there's an existential point, a kind of existential wall in this, which is: Beckett is dead. He no longer is. In fact, even the question—would he like it?— has no meaning. He hasn't lived in the decade in which the world itself has changed. He is no longer inhabiting our time. The writing can inhabit our time, but only if it is ignited by the people of our time. So of course I would, I'd love to do any of them.

   MC: Could I just say something about his no longer being here, at the risk of getting into a big fight with Fiona? You don't say, I think he'd like it, because you worry about whether he'd like it. You do listen sometimes to his instructions, because you think he might be right. Now, what if he's not right? There were certainly times in making the films when I wanted to be completely disobedient. For certain films, and what we were doing, his instructions for plays were wrong. I had no doubt about that. And I fought with the Estate on some of them. We just went ahead and did it. But there are times when you're doing them, and I've done the nineteen on stage three times and only once on film, when I have actually found that listening to the instructions is right. In that way that you know that the man suffered very greatly, and tested it, and wanted to do it. When it gets down to saying in *Breath*, it's got ten seconds, and then a blackout, and then five seconds of this, I actually agree with Fiona. I think that's when an actor can judge that and change it, not just for a production but change it night by night. There should be that freedom. But there are certain things within the work, where as a dramaturg and as a director I think he was right. And it wasn't in an ivory tower. His production of *Godot* that he did in 1975 in the Schiller Theater was a terrific piece of direction. He was a very good director.... Beckett had a very good instinct about what would work and what would not.

   FS: Can I comment on that? I don't think I could go into a room if I thought there was going to be a tree with two leaves in the middle, and two men with funny hats doing a play. The image is now so absorbed by the culture, it no longer has the theatrical necessity of newness. If someone says that there's a production of *Waiting for Godot*, and goodness knows what it will look like, I would be very excited about going. I think stage directions can sometimes become the Waterloo for the writer, who in essence is trying to guide productions at a moment that he is normally moving the form forward. Ibsen has a stage direction that says: "She slowly peels the pages from the book and one by one she puts them into a fire." Now I would just humbly say that a hundred years later, the rhythm of our lives is no longer that. And if you serve the stage direction, you are not serving the writer. I do think that Beckett was using the most modern aesthetic he could think of, when he was having grey tattered dresses moving across grey studio theaters. It's gone. He won't live in that, because we now have a different aesthetic. And we're not serving him, strangely, by obeying him. I suppose that will cause generations of debate.

MC: You are absolutely right that an aesthetic becomes dated and tired and overused. But there are times when the audience you're putting on a play for is not necessarily Michael Colgan or Dennis Kennedy or Fiona Shaw sitting in the front row. You can't say, I don't want to go into a room with two men in bowler hats and a tree, if you're doing the play for the first time in Western Australia, or if you're doing the play for the first time for people who have never seen it before. Or indeed, if you're doing it on film, where the majority of the people who would look at it on television actually haven't seen it before. And the people who went to the Irish Film Centre [where the nineteen Beckett films were premiered] came out and said: I never knew what *Krapp's Last Tape* was all about. They hadn't seen it. So in that version I think it's right to have the tape recorder, and not have, as somebody wanted to, when they were suggesting making the film, a video, and turn it into that new idea. So I think you're right, but I also think that there are some lasting images and the tree can work for a new audience.

FS: I think the Globe Theatre was built precisely for that purpose with Shakespeare, and it is death to the theater. It is fantastic as an educational tool, but I don't think Beckett, with respect to a university, should be hijacked by the academic world. It must continue to live.

MC: I'm not disagreeing with that either. I think you're right and I think that it shouldn't be hidebound. I can't bear the idea of productions that are in doublet and hose and all of that sort of thing. But I am just saying: there is no doubt that that is coming. Jérôme Lindon is dead. Edward [Beckett] is much freer than Jérôme was. There will be *Endgames* in abattoirs, no doubt about it. And there will be Winnies in hair-dressing salons. We know that's coming. What I was trying to do with the films was to go, as near as he could, given what the director wanted, to this different thing, and to put that down as a marker. But having said that, it's a testament to how I feel that I'd love to do it again.

Q: [A question about the precise use of stage directions as a guide for acting.]

FS: Brecht did say, didn't he, to one of his actors: now it's your turn, because you must be entertaining. How are you going to serve the story and the political necessity of the play? You must also serve your own needs. And he said in the contradiction between those two things, all energy flows. I think that's very true. There is always going to be a tension.

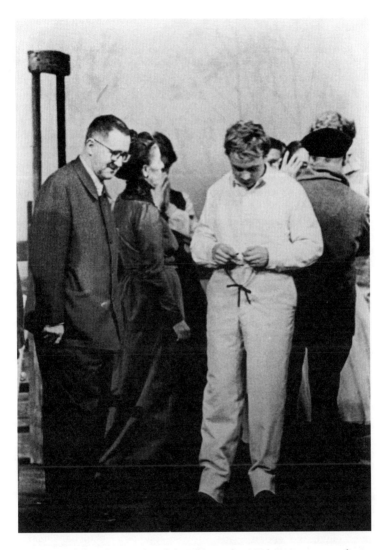

Bertolt Brecht probiert *Die Ziehtochter oder Wohtaten tuen weh* von Ostrowski. Berliner Ensemble 1955. Brecht, Helene Weigel, Lothar Bellag. Foto: Percy Paukschta.

Immer und immer wieder: Brechts und Becketts Echtzeit spielen im digitalen Zeitalter

Bertolt Brecht and Samuel Beckett can be made to represent two different and even oppositional traditions of twentieth century performance: the politically dedicated theater and the formal, removed one. Putting aside that simple, perhaps even rhetorical comparison, however, one can find in both their works a creative use of the very technologies that have come to represent central inventions and obsessions of the century: the audio technologies of radio and tape. Using the acoustic technologies of radio and tape, they separate the voice from the body in some of their work, thereby complicating the physiology of the performative and challenging any organicist notion of it. Although Brecht and Beckett can be coupled by their mutual investment in acoustic technologies, the technological nightmare of the twentieth century, World War II and its aftermath, divided their use and understanding of these apparatuses. It was their times that were different, both the times of their historical situations and the times they fashioned in their work.

Bertolt Brecht und Samuel Beckett können als zwei verschiedene, ja sogar entgegen gesetzte Traditionen im Theater des zwanzigsten Jahrhunderts dargestellt werden: das politisch engagierte Theater einerseits und das formalistische, distanzierte Theater andererseits. Jenseits einer solch vereinfachenden, vielleicht auch lediglich rhetorischen Gegenüberstellung aber findet man in beiden Lebenswerken einen schöpferischen Umgang mit genau den Technologien, die inzwischen als zentrale Erfindungen bzw. Obsessionen des vergangenen Jahrhunderts gelten: die Audio-Technologien Rundfunk und Tonband. Indem sie die akustischen Technologien Radio und Tonband benützen, trennen sie in manchen Arbeiten die Stimme vom Körper; dabei erschweren sie sowohl die Physiologie des Performativen als auch jegliche organische Vorstellung des Performativen. Obwohl Brecht und Beckett durch ihren gemeinsamen Einsatz für akustische Technologien gepaart werden können, trennt sie der technologische Albtraum des zwanzigsten Jahrhunderts: der zweite Weltkrieg und die Nachkriegszeit. Es waren ihre Zeiten, die anders waren, sowohl die geschichtliche Situation selbst als auch die Zeit, die sie sich in ihren Arbeiten erschufen.

Time and Time Again: Playing Brecht and Beckett's Real Time in the Digital Age

Sue-Ellen Case

When one thinks of the works and legacy of Bertolt Brecht and Samuel Beckett, it would seem they are more dissimilar than similar. Certainly, they can be made to represent two different and even oppositional traditions of twentieth century performance: the politically dedicated theater and the formal, removed one. Putting aside that simple, perhaps even rhetorical comparison, however, one can find in both their works a creative use of the very technologies that have come to represent central inventions and obsessions of the century: the audio technologies of radio and tape. Using the acoustic technologies of radio and tape, they separate the voice from the body in some of their work, thereby complicating the physiology of the performative and challenging any organicist notion of it. The term cyborg comes to mind, here, in their sense of acting as part machinic. Although Brecht and Beckett can be coupled by their mutual investment in acoustic technologies, the technological nightmare of the twentieth century, World War II and its aftermath, divided their use and understanding of these apparatuses. It was their times that were different, both the times of their historical situations and the times they fashioned in their work.

What time is it?

"What time is it?" the question favored by language teachers scattered across many time zones, takes on a different meaning in the digital age. The question has come to mean what kind of time is it, what register of time do you mean, what order of time is operating. The term "real time" in my title is prompted by the operations of a digital age, in which most time, the time of work, the time of communication, and the time of entertainment is virtual time. Time in the digital age is the world time of the internet, the speed time of Pentium IV chips, and the time of video capture techniques which allow rearrangements of events to occur within minute, rather than minute segments. In this age, "real time" is "distanced," as one member of our male couple, Brecht, would put it, from our quotidian experience of virtual time. "Real time" is no longer the ground of all experience, the necessary referent of representation, but a time out of the digital, with its separate, but no longer determining structuring of passage.

In the digital age, the notion of "time" is a diluvian one, made to float in the great confluence of media that fiber optics transport. The

Where Extremes Meet: Rereading Brecht and Beckett / Begegnung der Extreme. Brecht und Beckett: Eine Re-interpretation
Stephen Brockmann et al., eds., *The Brecht Yearbook / Das Brecht-Jahrbuch*
Volume 27 (Pittsburgh: The International Brecht Society, 2002)

differentiation of media, which were dedicated singly to the aural or to the optic now flow together through streaming techniques and broadband broadcasts. Time, once channeled by earlier critics into such tributaries as "narrative time," or "stage time," made to seem rich with the silt of scholarship, now flows into the great confluent of virtual time which, in contrast to earlier, well, times, is now the time of much labor, communication and fantasy; whereas "real time," that referent of production and social organization, recedes out of the great global flood into localized pools of temporal capital. "Real" time, then, is now merely one form of time, no longer primary. In fact, "real" signifies more a time out of the virtual than a foundational structure. Its new status has been created by the confluence of media and their quotidian uses in all sectors of labor, communication, and entertainment.

However, when the precursors of the digital media first began to appear, around the end of the Nineteenth century, at the dawning of what would become digital time, the media were perceived as storage banks of "real" time, either as re-producers of the "real" time of the documentary, or the real time of cultural performance. As Friedrich Kittler notes, in his book *Gramophone, Film, Typewriter*, these media were able to store time in a new way, for example, "time as a mixture of audio frequencies" (3). Before their invention, time had been stored in what Kittler calls the European tradition of texts and scores. Quoting Kittler again, texts and scores "whose time is (in Lacan's term) symbolic.... Whatever ran as time on a physical or (again in Lacan's terms) real level, blindly and unpredictably, could by no means be encoded. Therefore, all data flows, provided they were really streams of data, had to pass through the bottleneck of the signifier" (4). By this, Kittler means that before the acoustic medium was able to capture data as data, it could only be recorded through words or scores. These types of record were, by nature, an interpretation of acoustic data and thereby in the Lacanian sense, symbolic representations of time. There ruled an alphabetic monopoly, a grammatology, accompanied by its institutional accomplice, compulsory education (4). Kittler argues that merely capturing those sounds and reproducing them with a needle, as in the gramophone, took them out of that symbolic representational economy. As Kittler would have it, "Electricity itself put an end to this [rule]...." (10). As he insists, recording devices do not think. They are not conscious (33). Quoting Kittler again: "Ever since the phonograph, there has been writing without a subject" (44).

Free as this data was from interpretation, capable of floating as sound, or sight, into the space of the receiver, the instrument of capture and broadcast was dedicated to a single sense. The acoustic and the optic regimes each had their own technology of reproduction and distribution. Especially Brecht, but also Beckett, participated in those technologies that channeled the aural as separate from the optic. Each author used this separation in different ways. Brecht saw the division as not dissimilar to his sense of Epic theater, which also worked on the principle of individuation, in the service of binding theater with social commentary (Der Rundfunk 556). Beckett also used the division into acoustic and optic as a distancing device, but one that divided the character from him or herself—a personal and solipsistic relation. Both authors used images of acoustic technology to work in dialog with a live actor, but toward different ends. Brecht and Beckett staged the play that happens between acoustic technology and the listener, Beckett in *Krapp's Last Tape*, and Brecht in *The Flight of the Lindberghs*, or *The Ocean Flight*, Beckett through the recursive looping of tape and Brecht through the broadcasting potential of radio. Bound as I am to their comparison, I would like to focus on Beckett's project for a moment, in order to see how recursive acoustic technology and time as memory begin to accommodate one another.

Beckett's Mechanics of Memory

The new mechanical capture of time that was spreading through industrial nations at the turn into the 20th century induced an exploration of its opposite—an investment in subjective time and personal memory (Kittler 33). Freud was tinkering in his workshop of memory, while Edison was inventing the gramophone and a magnificent homosexual scaffolding of subjective time and memory was, well, being erected, by Proust into *Remembrance of Things Past*.

It is to that homosexual monument of subjective time that Beckett turned, as a young man, in the early 1930s, still tortured by teaching at Trinity College, and just beginning to imagine himself as an author. Interestingly, Beckett titled his monograph *Proust*, as if his critical investment resided more in authorial function than in the text as an independent artifact. Indeed, as John Pilling concludes in his study *Beckett Before Godot*, "For all Beckett's talk of a 'Proustian equation,' it is the possibility of a Beckettian equation which most concerns him" (37). Beckett gleans from Proust certain representational structures of subjective time and memory. Thus, he joins the investment in subjective time that swept across Europe in tandem with the development of new technologies. Beckett identifies two types of memory in *Remembrance of Things Past*: voluntary and involuntary. As he observes: "Voluntary memory (Proust repeats it ad nauseam) is of no value as an instrument of evocation, and provides an image as far removed from the real as the myth of our imagination or the caricature furnished by direct perception" (Proust 4). Two important associations with voluntary memory emerge in this sentence, each of them

165

representing Beckett's, not Proust's characterization of it: first, the distancing of the voluntary from the real and second, the assertion that direct perception and voluntary memory provide "caricatures," rather than representations of the real. He thus distances voluntary memory and direct perception, the volitional and the empirical, from the "real," as he terms it. Beckett also summarizes Proust's celebration of involuntary memory in words that mark his own investment in its relation to the real: "the experience is at once imaginative and empirical, at once an evocation and a direct perception, real without being merely actual, ideal without being merely abstract, the ideal real, the essential, the extratemporal" (56). Beckett then pithily concludes that, in the workings of involuntary memory "time is not recovered, it is obliterated" (56). Yet Beckett's interest is in time rather than its obliteration. His works do not structure the kind of agency that obliterates, residing in things such as madeleines. From his study of Proust, he gleans no conquest of time, but the notion that there are two possible structures of time in relation to memory that set up epistemological relations to the real. Proust offers a key to representing time and the real as effects of memory. Through these narrative inventions the categories of the real and real time, established through the tradition of empiricism, can then be tossed off as "caricatures" of conditions. [Just to note, here, parenthetically, that Beckett's ironic dismissal of will and the empirical constitutes a major and, I think obvious difference to Brecht, who would embrace them.]

Interested in the effects of the Proustian equation of the real, Beckett does not proceed to deploy the operations of involuntary memory, or any representations of the transcendent; instead, he stages the vicissitudes of voluntary memory in a way that ironizes the volitional through tropes of impotence. Of course, as many critics have already discussed, memory and impotence are signature interests in Beckett's work. But central to this study is the way in which Beckett sets up the very dialog of the early years of the twentieth century between voluntary memory and time that has been captured by the acoustic technology of tape. In numerous plays, he intricately weaves tape and memory into new patterns of play. I want to focus on two examples that I think illustrate how technology and memory work in Beckett: *Krapp's Last Tape* and *Rockaby*. In these plays, taped memory is staged in relation to "live" actors, who perform embodied actions related to voluntary memory. *Krapp's Last Tape* offers an early exploration of how tape signifies on stage and in relationship to the "live." Tape and its machinery are staged as fetish objects of voluntary memory, around which Krapp performs certain embodied acts that establish their fetish functions. Krapp dwells in a space dedicated to the storage and indexing of tape. Outside of that relationship, there is no other order of perception or retention, as Beckett specifies: "Table and adjacent area in strong white light. Rest of stage in darkness" (55). The stage lighting signifies the radiance of the fetish, the "aura" new technologies organize, in contrast to the aura of the real Benjamin mourned in its passing. The tapes are ordered as amulets of time captured. Krapp listens to them in rapt, motionless attention, evoking their seductive strength with the word "spooool." As he manipulates the tapes and the tape recorder, the phallic anxieties that prompt fetish relations appear in several ways. For example, one of his only embodied actions apart from tape management is to eat a banana. The phallic allusion is marked in the stage directions: "strokes banana, peels it, tosses skin into pit, puts end of banana in his mouth and remains motionless, staring vacuously before him" (56). To paraphrase Freud, a banana is not just a banana in this instance, but part of the play of potency and impotency that is embedded in the fetish relations to the technology of tape as voluntary memory. Further, Tape, as Beckett designates the recorded voice, sounds the memory of a sexual scenario, which forms the penultimate recursive structure of the play, driving it to its conclusion. Here is the concluding section of the play:

> TAPE: I lay down across her with my face in her breasts and my hand on her. We lay there without moving. But under us all moved, and moved us, gently, up and down, and from side to side. [Pause. Krapp's lips move. No sound.] Past midnight. Never knew such silence. The earth might be uninhabited. [Pause.] Here I end this reel. Box—[Pause]–three, spool—[Pause.] five. [Pause.] Perhaps my best years are gone. When there was a chance of happiness. But I wouldn't want them back. Not with the fire in me now. No, I wouldn't want them back. [Krapp staring motionless before him. The tape runs on in silence.] (63)

It is Krapp's LAST tape, as the title indicates and therefore the end of something. The title suggests that the play will conclude by somehow ending the recursive looping, which tape and memory represent in their very structures. The solution resides in the character's relation to sexual practice—specifically heterosexual practices.

Proust offered Beckett a monumental example of how to represent the drive to remember as a form of desire. Desire and memory together play the roles of captor and captive (the title of one of the novels) in relation to the object of desire. Yet the Proustian equation or lack of equation between desire/memory and object, the illusive captive, is driven by a homosexualization of representation in Proust, which drives him to the transcendence of the involuntary; while Beckett, inscribing the heterosexual regime, installs the engine of the voluntary. In his monograph, Beckett briefly alludes to the homosexual dynamic in the novel, but he does not perceive it as constituting perhaps the most painfully elusive quality of the object. Following his citation from Proust that "One only loves that which is not possessed, one only loves that in which one pursues the inaccessible," Beckett does turn to a discussion of the representation of homosexual relations in the novel. He recounts Dr. Cottard's "pompous" diagnosis of Marcel's object of desire, a woman who has lesbian affairs, as a "case of sexual perversion". But rather than turning to the force of social prohibition against homosexuality that drives Proust's cross-gender, inverted mapping of homosexual desire in the novel, Beckett ascribes the elusive quality to a fault of character, concluding that "Albertine is not only a liar as all those that believe themselves loved are liars: she is a NATURAL liar" (35). Of course, the word "natural" here has an unnatural ring, since her lies concern her lesbian relations.

What Beckett does not account for, in his reading of Proust, is the scopic economy of heteronormativity—one in which only heterosexual relations are visible, or representable. Teresa de Lauretis, in her article "Sexual Indifference and Lesbian Representation," argues that representations of heterosexual relations are "those very images which our cultural imaginary and the whole history of cinema have constructed as the visible, what can be seen, and eroticized" (35). De Lauretis continues to illustrate how any representation of homosexual relations dissolves back into the order of heteronormativity—cannot be seen. Proust traces this elusive quality of homosexual visibility through betrayals of the heteronormative regime. Homosexuality can only become visible through lies and the endless longing that cannot capture the love object. The only satisfaction comes through a sensory experience that stands in for the sexual. Involuntary memory is thus a displacement, or a metonymic symbol for any direct representation of homosexual desire, offering satisfaction through an effective recursive loop of memory.

In contrast, Beckett charts the recursive looping of voluntary memory—the iteration of heteronormative tropes. In his work on Proust, he consigns this normative order to the sense of the deadening repetition of "habit." As he puts it: "Habit then is the generic term for the countless treaties concluded between countless subjects that constitute the individual and their countless correlative objects" (8). Habit hides the object, he contends, in "a haze of conception—preconception" (11). Habit is Beckett's term for normative practices—the institutionalization and repetition of social codes. It is the installing, the institutionalization of the normative practice of heterosexual desire that drives the repetition of the tape in Krapp. Finally, representation is so overdetermined that he need only wordlessly mouth the tape's lines, as he listens. Its recursive loop is broken by him in the end, when he concludes that he no longer wishes to return to the satisfaction promised by the scenario of seduction. He performs a finalizing voluntary act, when he decides, "I wouldn't want them back. Not with the fire in me now" (63). This decision to stop the loop of desire that brings him back to the site of seduction brings about his final stillness and the tape to the silence that ends the play.

Currently, in an era in which tape is passing away, already a kind of antique, nostalgic form of acoustic reproduction, we might view this stage picture as fetish of the analog, in the time of the digital. But *Krapp's Last Tape* stages a relationship to tape near the beginning of its use, exploring how its capabilities may be made to signify on stage. Martin Esslin contends that *Krapp's Last Tape* owes its existence to Beckett's fascination with tape recording in the wake of the production of his first radio play, *All That Fall* (Esslin 203). Krapp was composed the year following the broadcast of the play. At the time, tape was just becoming a medium for recording and broadcasting for the BBC (Zilliacus 24). In fact, the use of tape in *All That Fall* was so innovative that it inspired the founding of a new workshop for the development of tape's capabilities, the BBC Radiophonic Workshop (Zilliacus 24). The innovative element in *All That Fall* resided in what Esslin calls "stylized realism". Sound effects, such as animal noises, and footsteps, needed somehow to be removed from the context of naturalistic reproduction, which most resources provided. So treating these effects electronically with changes in speed, fragmentation, and montage produced the sense that these sounds existed in a more removed space (Esslin 129). Esslin notes that the stylizing of the acoustic elements positions the piece "halfway between the objective events experienced and their subjective reflection within the mind of the character, who experiences them". In fact, Esslin insists that among all media, only radio can really effect this representation of the subjective, which is then received through and recreated by the subjective responses by the listener (131). Katherine Hayles, in her work on tape and artistic innovation, adds that tape provided a break between presence and voice in a more radical way than the phonograph and the radio, since it inscribed and yet could be manipulated (76). In other words, tape offered the capability to separate voice from body, consciousness from presence.

The ability of tape, or radio, to produce a voice in the room that goes on, as Kittler contends, without an inscription of it into a symbolic order, without a subject that produces it, informs much of Beckett's later works in which voices continue apart from the consciousness that is associated with them. In *Krapp's Last Tape*, the situation of the taped voice resides in a removed zone. Krapp listens to his own voice, but not as if it comes from within. It is a documentary recording of his memory, which he controls, rather than the voice, say, of his conscience, or unconscious, or any other display of his present interiority. In his later play, *Rockaby*, Beckett uses tape as the interior voice of the character on stage, which speaks when she does not, which she controls, to some extent, and which she sometimes joins in unison. The voice runs on, as in Krapp, and once again, the conclusion of the play is the act of stopping the taped voice. But in *Rockaby*, the end of the tape is the end of the character.

Tape, as the engine of voluntary memory, sketched out in the rites of fetish in Krapp, permeates the entire performance in *Rockaby*. As the director Alan Schneider put it: "Once we cut the track, there's no way out of it. The track then becomes the armature for the whole damn thing" (from the video). Rather than playing a role in the play, tape determines the play. The fragmentary residue of a subject position that Krapp embodies gives way to the object status of the technology of reproduction. The play stages what Marxist critics would identify as "reification," a condition in which objects determine human relations and, as Jameson explains it, "function like an institution" (Jameson 245). The woman, often the gender of object status in heteronormative discourse, sits nearly motionless in her chair. She does not even rock the chair herself. Beckett is careful to note that the rocking is "controlled mechanically without assistance from w" (274). The letter "w" stands for the woman and "v" for her taped voice. Any remnant of character has shrunk to the letter that holds the place of character, like a function in a system, or in an equation. Yet the place holder is not derived from the name of a character, but of her gender. The role of the gender Woman in the system, as an object, is signified here by the "w." The schematic quality of the play is also installed through stage directions that indicate a hyper-precision of definition. Even the blinks of w's eyes are prescribed. The directions determine the blinks to occur "about equal proportion section 1, increasingly closed 2 and 3, closed for good halfway through 4" (273). The pauses in the taped voice are specified in length, down to the second. Once again, the area in which the play takes place is strictly defined by light, with darkness beyond.

"W' is cast in the role of the faithful listener. In *Rockaby*, Beckett has staged the condition of the "listener" as it evolved throughout the twentieth century. "W" is reminiscent of the logo for RCA Victor, which pictures a dog sitting before the speaker, ears cocked, listening to "his master's voice." RCA Victor reported that the overwhelming popularity of the logo was as a figure of fidelity (Taussig 213) that Michael Taussig deems "the civilized man's servant in the detection, and hence selling, of good copy" (220). High fidelity, then, as loyalty and submissiveness in the technoculture. The conditions of the taped voice and the mechanics of the stage create an object-defined situation. As the twentieth century proceeded, the relations of power inverted: the character does not run the machine, but the machinized relations run the character. The taped voice is not located, but locates. The time is the time of the machines, sequenced out in strict parcels, shrinking back to units approaching the digital. The only time is recursive and mechanical. "Real" in any organic sense, is not the referent of any elements. The listener is disciplined by the technology. Beckett's "w" represents "high fidelity." To stop the tape is to stop herself.

Brecht Never Listens

Brecht foresaw the future of the listener, or the receiver of the new media in precisely this condition of passive bondage. For him, this condition was a probable outcome, rather than a necessary one, contingent upon the possibility for people to change their conditions. Nonetheless, he coined a new term for the receiver's condition: "inploitation" (Einbeutung). The receiver, or audience, in Brecht's terms, for the new media "formed a double character.... ambivalently split into exploiter and exploited" (Mueller 24). Thus, inploitation describes one's own exploitation of self. "W" in Rockaby seems caught in this relationship to herself, dominated by and dominating "v" or voice. Brecht perceived the issue within the terms of his time, trying to reconcile the relationship of productivity, which seemed active, and pleasure, which seemed passive. Indeed, his invention of the learning play was meant to bring these two functions together, so that the sender and the receiver were one, in an active sense.

In order to stage this problem, Brecht created a learning play about the new media entitled *Lindbergh's Flight* (*Der Lindberg-Flug*), which he later changed to *The Flight of the Lindberghs* (*Der Flug der Lindberghs*) and then retitled *The Ocean Flight* (*Der Ozeanflug*). The play was performed at the Baden-Baden Music Festival in 1929. The stage was split into two sides: on the left side was the live radio orchestra, singers, and signs of its technical apparatus; on the right side was the listener, who read the parts, including the score, hummed along, and sang the part of the pilot along with the orchestra. Brecht's major point, in the staging, was to offer a model of an active listener.

Yet Brecht's notion of the active listener included more than a sort of karaoke-like singing along with broadcast sounds. In his 1932 article, "Radio as a Communications Device" (Der Rundfunk als Kommunikationsapparat) he emphasizes the need to remake radio from an apparatus for distribution into one for communication—a site for disputation rather than dissemination (552, 554). Brecht was not for the so-called neutrality of media, but for everyone being able to participate in that sphere (Radio 218). Radio would consist of a huge network of channels that would send and receive. In this way, Brecht foresaw something more like the internet than the radio. Interactivity rather than distribution would offer a more participatory form of "tuning in," with the promise of participation for what he called the masses.

Let us return, for a moment, to *The Lindbergh Flight* as the model for how this new medium might be characterized. The story is about Lindbergh crossing the Atlantic, his progress tracked only by radio reports that, like him, complete a transatlantic crossing. Radio's capability of broadcasting the disembodied voice offers the possibility of having the forces of nature speak, such as the fogbank that obscures Lindbergh's way. But the hum of the new technology of flight, along with Lindbergh's heroic achievement, bring enlightenment to the primitives, "ignorant people," as Brecht puts it, who "glimpse God" (11). "Under the more powerful microscopes" he contends, God disappears (12). By conflation, the new media could be cast in an heroic role of participatory enlightenment. Like the world wide web, they etch out a sense of the global, conflating travel, distribution, and interactivity.

Yet Brecht is cautious about how this claim to the global will actually function. In his 1927 piece, "Radio—An Antedeluvian Discovery?" (Radio—eine vorsintfluchtliche Erfindung?) Brecht cautions:

> It is an old custom of ours to get to the root of all things, even the most superficial, when nothing is really there. We have an exceptional appetite for things that we can investigate.... The truth is that we are led around by the nose by POSSIBILITIES. These cities which YOU run around to explore, exhausting yourself in the process, make the bourgeois consumer, through his actions and inactions, unquestionably astonished... The bourgeoisie judge them purely on the basis of their prospects which, naturally, they will yield up to them. From this comes the over-estimation of all things and institutions in which these [so-called] "possibilities" reside. No one busies himself with results. Merely the possibilities. The results of radio are shameful, their possibilities are limitless. Thus the radio is a good thing. It is also a bad thing. (redaction, translation mine, from 217-219)

Thus explorations, scientific and touristic, airplane flights and electronic connections, seduce by the promise of new possibilities that will somehow pay off for the discoverer.

For Brecht, technology and commodification go hand in hand. In reflecting on the court trial over the filming rights to his *Threepenny Opera*, he wrote: "The author is being engulfed in the technological process and the latter is seen as commodity production" (Mueller 21). Brecht was prescient in noting that the new technologies would challenge the rights of intellectual property, as his was challenged in that case. Cultural producers who worked with the new media would discover that the technology produced commodities and their work would belong to that order of "thing." Brecht was not purely pessimistic about the new form of production; however, he imagined that it could be a progressive process, moving away from the property rights of the individual creator, foreshadowing socialism in a more collective process (Mueller 21). As Mark Poster has noted, the conditions of capitalist production are best suited to factories and most challenged by the organization of the internet, as demonstrated in the recent court case around Napster and the free trade of music—an acoustic medium (Poster, Chapter 6).

Brecht also saw the danger in new media's collusion with the profit motive, commodifying all relations (Mueller 20). The consequent reification of social relations would, indeed, make the rocking chairs rock the people. Machines have long served as an image of this condition, in which objects, or objectified relations appear to function, to perform. In our darkest imagination of the future, we might characterize internet performance in this way, where cartoon avatars act and software performs. We will be "rocked off" as Beckett put it, in our computers, our "static audiovisual vehicles."

The coupling of Beckett with Brecht offers at least a bifocal perspective on the digital age: either we are rocked off, or we become the active spect-actors, as Boal calls them, who will change the conditions—hacktivists rather than faithful listeners. What has changed is the new sex/gender relations produced in the digital realm. Brecht often typically ignores the role of sexuality. Possibly he would not want to name the homoerotic relations that pertain between men and their heroes. When gender does appear in Brecht and Beckett, it is caught in the stable gender divide of heteronormative institutions. It is precisely this assignation of gender to role that is one of the principle contestations the new cyber-feminism finds appropriate to web activism. In an "FAQ" on cyberfeminism, Alla Mitrofanova advises: "We don't occupy our time with criticizing male dominant economy... we look for multiplicities which dissolve claims of binary oppositions... Weirdly, cyberfeminism deals with performed bodies, recreating concepts of the feminine and the subjective in multiplicity" (12).

Cross-gender casting about on the web does seem to destabilize the old heteronormative order in a promising way. Transgender identifications are touted as one of the most pleasurable of web masquerades. However, it is important to remember who owns this technology—most upper management and owners are men—and who uses it—majority also men. Men have enjoyed cross-gender performances at least since classical Greek tragedy, and they did not seem to destabilize the institutions of gender or heteronormativity.

Yet new configurations of what constitutes a body are emerging that combine a sense of broadcast as prosthetic device and gender as performance, promising a different order in which sex, gender, and performance are ineluctably bound together. Sandy Stone, the male-to-female transgender author of much theory of cyberspace, speculates that perhaps "hetero phone sex" might offer a model of a new version of radio drama. (396) Stone argues that, in radio drama, the sound of fire was more persuasively produced by crumpling cellophane than by recording the sound of fire itself. So with phone sex and, by extension, cybersex, in which the signs of corporeal pleasure may actually reproduce them. The sound system, then, is more than a prosthetic device—it offers a new realm for bodies in relation to one another, with masquerade at its base.

Borrowing Brecht's notion of interactivity and Beckett's relation of tape/memory and subjectivity, we can imagine an acoustic and luminous realm of the digital that provides a recombinative body that re-mediates social and sexual intercourse. As Brecht foresaw, however, this digital body travels in a realm completely suffused with the corporate and commercial ownership of the data. The anterior realm of the private gives way to the commodity fetish, which actually transports gender and sexual identifications. The time of Beckett's recursive loop, or Brecht's model, already receding from the "real" in their own time, now enters a time of global branding: the time it takes to efficiently transport goods through signs of corporeality.

Works Cited

Beckett, Samuel. *Krapp's Last Tape. Collected Shorter Plays.* New York: Grove P, 1984. 53-63.

Beckett, Samuel. *Proust.* 6th ed. New York: Grove P, n.d.

Beckett, Samuel. *Rockaby. Collected Shorter Plays.* New York: Grove P, 1984. 271-82.

Brecht, Bertolt. *Lindbergh's Flight. Brecht Collected Plays,* v. 3. Ed. John Willett. London: Methuen, 1997. 1-19.

Brecht, Bertolt. "Der Rundfunk als Kommunikationsapparat," in *Werke: Grosse kommentierte Berliner und Frankfurter Ausgabe* 21. *Schriften* 1. Frankfurt am Main: Suhrkamp Verlag, 1992. 552-57.

Brecht, Bertolt. "Junges Drama und Rundfunk," in *Werke: Grosse kommentierte Berliner und Frankfurter Ausgabe* 21. Eds. Werner Hecht, Jan Knopf, Werner Mittenzei, Klaus-Detlef Mueller. *Schriften* 1. Frankfurt am Main: Suhrkamp Verlag, 1992. 189-90.

Brecht, Bertolt. "Radio—eine vorsintfluchtliche Erfindung?" in *Werke: Grosse kommentierte Berliner und Frankfurter Ausgabe* 21. *Schriften* 1. Frankfurt am Main: Suhrkamp Verlag, 1992. 217-19.

Brecht, Bertolt. "Vorschläge für den Intendanten des Rundfunks," in *Werke: Grosse kommentierte Berliner und Frankfurter Ausgabe* 21. *Schriften* 1. Frankfurt am Main: Suhrkamp Verlag, 1992. 215-17.

De Lauretis, Teresa. "Sexual Indifference and Lesbian Representation," in *Performing Feminisms: Feminist Critical Theory and Theatre.* Ed. Sue-Ellen Case. Baltimore: Johns Hopkins UP, 1990. 17-39.

Esslin, Martin. *Mediations: Essays on Brecht, Beckett, and the Media.* Baton Rouge: Louisiana State UP, 1980.

Hayles, N. Katherine. "Voices Out of Bodies, Bodies Out of Voices," in *Sound States: Innovative Poetics and Acoustical Technologies.* Chapel Hill: U of North Carolina P, 1997. 74-96.

Jameson, Fredric. *Marxism and Form.* Princeton: Princeton UP, 1971.

Kittler, Friedrich A. *Draculas Vermächtnis.* Leipzig: Reclam Verlag, 1993.

Kittler, Friedrich A. *Gramophone, Film, Typewriter.* Trans. Geoffrey Winthrop-Young and Michael Wutz. Stanford: Stanford UP, 1999.

Mitrofanova, Alla. "How to Become a Cyberfeminist," *next cyberfeminist international.* Hamburg: Old Boys Network, 1999. 12.

Mueller, Roswitha. *Bertolt Brecht and the Theory of Media.* Lincoln: U of Nebraska P, 1989.

Pilling, John. *Beckett Before Godot.* Cambridge: Cambridge UP, 1997.

Where Extremes Meet: Rereading Brecht and Beckett / Begnung der Extreme. Brecht und Beckett: Eine Re-interpretation

Poster, Mark. *What's the Matter with the Internet?* Minneapolis: U of Minnesota P, 2001.

Stone, Sandy. "Split Subjects Not Atoms: or, How I fell in Love with my Prosthesis," in *The Cyborg Handbook*. Ed. Chris Hables Gray. New York and London: Routledge, 1995. 393-406.

Taussig, Michael. *Mimesis and Alterity*. New York: Routledge, 1993.

Zilliacus, Clas. *Beckett and Broadcasting*. Abo, Finland: Abo Akademi, 1976.

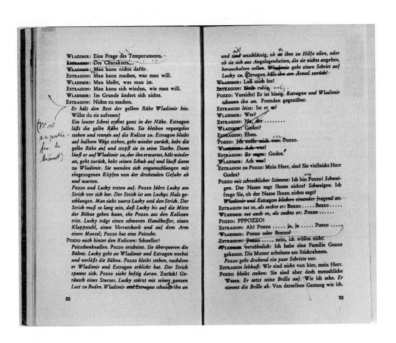

Samuel Beckett: *Warten auf Godot.* Berlin: Suhrkamp, 1955.
Nachlaßbibliothek Bertolt Brecht.

Feministisches Theater und Brechtsche Tradition: Ein Rückblick und eine Vorschau

After over thirty years of feminist theater practice, this article makes a retrospective examination of the critical reception and practical use of the Brechtian aesthetic by feminist theater theory and performance respectively. With specific reference to the main strands of feminist theory on female identity and representation and to some characteristic practices of Anglo-American theater groups, performers and playwrights, I endeavor to demonstrate that, despite some insidious strategies of suppression of the Brechtian influence, Brecht's legacy has on the whole been favorably received and has proved a useful expedient for the achievement of the targets of feminist theater.

Nach mehr als dreißig Jahren feministischer Theaterpraxis untersucht dieser Artikel retrospektiv sowohl die kritische Rezeption als auch den praktischen Gebrauch der Brechtschen Ästhetik durch die feministische Theatertheorie bzw. die feministische Aufführungspraxis. Indem ich auf die Hauptgedanken der feministischen Theorie in Bezug auf die weibliche Identität und deren Darstellung und auf einige charakteristische Praktiken angloamerikanischer Theatergruppen, Künstler, und Theaterschriftsteller eingehe, versuche ich zu zeigen, dass, trotz einiger schädlicher Strategien der Unterdrückung des Brechtschen Einflusses, die Erbschaft Brechts im großen und ganzen positiv rezipiert worden ist und sich als brauchbares Werkzeug zur Erreichung der Ziele des feministischen Theaters gezeigt hat.

Feminst Theater and the Brechtian Tradition: A Retrospect and a Prospect

Elizabeth Sakellaridou

I. Brecht and His Critics

How great a personality was Brecht? What were the real dimensions of his contribution to the formulation of contemporary dramatic and theatrical aesthetics? Who continued and who appropriated his work? Who admired or criticized him, deified or rejected him? Among artistic and intellectual circles there has been a strong ongoing debate around his personality and work for the last half of the past century. The centenary celebration for his birth (1898-1998) simply refueled the long-standing Brechtian ideological and aesthetic controversy. Commenting on the spirit of the German centennial festivities in Berlin, Antony Tatlow picks up the eloquent title "Brecht: 100 oder tot?" (Brecht: 100 or dead) from an article in *Theater Heute* as "the truest summary of this cultural discourse" and notes with humor that "if some had come to praise their erstwhile Caesar, most had come to bury him" (Tatlow 1).

The celebratory atmosphere of 1998, though useful and necessary for a systematic revision of the role of Brecht in the shaping of a new theater, also ran the risk of turning into an uncritical eulogy and a populist mystification of the man—symptoms which had already been detected in Brecht's eager appropriation by the exponents of postmodernism on the one hand (e.g. Elizabeth Wright) and in the fairly voyeuristic engagement by a number of scholars with aspects of his private life and affairs on the other (e.g. John Fuegi).[1] In her introduction to the volume *Re-interpreting Brecht: His Influence on Contemporary Drama and Film* (1990) Pia Kleber expresses annoyance at the "mythic proportions" Brecht has taken in our days (Kleber and Visser 1), while Manfred Wekwerth, one of the contributors to the volume, suggests the rescue of Brecht from dangerous distortions (Wekwerth 19). A similar defensive attitude can be detected in Marc Silberman's article "A Postmodernized Brecht?" (1993), which undertakes a stern but sober critique against the opportunistic character of many trends of postmodernism and concludes rather skeptically that we should first deconstruct our own postmodern critical position before

---

[1]   I am alluding to Fuegi's controversial book *The Lives and Lies of Bertolt Brecht* (1994). Olga Taxidou's article "Crude Thinking: John Fuegi and Recent Brecht Criticism" (1995) is a bold and illuminating critique of the pitfalls of Fuegi's intended revisionist approach to Brecht.

Where Extremes Meet: Rereading Brecht and Beckett / Begegnung der Extreme. Brecht und Beckett: Eine Re-interpretation
Stephen Brockmann et al., eds., *The Brecht Yearbook / Das Brecht-Jahrbuch*
Volume 27 (Pittsburgh: The International Brecht Society, 2002)

"working with Brecht through postmodernist theory" (Silberman 1993: 12). Loren Kruger's name should also be added to the list of scholars who oppose the popularization of the Brechtian tradition and resent the vulgarization of the Brechtian model. Kruger is dismissive of the postwar British misreadings of Brecht, which she attributes to limited knowledge of Brecht's complete oeuvre.[2]

All these reservations concerning the preservation of the integrity of the Brechtian legacy are of considerable value, whether they spring from an unavowed German possessiveness (Pia Kleber), or from a theoretical distrust of some postmodernist trends (Marc Silberman) or from complete devotion to pure marxist models (Loren Kruger). At the same time the opposite views, which favor the appropriation of Brecht in support of some new-emerging socio-cultural or ideological or intellectual movement, are of equal interest. In her book *Postmodern Brecht* (1989) Elizabeth Wright engages in a serious reevaluation of Brecht the dramatist and theorist from the point of view of postmodern theory and art. Sustaining a strong argument and a convincing analysis throughout, Wright proposes Brecht's early plays as precursors of postmodernism, and she discusses the fertile appropriations and transformations of the Brechtian aesthetic model by two distinguished German postmodern artists, the dancer and choreographer Pina Bausch and the dramatist Heiner Müller. Thus Wright highlights the doubly dynamic position of Brecht as a precursor of and a transformational model for postmodernism.

---

[2]   See her article "The Dis-Play's the Thing: Gender and Public Sphere in Contemporary British Theatre" (1990), p. 72. Kruger's main argument, which uncovers a real bibliographical problem till the beginning of the 1990s, is that access to Brecht's theoretical texts, for anglophone researchers who do not speak German, is practically limited to the selected translated pieces by John Willett, published in 1964. This argument reflects the general attitude to this issue of other contemporary theater critics, who believe that the French and Anglo-Saxon interpretation of Brecht is still inadequate (Kleber 10). This situation of scarcity of sources in translation has been improved through several new English editions of Brechtian texts in translation during the past decade. Of course the relationship of the contemporary German theater with Brecht is not considered satisfactory either. In her introduction to the volume *Re-interpreting Brecht*, Pia Kleber underlines on the one hand the West German mistrust of the work of Brecht and on the other hand the exhaustion of the East German Brechtian model and its need for renewal. In her reappraisal of Brecht's reception in the East Germany of the 1950s and 1960s, Christa Wolf also admits the misreadings of his work by the writers of her generation (Rechtien 199).

II. Women's Theater and the Brechtian Legacy

In the thirty years of its existence feminist theater, especially in the Anglo-American world, has formed a very close relationship with the Brechtian tradition both in the area of its performance practices and in the field of theory accompanying these practices. The historic visit of the Berliner Ensemble to London in 1956 was perhaps only of nominal importance for British feminist theater, which actually grew in the 1970s out of the political theater of the 1960s. But the Brechtian aesthetic had also infiltrated avant-garde cinema and the media and has been finding its way back to contemporary theater under disguise and through various other channels. If delving into the origins of the Brechtian influence on women's theater is a complex task, searching for the identity of the recipients of this influence is no easier matter. Independent women dramatists, collaborative schemes, female theater groups, individual performers and theater theorists and critics can hardly be accommodated under one homogeneous category with identical politics and ideological or sexual orientation. The multiplicity of origin and the polyphony of the feminist recipients of the Brechtian influence have inevitably created serious disagreement concerning the recognition of the Brechtian model as a suitable tool for the goals of feminist theater. The feminist debate over Brecht may seem to reflect the general controversy in Brechtian scholarship today, but it certainly has different ideological origins, and it mainly stems from feminist theorists rather than dramatists and theater practitioners. With reference to the controversial feminist theory of identity and representation on the one hand and to women's theater practices on the other, I shall endeavor to demonstrate that Brechtian theory has proved and will further prove a very useful expedient for the achievement of the targets of feminist theater.

III. The Theoretical Debate: The Materialist Position

A formal link between the orientations of feminist theater and the Brechtian method was first suggested by the American feminist critic Janelle Reinelt in her article "Beyond Brecht: Britain's New Feminist Drama" (1986). By analyzing the dramatic structure and the stage representation of selected contemporary plays by women, Reinelt pinpoints some of their morphological features, which she recognizes as Brechtian.[3] Based on a rather descriptive approach, she proposes a

---

[3]   In her later book *After Brecht: British Epic Theatre* (1994), in which she returns to the larger question of the Brechtian influence on contemporary British political theater, she postulates with conviction the emergence of "a hybrid British form of recognizably Brechtian theatre" (1). In this book Reinelt

productive dialog between feminist theater and Brechtian theory for the development of a new morphology for feminist dramatic texts and performance; however, she totally overlooks the problem of female spectatorship.

Investigation in this direction was continued and systematized—though quite independently—by another American theorist, Elin Diamond. In her ground-breaking article "Brechtian Theory/Feminist Theory: Toward a Gestic Feminist Criticism" (1988), Diamond discusses all the techniques of the Brechtian method (epic narrative, historicization, alienation, the Gestus, the "not, but") as ideal strategies for the feminist representation of gender, which has as its aim the subversion of traditional mimetic (i. e. realistic) representation. Despite Kruger's strong reservations about Diamond's radical position,[4] this article is still a useful theoretical expedient for tracing all subsequent developments of feminist stage poetics. Diamond proposes a cross-fertilizing synthesis of a feminist-Brechtian model, which would fill in the blanks of the Brechtian theater in gender issues and would furnish the feminist theater with the right aesthetic tool (that of anti-realism) for the dethronement of the solipsistic male gaze from gender representation.

Assuming the same assertive tone, another American theorist, Jill Dolan, discusses the advantages of the Brechtian method for women's theater in her book *The Feminist Spectator as Critic* (1988). Finding value in Diamond's proposition, Dolan devotes a whole chapter to a minute analysis of the methods of materialist feminism, which are based on aspects of Brechtian theory and the adoption of precise Brechtian terminology. In a special section of her book Dolan talks about the "Brechtian legacy" and places particular emphasis on the usefulness of the "not, but" technique for feminist (especially Lesbian) representations of gender.[5] Her theoretical position is

---

discusses in a separate chapter the work of Caryl Churchill as a model of a socialist feminist theater of Brechtian origins.

[4] In her polemical article "The Dis-Play's the Thing," Kruger attacks Diamond for her "abstract and ahistorical" Brechtianism in her "(In)Visible Bodies in Churchill's Theatre" (1988) although she seems curiously to ignore (strategically?) Diamond's other basic and most fundamentally Brechtian article "Brechtian Theory/Feminist Theory" (Kruger, n. 22, p. 72).

[5] The "not, but" is the technical term by which Brecht defines a specific acting method, in which the actor also implies that which s/he does not impersonate. The potential of this way of acting is that it allows the recognition of all other possibilities while the actor actually represents only one (Willett 1964: 137). Both Diamond and Dolan consider the Brechtian "not, but" as an

followed by extended reference to specific female theatrical texts and performances.

It is noteworthy that these three feminist theorists—Reinelt, Diamond and Dolan—continued to revert to Brechtian models in their later theoretical writings concerning problems of representation of gender and subjectivity. Dolan, showing an undisguised partiality for a Lesbian theater aesthetic in her article "Breaking the Code: Musings on Lesbian Sexuality and the Performer" (1989), rekindles the issue of "mimesis" and recommends once again the Brechtian technique "not, but" for structuring a Lesbian stage model. In a more recent and more polemical article, "Personal, Political, Polemical: Feminist Approaches to Politics and Theatre" (1992), she revisits the Brechtian techniques with even more intellectual vigor and stresses their high suitability for the revival of a radical women's theater for the 1990s.

In her article "Feminist Theory and the Problem of Performance" (1989) Reinelt also touches upon the problem of female representation and predicts the usefulness of the Brechtian Gestus for the developing feminist theories of gender and the representation of female subjectivity. But it is Elin Diamond who turns a more theoretically fresh look at the tough issue of mimesis and female representation. In her article "Mimesis, Mimicry and the 'True-Real'" (1989), she pinpoints the rupture between the deconstructionist subversion of mimesis and the referentiality of the real on the one hand and the political necessity of feminist theory for a more positive consideration of the possibilities of representation on the other. She then goes on to suggest engrafting the Brechtian method upon the psychoanalytic models of representation of the French theorists Luce Irigaray and Julia Kristeva for the creation of a viable feminist poetics of mimesis.

IV. The Psychoanalytic and Deconstructionist Mistrust

The bold invasion of Diamond, an acclaimed champion of materialist feminism, into the territory of deconstruction and psychoanalysis,[6] brings to the surface the serious problem of the complete neglect of Brecht by the feminist theorists who are followers

---

ideal method for the theatrical deconstruction of gender because it allows for the synchronic representation of the whole spectrum of gender differences as conceived by the French deconstructionist philosopher Jacques Derrida.

[6]   Sue-Ellen Case refers to Diamond as "correct[ing]" the essentialist tendencies of the psychoanalytic critique (Case 1990: 8).

of these last two strands of feminist thought.[7] The relevant comments of Reinelt and Dolan also attest to this strange anti-Brechtian prejudice in the work of the above mentioned group of feminist theorists, which has led to the paradoxical phenomenon of a mute acceptance of Brechtian terminology vis-à-vis an ostensible absence of the name of Brecht. Diamond and Dolan, for instance, note Laura Mulvey's failure, in her pioneering article "Visual Pleasure and Narrative Cinema" (1975), to mention Brecht despite her clear references to the alienation effect. A rereading of Mulvey's article along these lines reveals precisely an unacknowledged appropriation of Brechtian terms and methodology—a minor slip, perhaps, if it did not eventually develop into repetitive habit in the work of other, slightly later feminist theorists of the psychoanalytic and deconstructive schools.

Indeed the examination of the work of theorists such as Sue-Ellen Case, Teresa de Lauretis and Judith Butler, reveals a systematic suppression of the Brechtian influence (real or potential) at points where this admission appears a must. Especially Sue-Ellen Case, who has done systematic and thorough research on the issue of constructing a purely feminine theater aesthetics, seems to be a case in point for Elizabeth Wright's succinct comment about "a Brecht-reception without Brecht" (Wright 113). In a series of important theoretical essays, Case incorporates Brechtian terms and techniques without acknowledging the obvious loans, thus raising serious questions of epistemological ethos.[8] In her "Brecht and Woman: Homosexuality and the Mother," she squarely dismisses Epic discourse, and her only credit to Brecht is for the "discourse of desire and corporeality" brought up in his early "homosexual" plays (Case 1985: 69).

Equally questionable is the attitude of the French feminist writer and theorist Hélène Cixous in her theoretical article on the aesthetics of women's theater "Aller à la Mer" (1977). In this short article Cixous proposes new techniques for feminine representation,

---

[7] Tatlow notes in general "the narrowness, even the vituperation" in some psychoanalytic assessments of Brecht where "denial is so violent" (Tatlow 1). The existing gulf between the materialist and the psychoanalytic strands of feminism is graphically reflected in the difference of tone between Karen Laughlin's triumphant acceptance of "feminist theorists of theatre hav[ing] been quick to embrace the work of Bertolt Brecht as ripe for adaption to serve feminist ends" (Laughlin 1995: 14) and Sue-Ellen Case's pleased statement about the "prevalence" of psychoanalytic critique in the US and the parallel "isolation" of socialist feminist discourse (Case 1990: 8).

[8] See Sue-Ellen Case, "From Split Subject to Split Britches" (1989) and "Toward a Butch-Femme Aesthetic" (1989).

and she discusses the ones she uses in her own play *Portrait of Dora* (1976). Following a method similar to that of Laura Mulvey in both texts, Cixous subverts the male gaze in the production and reception of women's theater by appropriating Brechtian techniques without ever naming them.

Similarly, in her book *Alice Doesn't: Feminism, Semiotics, Cinema* (1984) Teresa de Lauretis, who takes as her starting point Mulvey's suggestions about the possibilities of destroying androcentric scopophilia, is entrapped in strict psychoanalytic models as she moves into deeper analysis of female subjectivity and the subversion of male visual pleasure. Although deeply preoccupied with the possibilities of female representations of gender, even in later texts like "The Technology of Gender" (1987), where she refers positively to the usefulness of Althusser's research in the domain between marxism and psychoanalysis, she is unable, on her part, to create a link with Brechtian theory when exploring the possibilities of representation of the in/out condition of female experience. Under the influence of Foucault's studies on sexuality and Althusser's work on the interrelationship between the individual subject and society, de Lauretis discusses the double position of women within and without the patriarchal symbolic order and ideology as representation/sign on the one hand and as historical subjects on the other. In an attempt to assume a more materialistic critical position towards psychoanalysis than Sue-Ellen Case and based on the deconstructive notions of rupture, emptiness, and absence, she places women at the periphery of representation, and she talks of the "space-off" and the "unseen" of the female vision (de Lauretis 1987: 25-26).

By making references to avant-garde cinema, whose remarkable achievement was to focus on scenes deliberately omitted from traditional filmic representation, de Lauretis appears particularly optimistic concerning the ability of female performance to apply similar methods in order to make visible women's own perspective ("a view from elsewhere," 25) in matters of gender and social identity. As becomes obvious from the titles of some of her other studies, "Sexual Indifference and Lesbian Representation" (1988) and "Eccentric Subjects: Feminist Theory and Historical Consciousness" (1993), her main concern is the shift of women away from their "ec-centric" or peripheral position and to the center of the symbolic order so that their different perception of the world can become visible. In fact, her aim, which is to sensitize the gaze of the spectator to another, so far invisible, aspect of gender difference, interestingly corresponds to the aim of Brecht's theater to render visible the class differences that were systematically concealed by the bourgeois realistic stage. The anti-realist techniques of Brecht's theater, especially the "not, but" (which is actually a technique of alterity), would be most suitable for the representation of the "space-off" and the "unseen" discussed by de Lauretis in her revisionist feminist theory of gender.[9] In fact her own positive references to Marxist thinkers like Louis Althusser (and Fredric Jameson) can be said to have provided the right ideological link to the Brechtian method.

Demonstrating gender differences is avowedly the major endeavor of feminist theater, and the possibilities of representing such differences have been thoroughly explored by the majority of women theorists and theater practicioners. Playwrights as diverse as Caryl Churchill, Pam Gems, Sarah Daniels, Timberlake Wertenbaker, Hélène Cixous, Marguerite Duras, Simone Benmussa, Maria-Irene Fornes, Adrienne Kennedy and Franca Rame—to mention only a few names from across culture—and theorists such as Elin Diamond, Jill Dolan and Sue-Ellen Case, theater groups like the Women's Theatre Group, Monstrous Regiment, Split Britches, and Spiderwoman, and performers like Karen Finley and Rachael Rosenthal have given their own answers to the problem. But more general philosophical issues such as the idea of gender as an ontology of sex or as a social construction of identity have not been part of their agenda. De Lauretis's relevant study on the "technologies of gender," as already discussed, and that of Judith Butler on gender performativity,[10] serve as a useful theoretical backdrop for all other women working in the domain of feminist theater. Just as de Lauretis seems reluctant to cross the boundaries of deconstruction and psychoanalysis, so too Butler, who moves in the field of philosophy (mainly phenomenology), does not seem eager to acknowledge any vital bond between her own theoretical quest and Brechtian theory. Although the title of her article "Performative Acts and Gender Constitution" and her ensuing analysis might suggest a sensitivity to theatrical praxis, she is, in fact, only using the theatrical role as a metaphor for the illustration of the social function of gender rather than taking a genuine interest in actual stage practice.

---

[9]   The kinship of the Brechtian theory on realism/anti-realism with the methods of avant-garde cinema is discussed in detail in Marc Silberman's article "The Politics of Representation: Brecht and the Media" (1987). See also his chapter "Brecht and Film" in Siegfried Mews, ed., *A Bertolt Brecht Reference Companion* (1997). Also Martin Walsh, "The Complex Seer: Brecht and Film" in Keith M. Griffiths, ed.,*The Brechtian Aspect of Radical Cinema* (1981).

[10]   See her book *Gender Trouble: Feminism and the Subversion of Identity* (1990) and her article "Performative Acts and Gender Constitution: An Essay in Phenomenology and Feminist Theory" (1990).

On the other hand, however, Butler seems to be thoroughly informed about the feminist theory of representation, especially the filmic one, and she has made repeated reference to the subversive techniques of avant-garde cinema.   Her familiarity with issues of feminist performativity is also proved by her preoccupation with female masquerade in the context of Lacanian psychoanalysis and its feminist variations (as elaborated by Luce Irigaray and Julia Kristeva).   The fact that her own preferred approach to the matter is rather abstract, since it passes through the channels of philosophy, is no obstacle to a feminist use of her research.   Butler's contention that the social dimensions of gender are only a series of performative acts can be almost automatically translated into the Brechtian theory of the Gestus, and it offers a very useful theatrical metaphor for immediate application on stage.   Her argument corresponds to the widely used stage tactic of female masquerade, which has become the major performing strategy of subversive feminist theater groups such as Split Britches and Spiderwoman.   In fact Butler's proposal for the destabilization of gender provides the theoretical backup for all activity in feminist representational art.   It is no exaggeration to say that Brechtian techniques, overtly or covertly employed in feminist theater practice, are inherent in Butler's theoretical texts, which talk about denaturalizing strategies (Butler, *Gender Trouble*, xii), or comment on the advantages of anti-realist acting in theater (Butler, "Performative Acts," 278), or make a vague reference to a "Brechtian sense" (Butler 1993: 223).

V. The Postmodernist Revision

From the above discussion we can conclude that the possibility of dissolving the anti-Brechtian prejudice of psychoanalytic and deconstructionist feminist theorists lies in their own texts, which brim with cryptic references to the Brechtian tradition.   Although the somewhat rigid position of the guardians of Brechtian orthodoxy can serve as a useful brake against uninhibited populist appropriations, it would go against any sense of epistemological spirit to allow such positions to inhibit a serious cross-fertilization of disciplines and theories that meet in the process of artistic creation and transmutation. The positive reception of Brecht by postmodernist critics and scholars, despite sporadic individual objections, moves in the right direction. When Iris Smith, in her article "Brecht and the Mothers of Epic Theatre" (1991), claims that "feminist criticism needs to *adapt* Brecht's ideas, not just adopt them" (Smith 491), she in fact repeats Heiner Müller's words that "to use Brecht without criticizing him is a betrayal" (Wright 122). These words precisely encapsulate all the essence of a fruitful assimilation of the Brechtian legacy by contemporary trends of the performance arts.

Regarding feminist theater, Iris Smith brings in new arguments in order to support the promising prospects of a feminist representation of gender through an injection with elements from Brechtian theory. After a cursory reference to Mulvey's, Diamond's and Dolan's familiar positions concerning the establishment of the female gaze, Smith takes one more decisive step into the domain of deconstruction and psychoanalysis by proposing the Brechtian Gestus as a technique "tailormade for feminist theatre" (Smith 493). Smith compares the marginalized female subject to the schizophrenic subject that Deleuze and Guattari discuss in *Anti-Oedipus* (1983), and she urges the feminist theater to "go beyond Brecht's 'not, but' and embrace the 'and' of excess, of schizophrenia" (Smith 504).[11] As an example of such feminist practice she presents and analyzes an avant-garde production of *The Good Person of Szechwan* at Indiana State University. Making a quick but firm critical survey of the latest developments in the domains of theater and theory, Smith provides feminist theory with the missing link between the political targets of women's theater and the dominant trends of deconstructive thought on issues of subjectivity and representation. Her analysis of a postmodern stage version of *The Good Person of Szechwan* is also an important revision of earlier views of Brecht that criticized his later works—those of his epic period—for their closed form and their firmly constituted characters.

In a more recent study of Brecht, "'Dragging' Brecht's Gestus Onwards: A Feminist Challenge" (1998), Meg Mumford discusses the importance of cross-dressing as a manifestation of the Brechtian Gestus. Mumford believes that Shen Te's transvestism in *The Good Person of Szechwan* proves the social construction of gender (Mumford 249) and that it therefore implies that the destination of woman is not dictated by anatomy—a view endorsed by feminists from Simone de Beauvoir to Judith Butler. What is more, Mumford highlights the simultaneous representation of male and female features in Shen Te's masquerade, which thus disrupts the bipolarity of gender (Mumford 25) by proposing an antithetical synecdoche as one more possible position for the deconstructed subject, shaped in the fashion of Smith's schizophrenic model. Mumford underlines Brecht's sensitivity to this way of representation of the fragmented human identity by quoting his own description of the disguised Shen Te as "a continual fusion and dissolution of two characters" (Mumford 250).

---

[11] Paraphrasing Brecht's term, I would suggest the name "not only, but also" for the extended model proposed by Smith.

Elizabeth Wright's earlier postmodernist revision of Brecht in her seminal *Postmodern Brecht* had already focused on the deconstructive elements inherent in his early plays *Baal* and *In the Jungle of Cities*, especially the presentation of fluid characters in the process of becoming. The fragmentation and gradual formation of human identity in these plays is a useful structural model for feminist dramaturgy, which conceives of female identity in a similar deconstructive and progressive manner. Smith's and Mumford's more recent revisions of the Brechtian oeuvre are out to prove that even the works of his mature period, which appear as more solid structurally, contain vital elements of a deconstructive representation of subjectivity and they can, therefore, operate, together with the early plays, as valid models for the formulation of a new feminist stage aesthetics, the Brechtian derivative "not only, but also" technique.

The contemporary revision of Brecht has also cast light on other, less known aspects of his work and has increased the possibilities for a further creative use of the Brechtian legacy. For instance Manfred Wekwerth, in his "Questions Concerning Brecht" (1990), discusses Brecht's use of the mixed (and contradictory) technique of empathy and alienation, which sets up a trap to the spectator before leading him/her to the shock of recognition (Wekwerth 34-37). This current reassessment of Brecht saves his work from monolithic interpretations and reveals the multi-layer potential of this theatrical instinct, which at points makes his theater surprisingly converge with Artaudian or Beckettian theater, his affirmed antipodes.[12]

The specific mixed method of identification and estrangement has already proved particularly successful in its theatrical application by feminist theater groups like Monstrous Regiment and the Women's Theatre Group. It is the work of this latter group that Loren Kruger takes up in order to argue that "those groups succeed best that engage their audience with a combination of the new and the familiar so as to then surprise them with critical theatre" (Kruger 64). Kruger, however, has many reservations about the canonical origins of the various subversive tactics of political theater, and she names the contemporary theorist and practitioner of "popular theatre" in Britain John McGrath rather than Brecht as the instigator of the "sentimental concessions" made in the performance practice of British political theater (Kruger 75-76). However, we cannot ignore the historical fact, also underlined by

---

[12]   Elizabeth Wright is strongly in favor of this compatibility, especially in the domain of recent experimentation with performativity (Wright 114-15).   On Brecht and Beckett, see also Antony Tatlow's essay in the present volume.

Wekwerth, that Brecht had already discussed and tried, in some of his own productions, the advantages of this mixed technique.

On the whole, the postmodern critique tends to view the Brechtian legacy as a non-closed system, by arguing that its very initiator considered it as open and under continuous revision. The fluidity and polysemy of the characters, the possibility of gradual change, the temporariness of the epic theater, the conflation of distance and emotion, all give the impression of a dynamic system under constant experimental testing and inquiry and, therefore, receptive to new configurations. Besides Heiner Müller, Christa Wolf has emphasized the deconstructive dimensions of Brecht's work, those which enhance "contradiction, disharmony and uncertainty" (Rechtien 199) and thus correspond to the latest cultural trends and artistic quests.

VI. Brecht and Feminist Theater Practice

Within the territory of British feminist theater practice, the adoption of the Brechtian method was much more direct and fertile. Women assimilated the Brechtian model to the needs of their theater without any theoretical reservation or ideological scruple. Gillian Hanna, an actress and a founding member of the well-known British feminist theater group Monstrous Regiment, stresses the need for women's theater to develop a mixed performance technique, "a kind of Brechtian acting, which doesn't deny Stanislavski but puts the emphasis elsewhere" (Reinelt 1986: 163). Hanna's view seems to reflect the general tendencies of British political theater, a major branch of which is women's theater.

Caryl Churchill, a prolific, protean dramatist, is justly considered the most dynamic voice of this new theater from both thematic and stylistic aspects. Among other works, her plays *Vinegar Tom* (1976), *Light Shining in Buckinghamshire* (1976), *Cloud Nine* (1979) and *Top Girls* (1982) are characteristic samples of a Brechtian feminist aesthetic. In these works, Churchill makes ample use of various Brechtian techniques, which she aptly adapts to the needs of her personal theatrical idiom. It is no accident that Reinelt and Diamond, as well as Kruger, refer to Churchill when they discuss the usefulness of the Brechtian theory for feminist theater practice. In a sense, this aspect of Churchill's work can be viewed as putting into practice and, consequently, validating Diamond's proposal for the constructive conjunction of the Brechtian/feminist model.

The artistic form of Churchill's theater in its further development in the 1980s and the 1990s gives the full spectrum of all the variants of the feminist stage aesthetic, comprising also the visionary poetics of the other camp of feminist thought, that of deconstruction and psychoanalysis. Without giving up the traces of her earlier Brechtian influence, Churchill continues her research for new forms in more recent plays such as *A Mouthful of Birds* (a collaboration with David Lan, 1986), *Mad Forest* (1991), *Lives of the Great Poisoners* (1991), *The Skriker* (1994) and *Hotel* (1997). Her new stage language bears obvious resemblance to the theoretical quest of Sue-Ellen Case, Teresa de Lauretis, Hélène Cixous and other feminist theorists. More particularly, her increasing sensitivity to the multiple manifestations of the corporeality of performance brings her very close to the Artaudian model promoted by another theater theorist, Josette Féral, in her article "Performance and Theatricality: The Subject Demystified" (1982). Féral belongs to the same territory of poststructuralism as de Lauretis and Cixous since her article is mainly based on Derrida's interpretation of Artaud as a model of non-representational performance.[13] What makes Féral's position more interesting is that, in contrast to other theorists of similar orientation, she does not hesitate to praise Brecht for the radical blow he brought to the illusionistic Stanislavski system and for his contribution to the ensuing liberation of the actor/performer and the spectator. In Féral's train of thought Brecht's name is closely associated with questions of performativity such as those that, in recent years, have increasingly attracted the interest of feminist theater groups and individual performers.[14]

Among the ranks of British women playwrights, Caryl Churchill (and more recently Timberlake Wertenbaker) presents the most exciting work in this direction, as she has focused systematically on the corporeality and the phenomenology of the stage and has expanded her aesthetic model into a mixture of Brechtian and Artaudian elements. The multivalence and dynamism of Churchill's theater

---

[13]   See Jacques Derrida, "The Theater of Cruelty and the Closure of Representation" (1978).

[14]   Wright quotes from Féral's article before introducing Pina Bausch's dance theater as a postmodern expropriation of Brecht (Wright 115). Beyond Féral's research on questions of performativity from within the field of French poststructuralism, Stanton B. Garner Jr, who also deals with the problematics of performativity but through the prism of phenomenology, discusses at length the Brechtian and post-Brechtian theater aesthetic in a separate chapter in his innovative book *Bodied Spaces: Phenomenology and Performance in Contemporary Drama* (1994). It is obvious that the recent resurgence of the theoretical interest in issues of performativity under the scope of the current sociocultural configurations has not marginalized the importance of the Brechtian canon and its legacy at all. By contrast it has validated once again its power for the continuous fertlization of dramatic and scenic experimentation.

discredits all Kruger's fears for an uncritical use of the Brechtian method (Kruger 53)[15]—a fear also voiced by the British feminist writer Michelene Wandor in her ironic (though also dubious) statement that the "feminist theatre suffers from too much Brecht" (Kruger 72, n.24). Significantly, Kruger herself makes of Churchill a notable exception from her indictment of uncritical feminist appropriations of Brecht and she gives particular praise to her play *Light Shining in Buckinghamshire* as an extraordinary text engaged in a critique of its own strategies (Kruger 61).

Another contemporary feminist playwright, the British (of Cypriot descent) Nina Rapi, makes a useful revision of the development of a female theatrical aesthetic in her article "Hide and Seek: The Search for a Lesbian Theatre Aesthetic" (1993). In her retrospective assessment of the progress of feminist theater theory and practice through the prism of the experiences of the 1990s, Rapi is especially attracted by the Brechtian orientation of the theater experiments of two other feminist theater practitioners, Monique Wittig and Zande Zeig. The focus of these two women's performance project is the synecdochic representation of gender beyond the masculine/feminine bipolarity through a complex system of gestures. Although Rapi's obvious placement in the discourse of deconstruction and psychoanalysis does not permit her overt references to Brecht, the analytic framework of her discussion of Zeig's and Wittig's gestural system evidently converges with the Brechtian paradigm of Gestus and, additionally, confirms once again the operative value of Smith's post-Brechtian performance model.

On the other side of the Atlantic the most systematic and innovative expression of consciously subversive feminist theater seems to derive from the collective work of female theater groups and performers rather than from individual women playwrights. It is true that in her article "Brechtian Theory and American Feminist Theatre" (1990), strangely echoing Reinelt's earlier exploration of British feminist theater, Karen Laughlin has ventured an assessment of some female American plays and playwrights from the perspective of the Brechtian aesthetic. The American dramatist Maria-Irene Fornes has also been particularly associated with the Brechtian Gestus.[16] However, the interest and the hopes of most feminist theorists for the formulation of a

---

[15]   In a bracketed note at the end of her above-mentioned article, Kruger carps about the "insufficiency and thinness of some feminist uses of Brechtian techniques" (Kruger 69).

[16]   See Deborah R. Geis, "Wordscapes of the Body: Performative Language as *Gestus* in Maria Irene Fornes's Plays" (1990).

consciously feminine/feminist theater aesthetic, largely inspired by the Brechtian method, has centred upon the collective work of the all-female groups Split Britches and Spiderwoman. In particular, Split Britches hold a central position in the theoretical analyses of Sue-Ellen Case, Jill Dolan and Janelle Reinelt.

The group Split Britches, based at the WOW Café in New York, consists of three women of different class, race and sexual preference who theatricalize their multiple difference in a variety of ways on stage and also in street performances. By using extravagant costume, mock cross-dressing, and gesture they try to undermine the bipolar stereotypes of gender while, by quick role changes, they set out to detach the actor and the spectator from identification with one specific character. Through such strategies they manage to construct a collective female subject, which has been precisely the target of female representation in the theories of Teresa de Lauretis and Sue-Ellen Case. It is obvious that their performance strategies of masquerade and gesture have a close relationship with the Brechtian concept of the Gestus, while their specific modes of staging the collective subject correspond directly to the new model of female representation which I have tentatively named "not only, but also" after Iris Smith's analysis.

The performance tactics of the other alternative all-female theater group, Spiderwoman, move in a similar direction. This group consists of three sisters of Indian origin, who build their performances on elements drawn equally from high and pop culture, from Brechtian as well as from ritual theater. However despite the mixture of heterogeneous acting and staging styles, they never lose the line of Brechtian alienation, which permits them to establish a firm critical attitude to myth and action and also to the theatrical techniques they have appropriated. The effectiveness of their methods has been praised by Jill Dolan, who claims that the work of Spiderwoman can form an excellent aesthetic model for the revival of a radical feminist political theater (Dolan 1992: 60-61).

Likewise, the solo performances of the American feminist performance artist Karen Finley seem to be based on the possibility of a synchronic representation of pluralistic subject positions. During performance Finley lets herself enter a quasi-schizophrenic situation, thus developing a strategy which she describes in the following words: "During a performance I try to let all the different voices going on inside my head be heard. I say what is usually left unspoken in a performance—what is on my mind at the moment. I don't censor myself. ... Sanity for me is the ability to let yourself go—to release yourself—and then to pull yourself back in again" (Reinelt 1989: 55). Finley's technique is closely related to the deconstructionist reading of the Brechtian subject as one "in process" and the Brechtian/feminist schizophrenic model fashioned by Iris Smith.

Closing this selective review of recent feminist theater activities and recalling also the reservations and objections of the conservative guardians of the Brechtian heritage, we should admit that what is often regarded as an ad hoc Brechtian influence is perhaps much looser and more diffuse than the feminist theorists of the materialist camp would have wished for. The Brechtian aesthetic has already been part of the inevitable postmodern process of the diffusion of art and its uninhibited mixture with popular culture and consumerist practices. Brechtian ideas have been infiltrated in the industry of the image and the media, and they travel back to performance arts in new hybrid forms. What we should also concede is that many of the ideas and stage techniques which look Brechtian to us undoubtedly existed in earlier, pre-Brechtian forms of art. Brecht would never conceal the origins of his own inspiration and sources of influence. Nevertheless, whatever the doubt concerning the absolute originality of his method and theory, what cannot be doubted is the value of a systematized model of theatrical aesthetics, which is multivalent and open to new experimentation and transformational renewal. Brecht himself had noted the progressive dynamism of his theater, and this is the best way to preserve its potential for future use even if its influence often comes as second-hand knowledge, popularized or mythified or transformed through the aesthetics of a related art like that of avant-garde cinema, or from the show business apparatus from which the feminist theory of the spectacle has drawn many of its basic positions.

In his recent book *Brecht and Method* (1998) Fredric Jameson, another rescuer of Brecht from the "Brecht fatigue," ventures the rather extreme statement that Brecht would be delighted to be remembered as "a proposer of proposals" (Jameson 1). Although one can detect here a reductionist tendency to emblematize Brecht, to turn him into a more or less abstract icon of constant praxis and productivity (Jameson 178), there is also something very positive in restoring the total image of the man as a versatile and indefatigable arbiter of the theater with a clear but also flexible agenda for the empowerment of contemporary theater activists and enthusiasts of all kinds.

Select Bibliography

Brater, Enoch, ed. *Feminine Focus: The New Women Playwrights.* New York and Oxford: OUP, 1989.

Brecht, Bertolt. *Journals 1934-1955.* Trans. Hugh Rorrison. Ed. John Willett. London: Methuen, 1993.

Brecht, Bertolt. *Letters 1913-1956.* Trans. Ralph Manheim. Ed. John Willett. New York and London: Routledge and Methuen, 1990.

Butler, Judith. *Bodies That Matter: On the Discursive Limits of "Sex."* New York and London: Routledge, 1993.

Butler, Judith. *Gender Trouble: Feminism and the Subversion of Identity.* New York and London: Routledge, 1990.

Butler, Judith. "Performative Acts and Gender Constitution: An Essay in Phenomenology and Feminist Theory." In Case, ed., *Performing Feminisms: Feminist Critical Theory and Theatre,* 270-82.

Case, Sue-Ellen. "Brecht and Women: Homosexuality and the Mother." In Fuegi, ed., *Brecht: Women and Politics,* 65-74.

Case, Sue-Ellen. "From Split Subject to Split Britches." In Brater, ed., *Feminine Focus: The New Women Playwrights,* 126-46.

Case, Sue-Ellen, ed. *Performing Feminisms: Feminist Critical Theory and Theatre.* Baltimore and London: Johns Hopkins UP, 1990.

Case, Sue-Ellen. "Toward a Butch-Femme Aesthetic." In Hart, ed., *Making a Spectacle: Feminist Essays on Contemporary Women's Theatre,* 282-99.

Churchill, Caryl. *Cloud Nine.* In Caryl Churchill, *Plays: One* (London and New York: Methuen, 1985), 243-320.

Churchill, Caryl. *Hotel.* London: Nick Hern, 1997.

Churchill, Caryl. *Light Shining in Buckinghamshire.* In Caryl Churchill, *Plays: One* (London and New York: Methuen, 1985), 181-241.

Churchill, Caryl (with Orlando Gough and Ian Spink). *Lives of the Great Poisoners.* London: Methuen, 1993.

Churchill, Caryl. *Mad Forest.* London: Nick Hern, 1990.

Churchill, Caryl (with David Lan). *A Mouthful of Birds.* London: Methuen, 1986.

Churchill, Caryl. *The Skriker.* London: Nick Hern, 1994.

Churchill, Caryl. *Top Girls.* London: Methuen, 1982.

Churchill, Caryl. *Vinegar Tom.* In Caryll Churchill, *Plays: Two* (London and New York: Methuen, 1985), 127-79.

Cixous, Hélène. "Aller à la Mer." Trans. B. Kerslake. *Modern Drama,* 27.4 (1984): 546-8. First published in *Le Monde,* 28 April 1977, 19.

Cixous, Hélène. *Portrait of Dora*. Trans. Anita Barrows. In *Benmussa Directs: Portrait of Dora and The Singular Life of Albert Nobbs* (London: John Calder, 1979), 27-67. First published in French as *Portrait de Dora* (Paris: Editions de femmes, 1976).

de Lauretis, Teresa. *Alice Doesn't: Feminism, Semiotics, Cinema*. Bloomington: Indiana UP, 1984.

de Lauretis, Teresa. "Eccentric Subjects: Feminist Theory and Historical Consciousness." *Feminist Studies*, 16.1 (1990): 115-50.

de Lauretis, Teresa. "Sexual Indifference and Lesbian Representation." In Case, ed., *Performing Feminisms; Feminist Critical Theory and Theatre*, 17-39.

de Lauretis, Teresa. *Technologies of Gender*. Bloomington and Indianapolis: Indiana UP, 1987.

de Lauretis, Teresa. "The Technology of Gender." In Case, ed., *Technologies of Gender*, 1-30.

Deleuze, Gilles and Félix Guattari. *Anti-Oedipus: Capitalism and Schizophrenia*. Minneapolis: U of Minnesota P, 1983.

Derrida, Jacques. "The Theater of Cruelty and the Closure of Representation." In Jacques Derrida, *Writting Differences* (Chicago: U of Chicago P, 1978), 232-50.

Diamond, Elin. "Brechtian Theory/Feminist Theory: Toward a Gestic Feminist Criticism." *The Drama Review*, 32.1 (1988): 82-94.

Diamond, Elin. "(In)visible Bodies in Churchill's Theater." In Hart, ed., *Making a Spectacle: Feminist Essays on Contemporary Women's Theatre*, 259- 81.

Diamond, Elin. "Mimesis, Mimicry and the 'True-Real'." *Modern Drama*, 32.1 (1989): 58-72.

Dolan, Jill. "Breaking the Code: Musings on Lesbian Sexuality and the Performer." *Modern Drama*, 32.1 (1989): 146-48.

Dolan, Jill. *The Feminist Spectator as Critic*. Ann Arbor and London: UMI Research P, 1988.

Dolan, Jill. "Personal, Political, Polemical: Feminist Approaches to Politics and Theatre." In Holderness, ed., *The Politics of Theatre and Drama*, 44-65.

Féral, Josette. "Performance and Theatricality: The Subject Demystified." *Modern Drama*, 25.1 (1982): 170-81.

Fuegi, John. *The Lives and Lies of Bertolt Brecht*. London: Harper Collins, 1994.

Fuegi, John et al. eds. *Brecht: Women and Politics*. The Brecht Yearbook 12. Detroit: Wayne State UP, 1985.

Garner, Stanton B., Jr. *Bodied Spaces: Phenomenology and Performance in Contemporary Drama*. Ithaca and London: Cornell UP, 1994.

Geis, Deborah R. "Wordscapes of the Body: Performative Language as *Gestus* in Maria Irene Fornes's Plays." *Theater Journal*, 42.3 (1990): 291-307.

Giles, Steve and Rodney Livingstone, eds. *Bertolt Brecht: Centenary Essays*. Amsterdam and Atlanta, GA: Rodopi, 1998.

Griffiths, Keith M., ed. *The Brechtian Aspect of Radical Cinema*. London: BFT Publishings, 1981.

Hart, Lynda, ed. *Making a Spectacle: Feminist Essays on Contemporary Women's Theatre*. Ann Arbor: U of Michigan P, 1989.

Holderness, Graham, ed. *The Politics of Theatre and Drama*. Houndmills, Basingstoke, Hampshire: Macmillan, 1992.

Jameson, Fredric. *Brecht and Method*. London and New York: Verso, 1998.

Keyssar, Helene, ed. *Feminist Theatre and Theory*. Houndmills, Basingstoke, Hampshire: Macmillan, 1996.

Kleber, Pia and Colin Visser, eds. *Re-interpreting Brecht: His Influence on Contemporary Drama and Film*. Cambridge: CUP, 1990.

Kruger, Loren. "The Dis-Play's the Thing: Gender and Public Sphere in Contemporary British Theatre." In Keyssar, ed., *Feminist Theatre and Theory*, 49-77.

Laughlin, Karen. "Brechtian Theory and American Feminist Theatre." In Kleber and Visser, eds., *Re-interpreting Brecht: His Influence on Contemporary Drama and Film*, 147-207.

Laughlin, Karen and Catherine Schuler, eds. *Theatre and Feminist Aesthetics*. London: Associated UP, 1995.

Mews, Siegfried, ed. *A Bertolt Brecht Reference Companion*. Westpoint Conn and London: Greenwood P, 1997.

Mulvey, Laura. "Visual Pleasure and Narrative Cinema.." *Screen*, 16.3 (1975): 6-18.

Mumford, Meg. "'Dragging' Brecht's Gestus Onwards: A Feminist Challenge." In Giles and Livingstone, eds., *Bertolt Brecht: Centenary Essays*, 240-57.

Rapi, Nina. "Hide and Seek: The Search for a Lesbian Theatre Aesthetic." *New Theatre Quarterly*, 9.34, (1993): 147-58.

Rechtien, Renate. "Relations of Production? Christa Wolf's Extended Equipment with the Legacy of Bertolt Brecht." In Giles and Livingstone, eds., *Bertolt Brecht: Centenary Essays*, 196-210.

Reinelt, Janelle. *After Brecht: British Epic Theater*. Ann Arbor: U of Michigan P, 1994.

Reinelt, Janelle. "Beyond Brecht: Britain's New Feminist Drama." *Theater Journal*, 38.2 (1986): 154-63.

Reinelt, Janelle. "Feminist Theory and the Problem of Performance." *Modern Drama*, 32.1 (1989): 48-57.

Silberman, Marc. "Brecht and Film." In Mews, ed., *A Bertolt Brecht Reference Companion*, 197-219.

Silberman, Marc. "The Politics of Representation: Brecht and the Media." *Theater Journal*, 39 (1987): 448-60.

Silberman, Marc. "A Postmodernized Brecht?" *Theater Journal*, 45 (1993): 1-19.

Smith, Iris. "Brecht and the Mothers of Epic Theatre." *Theater Journal*, 43 (1991): 491-505.

Tatlow, Antony. "Ghosts in the House of Theory: Brecht and the Unconscious." *The Brecht Yearbook*, 24 (1999): 1-13.

Taxidou, Olga. "Crude Thinking: John Fuegi and Recent Brecht Criticism." *New Theatre Quarterly*, 11.44 (1995): 381-84.

Walsh, Martin. "The Complex Seer: Brecht and the Film." In Griffiths, ed., *The Brechtian Aspect of Radical Cinema*, 5-21.

Wekwerth, Manfred. "Questions Concerning Brecht." In Kleber and Visser, eds., *Re-interpreting Brecht: His Influence on Contemporary Drama and Film*, 19-37.

Willett, John, ed. *Brecht on Theatre: The Development of an Aesthetic.* New York: Hill and Wang/London: Methuen, 1964.

Willett, John, ed. *Brecht in Context: Comparative Approaches.* London: Methuen, 1998.

Wright, Elizabeth. *Postmodern Brecht.* London and New York: Routledge, 1989.

Book Reviews

Furio Jesi. *Spartakus: Simbologia della rivolta.* Ed. Andrea Cavalletti. Turin: Bollati Boringhieri, 2000. xxviii + 107 pages.

"Mir kommt grad eine komische Idee, weißt du: Spartakus...," Murk interjects in the first act of *Trommeln in der Nacht*, and the late Italian Germanist Furio Jesi's *Spartakus: Simbologia della rivolta* is dedicated to the study of the Spartakus revolt and the "komische Idee" that it remains. Jesi presents the task of his *Spartakus* as "the clarification of the contingent reality of certain insurrectionary phenomena of yesterday and today," and much of his book investigates the specific temporality of the revolt and its distinction from the temporality of revolution. The third chapter offers a reading of *Trommeln in der Nacht* and the place of the Spartakus revolt in Brecht's play.

Furio Jesi (1941-1980) is known for his work on the relations of literature and culture to myth; he is the author of monographs on Thomas Mann, Rilke, Kierkegaard, Rimbaud, and Brecht as well as studies on myth (such as *Germania segreta: Miti nella cultura tedesca del '900*). His *Cultura di destra* was published in German as *Kultur von Rechts* by Stroemfeld/Roter Stern in 1984, and his correspondence with Kerényi appeared in Italian in 1996. Jesi was also a poet, novelist, and political activist, and he insisted that *Spartakus* "absorbed" the essential elements of his many types of writing, "from the mythological tract to union articles to poetry to the vampire novel." This "absorption" can be traced as the book gradually reveals the close links between epiphany, myth, and the revolt. Jesi submitted the manuscript of *Spartakus* to a publisher in 1969, but it was never printed; recently it was found among Jesi's papers by the book's editor, Andrea Cavalletti, whose introduction is a valuable addition to Jesi's text.

Spartakus offers a sustained investigation of the difference between revolt and revolution. For Jesi, revolution entails "the complex of long-term and short-term actions that are performed in view of changing, in historical time, a political, social, and economic situation." Its organizers "elaborate their tactical and strategic plans by taking into consideration, in historical time, the relation of cause and effect in the longest possible perspective." It is the work of a party and unions. In contrast, the revolt is a "suspension of historical time" that is "circumscribed by precise boundaries in historical time and space" and that is the work "not of a party but of a group formed by a revolting

Where Extremes Meet: Rereading Brecht and Beckett / Begegnung der Extreme. Brecht und Beckett: Eine Re-interpretation
Stephen Brockmann et al., eds., *The Brecht Yearbook / Das Brecht-Jahrbuch*
Volume 27 (Pittsburgh: The International Brecht Society, 2002)

class." The revolution works for a tomorrow; the revolt "provokes the anticipatory epiphany of the day after tomorrow." The final chapter presents the "untimeliness" of the revolt in a reading of Mann, Nietzsche, and Eliade, closing with the "legitimate conclusion that revolution creates and revolt destroys."

An extended reading of *Trommeln in der Nacht* forms the center of the book. It begins with a discussion of the claim that has been crucial for the reception of *Trommeln* since its first performance: Brecht does not bring together the play's two "levels" (the personal story of Kragler and Anna and the historical events surrounding the Spartakus revolt). In a comparison of the treatment of the Spartakus revolt in *Trommeln in der Nacht* and in Mann's *Doktor Faustus*, Jesi shows how the "bracketing" of Spartakus in *Trommeln in der Nacht* is not a failure on Brecht's part but an aspect of the exceptional temporality of the revolt itself, the way in which it "suspends" historical time.

Jesi's study places Brecht's play in its historical and literary contexts: he presents the historical debates about the Spartakus revolt and the decision of Rosa Luxemburg and Karl Liebknecht to remain in Berlin; and the interpretation takes account of the German and European literary tradition in discussions of Thomas Mann, Storm, Dostoevsky, Hans Christian Andersen, Rimbaud, Büchner, Rilke, Kassner, and Piscator. This short book succeeds in showing the limitations and possibilities of the revolt and its "essential untimeliness." *Spartakus: Simbologia della rivolta* offers a valuable reading of Brecht's play and the 1919 revolt as well as a rich meditation on their relation to the literature, myths, and thought of nineteenth and twentieth-century Europe.

Patrick Greaney
University of Colorado

***

Cornelius Partsch. *Schräge Töne. Jazz und Unterhaltungsmusik in der Kultur der Weimarer Republik.* Stuttgart und Weimar: Metzler, 2000. 305 Seiten.

Neil Edmunds. *The Soviet Proletarian Music Movement.* Oxford: Peter Lang, 2000. 407 pages.

Those seeking to deepen their knowledge of music as a popular medium, movement, and commodity in interwar Europe will find ample material in these two engaging and readable studies. Partsch surveys highbrow and popular literature, memoirs, and journalism as he analyzes several definitive episodes in the German history of jazz and its related "primitive" and popular forms during the 1920s and early 1930s. Based on readings of texts by and about the composers, teachers, and music club members who comprised the Proletarian Music Movement, Edmunds offers a historicist account of the conditions, practices, and effects of the groups who aspired to catalyze an ideologically guided, musical mass movement in the early years of the USSR. Read in tandem, the books open fruitful perspectives on the political dimensions of musical life in these rich, socio-historical contexts.

Partsch's general objective is to integrate textual, institutional, and ethnographic analyses in a study of jazz and pop's political economy, cultural significance, and ritualized functionalization during the Weimar years (3). He begins not in Germany but in Zürich, at the Cabaret Voltaire, where he traces the Dadaists' mobilization of "The Primitive" in their provocative spectacles. Tzara, Huelsenbeck, Ball, et al. tied this notion more strongly to Africa than to African-America, but Partsch demonstrates how the Dadaists' simultaneous deployment of "African" masks, drums, and chants and quasi-Futurist ("bruitist") mechanized noise prefigures the later images of jazz as both ultra-modern and ultra-primitive. Drawing on performance theory, Partsch frames the spaces, sights, and sounds of the Dada cabaret as both cultural objects and modalities of identity demarcation.

Having followed Dada to Berlin at the end of chapter one, Partsch offers a thorough overview of early jazz reception in that city in chapter two. He addresses several factors that impeded jazz's introduction and/or embrace in postwar Germany. These range from unavailability of American recordings (a result of recording industry tactics on both sides of the Atlantic that left German musicians fumbling to develop jazz skills) to the occupation of German territory by African colonial soldiers under French command, the so-called *schwarze Schmach* that triggered an avalanche of rape-and-pillage legends in the German popular imagination. The blackness of each linked jazz with the animalized occupiers. This was grounds for widespread yet anything but total rejection. Partsch also discusses, for example, Expressionism's interest in primitivism, which spawned a popular tendency to identify jazz as Expressionist music and vice versa.

Chapter three follows jazz's conscription by the popular entertainment apparatuses of the economically stable mid-decade. Here Partsch distinguishes between the discursive construction of jazz as an embodiment of Americanism (understood as cultural rationalization and symbolized by the Tiller Girls) and as a vehicle of savage blood that, once injected into the German body, would spell its ruin—or its rebirth, depending on one's cultural politics.   Here Josephine Baker provides the counter-image to the Tiller Girls, and Partsch assembles an array of sensational descriptions of the American dancer's ostensible wild gifts and rapacious appetites.   Baker's (the Other's) presence in Germany triggered anxious and interlocked examinations of "authentic" cultural/national identities, American/ African as well as German.   Chapter three closes with an account of New Music composers' efforts to harness jazz in their attempt to create an artistically valuable and socially accessible *Gebrauchsmusik* in the latter half of the decade.   *Jonny spielt auf*, Krenek's *Zeitoper*, and similar projects are read here less as paeans to a utopistic America than as attempts to energize a base of support for a musical movement whose popular audience never materialized.

Chapter four takes us through and beyond the years of collapse, covering the social-economic fates of musicians (including the 1931 national ban on black performers) and surveying critical responses to jazz. Here Partsch pays particular attention to Brecht and Eisler's attempt in *Die Maßnahme* to re-functionalize the music that for them had become a nearly irretrievable component of affirmative bourgeois culture.   On the heels of this examination of jazz's positive/subversive potential, one senses the inevitability of Adorno's entrance.   That Partsch turns in closing to the theorist generally regarded as jazz's greatest assailant is unsurprising, but his sober and insightful overview of Adorno's jazz writings is refreshing.   Without losing sight of the tenuous aspects of the arguments (particularly Adorno's neglect of the inherent dynamism in the performance/reception process), Partsch argues that the referent of his signifier "jazz" encompasses the popular music industry as well as the musical idiom itself. In addition to considering Adorno's critique in the context of Nazi-era exile, he suggests, we are thus well advised to locate Adorno's characterization of jazz in a broader characterization of the increasingly sophisticated culture industry that has evolved as a function of advanced capitalism.

Adorno had international compatriots in his rejection of jazz's critical (not to mention revolutionary) potential.   Indeed, German musical nationalists who condemned jazz as *Musikbolschewismus* would have been quite disheartened to hear what actual Bolshevists had to say about the African-American music.   Early in his first chapter, Edmunds recounts how the manifesto of the Russian Association of Proletarian Musicians (RAPM) classified jazz as an example of the bourgeois influence that was still "poisoning the workers' minds" (20) even as the Revolution enjoyed its initial triumphs. Maxim Gorky was more colorful, calling jazz the "music of the fat," which echoed through the "splendid pigsties of capitalist countries" (23). The balance of the chapter provides an overview of the ideas and programs of the main organizations that comprised the Proletarian Music Movement (a term used at the time as well as in historical accounts). In addition to RAPM, these included the Association of Revolutionary Composers and Musical Activists (ORKiMD), the Production Collective of Moscow Conservatory Students (Prokoll), and the music departments of the Ministry of Culture and Education (Narkompros) and the Proletarian Educational-Cultural Groups (Proletkult).

Edmunds's second chapter, "First Steps," traces the movement's early attempts to find appropriate balances: first between avant-gardism and tradition (both classical and folk) in its aesthetic program (here Beethoven and Mussorgsky vie with Futurist noise music and sailors' songs); second, between long-standing and radically new modes of teaching and performing music. The Association of Contemporary Music (ASM) engaged during this time in critical dialog with Narkompros and Proletkult about such topics as the value of integrating modern technology with musical performance and how exactly to program and stage concerts "for the people."

Chapter three focuses on the major Russian/Soviet conservatories as crucial components of the new musical apparatus that the movement was working fervently to assemble. As the venerable institutions played host to a confrontation between the establishment and the new faction of Red Professors, the very nature of the gateway to musical education was at stake. The solutions to the conflict were not as radical as RAPM, for example, might have hoped. Plans for transforming the conservatories into more broadly accessible musical universities remained on the drawing board, but this was compensated somewhat by the establishment of workers' faculties (*rabfaky*) for those traditionally excluded from studies and pedagogical faculties (*pedfaky*) for high-caliber students who wished to focus on popular education and agitation through music.

The next chapter examines the bold visions and everyday practical aspects of such "mass musical work." Edmunds pays particular attention to the organizational methodology of workers' musical clubs and amateur group performances, and he closes with an account of music's role in state holiday celebrations. Again, he provides insight into the hopes and fears that attended the growing awareness of music's social power: movement ideologues embraced such projects as Nikolay Demyanov's choral/theatrical *Uprising in Song* even as they rejected similar efforts as "unhealthy musical influence"

(118). Indeed, the inconsistencies between and even within various movement organizations strike one throughout Edmunds's account.

Chapters five and six are devoted primarily to composer case studies. While brief, these are generally fruitful: they illustrate the artists' often perilous exposure to the political vicissitudes that marked the 1920s and early 1930s, and they provide detailed snapshots (including score excerpts) of the composers' ideological and practical struggle to fuse popular and high musical art in their ideas and products. Aleksandr Davidenko, the guiding figure of Prokoll, seems to have stood out among the few composers who could, in the words of Kurt London, "use their political convictions to really artistic effect" (241). But as Edmunds's study implies, contemplating the conditions and ramifications of the obsession with preserving the "art" in art for the people is ultimately more interesting than attempting to separate retrospectively musical wheat from musical chaff. Throughout the book one notes the movement's distinctly bourgeois tendency to lament the alleged sacrifice of aesthetic achievement in much of the music that gains significant appeal.

1932 saw the end of the organizations that Edmunds covers. Their ideological and practical complications made them ripe for streamlining, and as Edmunds chronicles the dispersal and the resonance of various groups and individuals in chapter seven, one reflects again on the tension inherent in the movement's characteristic impulse to catalyze mass musical action through cultural micromanagement (RAPM, at one point, proposed installing proletarian musical activists [*rabkory*] in every record shop in the Union [43]). It is telling, perhaps, that "popular"—with its vexing connotation of "from/of the people"—is a word used infrequently in the texts Edmunds cites throughout his study (see 209). One wonders about the extent to which the movement that sought to capture and reflect the "rich, full-blooded psychology of the proletariat" (31) ever took on a widespread, grass-roots energy of its own. In his conclusion Edmunds argues that the movement did, in Lebedinsky's words, begin effectively to transform itself from "an object of music history to its subject" (303), but the temptation is great to argue the opposite (using the very evidence Edmunds so thoroughly marshals). This is not to insist that Edmunds's claims are invalid; it is simply to indicate that most of the questions raised by the movement itself and elaborated in Edmunds's study (e.g., "What is the nature of proletarian music?") resist authoritative answers.

Critical notes to each author can be brief. Partsch's study ends somewhat abruptly and could benefit from a conclusion that synthesizes from his analyses of the disparate musical, textual, and historical moments some general assertions (or demonstrates their impossibility). Edmunds's readers (non-specialists in particular) would be well served by an index of acronyms (they proliferated to a point of unwieldiness in the movement itself, a phenomenon the study faithfully reflects). Overall the books are well structured, the primary textual material is extensive and effectively presented, and the analytical insights contribute to a more sophisticated understanding of the subjects at hand. Reading each study should thus prove worthwhile for both specialists and the casually curious.

Theodore Rippey
Bowling Green State University

***

Taekwan Kim. *Das Lehrstück Bertolt Brechts: Untersuchungen zur Theorie und Praxis einer zweckbestimmten Musik am Beispiel von Paul Hindemith, Kurt Weill, und Hanns Eisler.* Frankfurt am Main: Peter Lang, 2000. 226 Seiten.

B recht's *Lehrstücke*, constructed between 1928 and 1935 and spanning *Der Lindberghflug* to *Die Horatier und die Kuriatier* as well as the fragments that comprise his *Lehrstück* theory, have always occupied a problematic position within Brecht scholarship. Interpretations of the *Lehrstück* have followed four main avenues: 1) a dogmatic and inferior Marxist theater in relation to the classic oeuvre; 2) a transitional phase between the early and the mature Brecht; 3) an integral element of his theatrical and political practice; and 4) a textual-musical nexus for addressing issues of the *Gebrauchsmusik* and *Neue Musik* movements of the late Weimar period. After the relative renaissance of *Lehrstück* scholarship in the 1970s and 1980s, recent Brecht scholarship has turned to issues more suitable to a postmodern state of mind. Into this fray jumps the musicologist Taekwan Kim and his *Lehrstück* monograph, which allows the reader an opportunity to revisit the *Lehrstück* debates in a twenty-first-century context.

Lehrstück scholarship has been defined by two works: Reiner Steinweg's *Das Lehrstück: Brechts Theorie einer politisch-ästhetischen Erziehung* (1972) and Klaus-Dieter Krabiel's *Brechts Lehrstücke: Entstehung und Entwicklung eines Spieltyps* (1993). Steinweg's text resuscitated the *Lehrstück* within the secondary literature corpus; indeed, it elevated the genre to the center of Brecht's aesthetic theory and praxis. Steinweg provided a unified aesthetic theory behind the *Lehrstück*, and in later scholarly works as well as theater pedagogy seminars explored the concrete performative aspects of this theory within contemporary society. Krabiel's monograph was an explicit critique of Steinweg's influential work. Instead of a coherent aesthetic theory and theatrical praxis, Krabiel emphasized the historical context in which the *Lehrstück* evolved and focused on the genre's musical rather than theatrical components. Most significantly, Krabiel stressed the *Gebrauchsmusik* and *Neue Musik* movements of the late Weimar period as they were articulated by Brecht's *Lehrstück* collaborators Paul Hindemith, Kurt Weill, and Hanns Eisler.

Kim's work seeks to negotiate a balance between these scholarly pillars. On the one hand, his musicological background grants him the expertise to ground and extend Krabiel's argument; on the other hand, he does not want to dismiss Steinweg's theatrical initiative. Concentrating on the four earliest *Lehrstücke (Der Lindberghflug, Das Badener Lehrstück, Der Jasager,* and *Die Maßnahme)*, Kim devotes a chapter to each piece, supplying background information concerning origins, premieres, and performances as well as textual-musical analysis. His work breaks new ground and engages the scholarly reader in the musical analysis. Beginning with biographical and theoretical information on Hindemith, Weill, or Eisler, he proceeds to show how the music of each collaborator amplified or illuminated the Brechtian text. To accomplish this, Kim supplies musical notation and a relatively jargon-free analysis of the notation. Since the music is not being played as we read and since most literary scholars, such as myself, do not have a deep background in music composition or theory, this is no small achievement. I found this analytical method particularly useful in the chapter concerning *Die Maßnahme*, where Kim artfully intersects Eisler's use of rhythm, repetition, and dissonance with Brecht's application of alienation effects. For the first time in my scholarly career I actually heard the music through reading a scholarly treatise on Brecht.

Whereas Kim's analysis points *Lehrstück* scholarship in an important direction, there is not enough to satisfy the Brecht scholar. He spends far too much time on contextualizing Brecht's theoretical ideas and the rise of the *Gebrauchsmusik* movement. This, of course, is interesting, but Steinweg and Krabiel have already covered this material; Kim adds nothing new to the historical scholarship. It would make more sense, and indeed be more valuable, if he had spent more time distinguishing his approach through an extensive critique of Steinweg and Krabiel. Moreover, Kim's musical-textual analysis could be deepened and more relevant, if it were to integrate aspects of music philosophy, especially recent discussions of Adorno. Kim does include Adorno in his work, but with little theoretical finesse; yet Adorno would provide an important component toward the musical-theatrical dialog Kim is trying to create. In general, Kim's work is a competent dissertation which provides a handy, readable introduction to the *Lehrstück* and points to a potentially fruitful new direction in *Lehrstück* scholarship.

Norman Roessler
Temple University

***

Ronald Speirs, ed. *Brecht's Poetry of Political Exile*. Cambridge, UK: Cambridge University Press, 2000. 257 pages.

Dedicated entirely to aspects and contexts of the *Svendborger Gedichte* (Svendborg Poems, 1939), the volume at hand began as a series of workshops—instigated by the late scholar of Brecht's poetry, Philip Brady—which were conducted at Birbeck College in London and at the University of Birmingham. While the contributions retain to differing degrees the atmosphere of the oral presentation and do contain a few avoidable redundancies, they have been helpfully cross-referenced and supplied with an index and a (selective) bibliography.

Following David Midgely's brief historical overview of Brecht's Svendborg exile in Chapter 1 is David Constantine's consideration of the poet's concept of "The Usefulness of Poetry," in which the author references the pertinent (and familiar) fragments by Brecht on poetry ("On Rhymeless Verse with Irregular Rhythms," "Short Report on 400 Young Poets," etc). The image of Brecht the poet that emerges from the discussion of poetry's "use value" is a somewhat tempered one. Against Brecht's radical claim—in a fragment not cited by the author—that the reception of a poem is an active operation just like seeing or hearing, Constantine closes by assimilating Brecht's poetic strategies to "traditional lyric aims and achievements." In Chapter 3, "'Visit to a Banished Poet:' Brecht's *Svendborg Poems* and the Voices of Exile," Tom Kuhn, co-editor of a pending book on Brecht's poetry featuring several of the authors in this volume (*Empedocles' Shoe*, London: Methuen, 2002), identifies the cultural context of exile as Brecht's defining aesthetic posture and the organizing communicative impetus of his poetry. Moving on to a different geographic site, Katherine Hodgson examines in Chapter 4 the place and function of the Soviet Union in the cycle, underscoring Brecht's difficult and ambiguous relationship to the situation of poets under a regime that has betrayed its founding ideals. In Chapter 5 Tony Davies asks "Is There an English Brecht?" and focuses on Auden and the discourse on poetry and politics in the tradition of English literature. For both poets the author discerns a commitment to "strength," "clarity," and "the true democratic style." Chapter 6, "Satire as Propaganda," fixes on the "original" context of the *Deutsche Satiren*, which were conceived for radio broadcast by the anti-fascist German Free Radio, on the way toward approaching the slippery relationship between satire and propaganda. Brecht's satires make for weak propaganda, argues author Micheal Minden, but this is what makes them most Brechtian.

In Chapter 7 Joyce Crick delves into various dimensions of Brecht's problems with the truth, referring to the key essay "Five Difficulties in Writing the Truth." The analysis addresses Brecht's vetting of poems to be included in the *Svendborger Gedichte* collection and the relevance of the formalism debate in the Soviet Union. Chapter 8 argues for the usefulness of classical rhetoric in defining Brecht's lyric strategy in the cycle, seeking to understand its complex structure as a rounded aesthetic work. Author Anna Carrdus's formalist approach elaborates how Brecht appropriated and transformed classical rhetorical arrangements for specific circumstances and wed them to an "aesthetics of sobriety, brevity, concision and subterfuge." In Chapter 9 Elizabeth Boa returns to the situation of exile and the triple strategy mobilized in the *Svendborger Gedichte* to "ward off the anxiety of impotence" felt by the poet cut off from his readers. This strategy involves constructing a readership, appealing to a historical tradition of author-exiles, and connecting the two in a poetic discourse that mediates between intellectuals and workers, historical contexts, and theory and praxis. The volume's three final essays engage issues of time, history, and memory. Concentrating on one section of the *Svendborger Gedichte*, in Chapter 10 Anthony Phelan takes Benjamin's notion of history as a point of departure for exploring issues of memory, commemoration, and self-reflexivity in "Figures of Memory in the *Chroniken*." In Chapter 11, "The Poet in Time," editor Ronald Speir (author of *Brecht's Early Plays*, Atlantic Highlands, NJ: Humanities Press, 1982; and *Bertolt Brecht*, New York: St. Martin's Press, 1987) reads the *Svendborger Gedichte* against the earlier *Manual of Piety* (1927) to elaborate on the particular and double-edged time-boundedness of political poetry. The volume concludes with Karen Leeder's marvelously titled and helpful "Those Born Later Read Brecht: The Reception of 'An die Nachgeborenen,'" which charts how figures such as Helmut Preißler, Heiner Müller, Johannes R. Becher, and Erich Fried responded to the most famous of Brecht's poems from the cycle.

With the *Svendborger Gedichte*, the contributors have clearly fixed on an essential cycle in Brecht's lyric production. Although the authors may have had a somewhat different goal, the primary value of this volume is as an introduction to Brecht's poetry as a whole for non-German-speaking students and as a point of departure for re-examining the tensions of poetry and politics in the twentieth century. Brecht specialists, on the other hand, will inevitably note the absence of substantially new perspectives on or approaches to Brecht's lyric production and in a number of instances will wish for a more comprehensive (or any) consideration of the secondary literature. Nonetheless, this is a useful volume—much better than Helmut Koopmann's recent and largely superfluous edited collection (*Brechts Lyrik—neue Deutungen*, Würzburg: Könighausen & Neumann, 1999), for example—and a source to which this reviewer will thankfully refer when teaching Brecht's poetry in English.

Stefan Soldovieri
Northwestern University

* * *

Albrecht Riethmüller, Hrsg. *Brecht und seine Komponisten.* Laaber: Laaber-Verlag, 2000. 223 Seiten.

"Die Musik ist keine Arche, auf der man eine Sintflut überdauern kann."
(Brecht an Paul Hindemith, zitiert in Kowalkes Beitrag)

Brechts Musikalität ist bekannt, und über seine Zusammenarbeit mit Komponisten liegen viele Veröffentlichungen vor. Unter ihnen sind Dümlings *Laßt euch nicht verführen: Brecht und die Musik* (1985) und Lucchesi/Shulls *Musik bei Brecht* (1988) die ausführlichsten Sammeldarstellungen. Seitdem widmen gerade im letzten Jahrzehnt Literatur- und Musikwissenschaftler dieser lange vernachlässigten Thematik ihre Aufmerksamkeit. Der vorliegende Band basiert auf Referaten, die auf einer von der Deutschen Forschungsgemeinschaft unterstützten Tagung in Berlin über Brecht *und die Musik* vorgetragen wurden. Die Konferenz fand im Mai 1998 statt, aus Anlass des 100. Geburtstages von Brecht und Eisler. Kompositionen von Hanns Eisler bilden somit einen Schwerpunkt dieses Bandes; drei der zehn Beiträge beschäftigen sich mit Eisler. Kurt Weill, der sonst meistdiskutierte "Brecht-Komponist" (7), ist mit zwei Artikeln vertreten; und über Paul Dessau, der als dritter Komponist oft in diesem Kreis genannt wird, enthält der Band einen Artikel. Die weiteren Aufsätze widmen jeweils einen Beitrag Musikern, die sonst eher am Rande des Spektrums stehen: Paul Hindemith, Carl Orff, Rudolf Wagner-Régeny und Benjamin Britten.

Giselher Schuberts Artikel, "'Hindemiths Musik stört kaum.' Zu Hindemith und Brecht," eröffnet die Sammlung. Das spannungsreiche Verhältnis zwischen Brecht und Hindemith steht hier im Vordergrund. Hindemith, ein bedeutender Komponist, spielt in der Brecht-Literatur eher eine zwiespältige Rolle. Das *Lehrstück*, Hauptprodukt der Zusammenarbeit beider Künstler, führte gleichzeitig zu ihrem Bruch, da Hindemith Brechts ideologischer Neuinterpretation des Stücks als *Das Badener Lehrstück vom Einverständnis* nicht folgen konnte. Schubert spürt den Gründen für Hindemiths Vernachlässigung in der Brecht-Forschung nach und bemüht sich, den Dissens zwischen beiden Künstlern zu erhellen. Dabei beschränkt er sich auf eine positivistische Materialsammlung der Korrespondenzen und Kontakte. Ansätze zu einer Werkanalyse, die seine interessante Fragestellung erörtern könnte, ob "Wirkungen des Brechtschen Textes von der Hindemithschen Musik" ausgehen (12), liefert er selbst nicht.

Gerade eine solche faszinierende Verbindung von musikalischer Analyse, politischer Bewertung und neuen biographischen Fakten bietet Kim Kowalke in seinem Aufsatz, "Carl Orff and His Brecht Connection," dem einzigen englischsprachigen Beitrag des Buches. Weit mehr noch als im Falle Hindemiths war Orffs Affinität zu Brecht lange unbekannt. Zwar kam es nie zu einer Zusammenarbeit zwischen Brecht und Orff, trotz Brechts gescheitertem Versuch 1952, Orff für seinen *Kaukasischen Kreidekreis* zu gewinnen; doch schrieb Orff Musik zu Texten Brechts, sowohl in den dreißiger als auch in den siebziger Jahren. 1975, als achzigjähriger, komponierte Orff *Sprechstücke für Sprecher, Sprechchor und Schlagwerk* nach Texten Brechts. In den sechziger Jahren veröffentlichte er zwei Kompositionen nach Brecht, die er 1930-31 komponiert hatte und die lange vergraben lagen: *Vom Frühjahr, Öltank und vom Fliegen* (ursprünglich 1932 erschienen) und *Von der Freundlichkeit der Welt* (bis dahin unveröffentlicht). Orff hatte Brecht und Neher schon 1924 in München kennengelernt, bei der Premiere von *Leben Eduard II von England*, und war von dem innovativen Theaterstil der Neuen Sachlichkeit begeistert. Orffs Kompositionen der frühen dreißiger Jahre bezeugen Brechts Einfluss. Da Orff jedoch unter den Nationalsozialisten gleichzeitig eine dubiose und opportunistische Rolle spielte, veröffentlichte der Schott Verlag diese Kompositionen nicht bzw. zog alle vorhandenen Drucke vom Umlauf zurück. Kowalke schildert ein komplexes Bild des Komponisten Orff und seiner Gratwanderung zwischen Brechtscher Ästhetik und Mitläufertum bzw.

Überlebensdrang unter den Nazis. Er wirft die Frage auf, ob politische Einstellungen sich auch in einer musikalischen Ästhetik manifestieren könnten, eine Frage, die in den letzten Jahren besonders im Hinblick auf Richard Wagner und seinen möglicherweise schon in seiner Opernästhetik ersichtlichen Antisemitismus gestellt wurde. Gerade hier jedoch sieht Kowalke Möglichkeiten, Orff zu verteidigen; denn seine musikalische Ästhetik, selbst in seinem Hauptwerk, *Carmina Burana*, teilt in ihrem rationalen und verfremdenden Ton wie auch in ihrer "gestischen" Beziehung von Text, Musik und Bild viele Elemente mit Brechts Theatertheorie.

Die beiden folgenden Artikel beschäftigen sich mit Kurt Weill. Michael Katers Aufsatz, "Weill und Brecht. Kontroversen einer Künstlerfreundschaft auf zwei Kontinenten," bietet einen Überblick über die künstlerischen, menschlichen und finanziellen Verhältnisse zwischen Weill und Brecht von ihrem ersten Kennenlernen 1927 nach dem Fest der Neuen Musik in Baden-Baden bis zum endgültigen Scheitern ihrer Zusammenarbeit im amerikanischen Exil, das Kater eingehend anhand der nicht zustandegekommenen Aufführung einer afro-amerikanischen *Dreigroschenoper* darstellt. Wie der erste Aufsatz im Falle Hindemiths geht Kater gerade auf die spannungsgeladenen Elemente dieser Künstlerfreundschaft ein; und Brecht entpuppt sich einmal mehr als taktischer und selbstbezogener Verhandlungspartner. Der Weillforschung sind diese Fakten—etwa Weills vertragliche Benachteiligung bei der *Dreigroschenoper*—nicht neu. Aufschlussreich und anregend ist Katers Analyse von Weills jüdischem Selbstverständnis als Sohn eines Kantors in Dessau, eine Stadt mit einer Tradition des aufgeklärten Judentums. Aus dieser Tradition erklärt Kater Weills musikalischen Stil und auch seine linkspolitische Haltung, die nicht erst durch Brecht geweckt wurde.

Jens Malte Fischers Beitrag, "*Happy End*—aber nur für Kurt Weill," konzentriert sich auf das von Elisabeth Hauptmann, Brecht und Weill konzipierte Stück *Happy End*. Dieses satirische Drama über die Heilsarmee, das am 2. September 1929 uraufgeführt wurde, war nach dem Erfolg der *Dreigroschenoper* zum Scheitern verurteilt. Fischer erläutert die Umstände der Entstehung des Stücks und weist auf die Schwäche des Textes und im Gegensatz dazu den leuchtenden Wert der Musik Weills. Dabei zeigt er interessante Verbindungen auf, z.B. zwischen Brechts Text zum "Hosannah!" Finale, eine Satire auf die nahezu religiöse Verehrung des Kapitals, und Walter Benjamins Fragment *Kapitalismus als Religion*. Er hebt Weills Innovationen in der Musik hervor, die längst nicht nur in den beiden berühmten Liedern "Bills Ballhaus in Bilbao" und "Surabaya-Johnny" ersichtlich sind. Weill wollte in *Happy End* über den Nummern- und Songcharakter der *Dreigroschenoper* hinausgehen, und im "Heilsarmeemarsch" oder im

"Matrosenlied" erkennt Fischer Anlehnungen an Mahler und Schönberg. Albrecht Dümlings Aufsatz, "Eisler/Brecht oder Brecht/Eisler? Perspektiven, Formen und Grenzen ihrer Zusammenarbeit," bildet den ersten der drei Beiträge zu Eisler. Mit Eisler unterhielt Brecht unter den Komponisten die freundschaftlichste Beziehung. Ruth Berlaus Anekdote über ein Schachspiel, in dem Eisler das Schachbrett einfach umdrehte, wenn Brechts Lage schlecht stand, belegt metaphorisch das kooperative und nicht konkurrierende Verhältnis zwischen beiden Künstlern. Brecht lernte von Eisler viel: er profitierte von Eislers Erfahrung in der Arbeitermusikbewegung, und er schätzte Eislers literarischen Sinn, da er dessen Änderungsvorschläge etwa im *Hollywooder Liederbuch* gern aufnahm. Umgekehrt beeinflusste Brecht Eislers musikalischen Geschmack, indem er z.B. Eisler, für den bis 1930 Beethoven als Modell galt, stattdessen die Genialität Bachs und gerade seiner h-moll-Messe nahelegte. Gelegentlich kam es zu kleinen Zwistigkeiten, wenn etwa Eisler für den Balladensänger in der zehnten Szene von *Leben des Galilei* einen singenden Tenor wünschte und Brecht hingegen, in der Tradition der Augsburger Zeitungssänger, die Sprechstimme eines Schauspielers forderte. Doch erreichte Brecht mit Eisler eher als mit anderen Musikern eine produktive künstlerische Symbiose, in der laut Dümling Genuss und Denken eine Einheit bilden.

Jost Hermands Artikel, "'Manchmal lagen Welten zwischen uns!' Brecht und Eislers *Deutsche Symphonie*," betont feine künstlerische Unterscheidungen zwischen Brecht und Eisler und zeigt diese konkret. Eisler konzipierte dieses großangelegte antifaschistische Werk um 1935 als *Konzentrationslagerkantate*—eine Bezeichnung, in der sich Bachsche Formen und linkspolitisches Engagement miteinander vereinen. Die Uraufführung unter dem Titel *Deutsche Symphonie* fand 1959 in der DDR statt, nach Brechts Tod; und Hermand nimmt an, dass Brecht das Werk aus verschiedenen Gründen missfallen hätte: er hätte wohl das Wort "deutsch" mit seinen nationalen Beiklängen im Titel vermieden; er hätte die schwere düstere Stimmung der Symphonie nicht gemocht, die wenig verfremdet und eher auf einer bürgerlichen Einfühlungsästhetik beruht; er stand dem Expressionismus wie auch jeder subjektiv expressiven Musik negativer gegenüber als Eisler; und er hätte wenig Sinn für Eislers "Schönbergisieren" gehabt und stattdessen eher eine einfache, balladeske, oder komisch-moritathafte "Misuk" empfohlen. Hermand deckt kenntnisvoll kleine Diskrepanzen zwischen Brecht und Eisler auf. Hingegen könnte man argumentieren, dass selbst ein Gedicht Brechts, das Eisler in Auszügen hier vertont ("Oh Deutschland, bleiche Mutter"), ebenso tragisch expressive Züge trägt wie Eislers Musik. Interessant wäre ein kontrastierender Vergleich zwischen Eislers Musik für die *Deutsche Symphonie* und Alain Resnais' Film *Nacht und Nebel*.

Claudia Alberts Aufsatz, "Dirigenten und Oberkellner: Eislers Kritik der musikalischen Verhältnisse," bildet eine Ausnahme in dieser Sammlung, da die künstlerische Partnerschaft mit Brecht nier nicht thematisiert wird. Dagegen zieht die Autorin interessante Querverbindungen zwischen Eisler und Adorno wie auch Eisler und Schönberg, und sie erklärt Eislers Materialästhetik. Als Gegenpol zu Adornos beinahe kulthaften Kultur- und Musikanalysen setzt Albert als Leitgedanken für ihren Artikel ein Zitat Eislers, das die Arbeit des Dirigenten mit der eines Oberkellners vergleicht und eine unpathetische, schlichte Form der Darstellung fordert.

Tilo Medek, Komponist und Schüler Wagner-Régenys, schreibt über das Thema "Wurden die Komponisten durch Brecht besser? Zu Rudolf Wagner-Régeny." Nach den Schilderungen von Brechts Reibereien mit Weill und seinen gelegentlichen Diskrepanzen mit Eisler ist die Antwort auf Medeks Frage in Wagner-Régenys Fall ein uneingeschränktes Ja. Wagner-Régeny, der Brecht erstmals 1930 als Berater für Pabsts Verfilmung der *Dreigroschenoper* kennenlernte, vertonte Lieder von Brecht und verfasste eine besonders gelungene Bühnenmusik zu *Pauken und Trompeten*, einer späten Stückbearbeitung Brechts, die die Bedeutung der Musik schon in seinem Titel betont. Caspar Neher wirkte als Librettist für vier Opern Wagner-Régenys, und Medek berichtet im Detail über die Entstehung einer von ihnen, *Der Darmwäscher*, die lange unvollendet blieb, Brechts Begeisterung fand und mit Brechts Hilfe 1950 fertiggestellt wurde. Doch wurde sie nur einmal 1963 in Rostock aufgeführt. Ein ähnliches Schicksal erlitt Wagner-Régenys Musik später bei der Universal-Edition, als Medek dort für den Druck einer Partitur seines Lehrers warb und abgewiesen wurde.

In "Dessau und Brecht" bietet Frank Schneider einen ausgewogenen Überblick über Dessaus Kompositionen für Brecht. Dessau, der schon 1936 in Paris eine Musik zu *Die heilige Johanna der Schlachthöfe* komponiert hatte, lernte Brecht erst 1943 in New York näher kennen. Zwischen 1944 und 1947 entstand das *Deutsche Miserere*, ein Oratorium nach Gedichten aus Brechts *Kriegsfibel*. Dessau schrieb wichtige Bühnenmusiken zu *Mutter Courage, Der gute Mensch von Sezuan, Der kaukasische Kreidekreis, Puntila, Mann ist Mann, Die Ausnahme und die Regel* und *Lukullus*. Besondere Aufmerksamkeit widmet Schneider einem Orchesterwerk, das Dessau 1956/57 in Erinnerung an seinen Freund schrieb: *In memoriam Bertolt Brecht*. Schneider charakterisiert Dessau als "Schüler Brechts" (181), dem Brecht zum Konzept einer "andersartigen Avantgarde" weiterverholfen habe (184). Dabei ist das Verb "dienen," das hier in

Bezug auf Dessaus Verhältnis zu Brecht gleich zweimal fällt (171, 184), vielleicht einen Hauch übertrieben.

Guido Heldts Artikel, "'... among them a drummer-boy'— Brittens Brecht," stellt ein selten besprochenes Werk vor: *Children's Crusade*, Benjamin Brittens 1969 uraufgeführte Vertonung von Brechts 1941 entstandenem Gedicht *Kinderkreuzzug.* Dieses Musikstück unterscheidet sich von anderen in der Sammlung diskutierten dadurch, dass es nicht aus der Zusammenarbeit Brechts mit einem Komponisten entsprungen ist, sondern eine postume Rezeption Brechts durch Britten darstellt. Der für seinen Pazifismus bekannte Britten schrieb die Musik zu *Children's Crusade* für das 50jährige Jubiläum des Save the Children Fund. Heldt berichtet ausführlich über die Umstände der Entstehung, die 1969 mit den Vietnam-Protesten zusammenfallen, ebenso wie mit dem im gleichen Jahr veröffentlichten Roman *Slaughterhouse Five* von Kurt Vonnegut, der den Untertitel *or The Children's Crusade* trägt. Wir erfahren im Detail von den ironischen Umständen der Uraufführung von Brittens *Children's Crusade* in einem ökumenischen Dankesgottesdienst in Londons St. Paul's Cathedral, den Britten selbst als "curious" bezeichnete (195). Heldt bietet eine musikwissenschaftlich fundierte Analyse des Verhältnisses von Text und Musik im Stück. Er vergleicht den historischen, mittelalterlichen Kinderkreuzzug 1212 mit Brechts modernem aus dem Jahre 1939, bespricht literarische und musikalische Konstruktionen des Kindlichen, die Rolle der Dissonanzen als Verunsicherungsstrategie, ein dialektisches Verhältnis von Ordnung und Störung, den Status der Zwölftönigkeit, bis zu Details wie der Rolle der großen Sekunde in dieser Musik. Es bleibt das Bild einer komplexen Komposition, die Brechts Lyrik über den Leidensweg der Kinder klanglich neu rezipiert.

Die Sammlung erhält besonderen Wert durch solche Artikel, die Komponisten vorstellen, die sonst im Umkreis Brechts weniger besprochen werden—wie etwa Britten, Orff, Wagner-Régeny oder Hindemith. Doch auch indem sie eine vertiefende Kenntnis der drei in diesem Zusammenhang häufig erforschten Komponisten—Weill, Eisler, Dessau—bietet, gewinnt sie an Interesse für allgemeine Leser und Fachspezialisten zugleich. Musik mag für Brecht keine "Arche" zum Überleben der Sintflut gewesen sein, jedoch als immanenter Bestandteil seiner Lyrik und seines Theaterschaffens bleibt sie fortdauernd bestehen.

Vera Stegmann
Lehigh University

***

Sarah Bryant-Bertail. *Space and Time in Epic Theater: The Brechtian Legacy.*   Rochester: Camden House, 2000.   245 pages + illustrations.

Peter Yang. *Play is Play: Theatrical Illusion in Chinese Wall by Frisch and Other "Epic" Plays by Brecht, Wilder, Hazelton, and Li.* New York: University Press of America, 2000. 173 pages.

As early as in 1939 Walter Benjamin recognized the radical quality of Brecht's theater in his re-definition of the audience-stage relationship. Benjamin applied the term "dialectic" to this style, and Brecht himself came to prefer the term "dialectic" over "epic" to describe his theater in the late stages of his career, noting that epic was a prerequisite for but not the ultimate aim of a productive political theater. Brecht's preference for this term implies the recognition on his own part that the ultimate legacy would lie in his theatrical practices—the arresting of dramatic action in politically charged tableaux and the translation of political perspective into the theatrical gestus—and not simply in his innovative approach to story-telling and narrative structure.

Two recently published books revisit the issue of the fundamental qualities of Brecht's concept of the theater. Sarah Bryant-Bertail's *Space and Time in Epic Theater* is a useful critical analysis of selected performances, including Brecht's own productions and those of key contemporary directors such as Peter Stein, Rustom Bharucha, JoAnne Akalaitis, and Ariane Mnouchkine.   Understanding the significance of the dialectic in Brecht's theater, she argues that its power and that of his followers lie in their handling of theater's time-space configuration. In contrast, Peter Yang's *Play is Play* proposes a rethinking of epic theater through a comparative analysis of how authors such as Max Frisch, Bertolt Brecht, Thornton Wilder, George Hazelton, and Li Xingdao script the performer-spectator relationship in the text.

Bryant-Bertail draws on a number of theoretical approaches to capture the spatio-temporality of Brecht's theater, taking a different route than Brecht's own of defining the epic theater by delimiting it from the naturalist theater and traditional drama.   Following the semiotic approaches of Patrice Pavis and Anne Ubersfeld, who assume a much more complex mode of theatrical communication than earlier semiotics, Bryant-Bertail thinks of theater as a complex performance text in which the artist must fill the "blank expanse" of theater space and develop a "performance continuum" of "blocks of meaning" and "chains of episodes" (18). She weaves together concerns of cultural semiotics and materialist feminism by insisting that the codes of meaning are historically determined and express ideologies. She asserts that Brecht manipulated the temporal and spatial codes of the theater and that his "epic theatre relentlessly exposes the volatility of these codes" (7). From this theatrical perspective Brecht's gestus becomes the central organizing principle of the spatio-temporality in his dialectical theater, while the actor's body is the nexus marking real and fictional bodies constructed as signifiers. Throughout the book Bryant-Bertail also reads Brecht's theater through the eyes of Barthes, Bakhtin, de Certeau, Eco, Derrida, materialist feminism, and many other theorists. This surfeit of theoretical perspectives, while engaging and occasionally insightful, often diverts attention from the author's central methodological approach.

The book essentially offers two narrative strands. Historically the chapters are organized chronologically to emphasize the breadth of Brecht's influence: chapters 1-3 focus on the development of epic theater in Piscator's production of *The Good Soldier Schwejk* (1928) at the Piscator Bühne (treated as the prototype of epic theater), in Brecht's *Mother Courage* (Brecht's most influential production, widely seen in Europe on a tour by the Berliner Ensemble and critically lifted to prominence by Roland Barthes), and in Lenz's *The Tutor* (discussed as an exemplary performance developing Brecht's fundamental concept of gestus). Chapters 4-6 examine influential directors who have applied Brechtian strategies. This layout creates a historical narrative of precursor, master, and influence that is surprisingly traditional, especially considering the author's extensive use of theorists who advocate alternative historiographical schemes. Thematically Bryant-Bertail uses each chapter to associate a performance with a contemporary theoretical issue: she examines a post-colonial performance approach in Bharucha's production of Ibsen's *Peer Gynt*; she frames Ariane Mnouchkine's production of Aeschylus's *The Oresteia* through a discussion of gender issues; and she discusses JoAnne Akalaitis's production of Büchner's *Leonce and Lena* within the context of postmodern staging approaches to show that postmodernism and epic theater are not mutually exclusive styles.

Bryant-Bertail's methodological scheme has advantages and disadvantages. The chapters provide detailed and engaging analyses of critically acclaimed productions by first-rate directors. Also, by reading Brecht's theater through critics who have clearly defined interests in performance issues themselves, Bryant-Bertail avoids treading the well-worn path of interpreting Brecht's concepts of alienation and epic theater against the background of theatrical realism, traditional plot construction, or the Wagnerian *Gesamtkunstwerk*. Specifically, her engagement with Michael de Certeau's concept of "tactics" throughout the discussion of Piscator's and Brecht's performances applies a poststructuralist concept to Brechtian performance and, conversely, provides de Certeau's theory with a concrete and effective example.

Still, the range of critics whose theories are being used to understand the epic in light of the contemporary performance context is often disorienting. While stimulating, the diverse approaches, references, and insights sometimes make the work seem unfocused. Although Bryant-Bertail is careful to provide the cultural context for her semiotic analysis, the contextualization is often brief and not fully integrated into her analysis. Hence, she fails to capture the complexity of the concrete performer-spectator relationship within a specific historical situation. This is especially problematic given the broad scope of the book—she covers performances from multiple cultures and political situations as diverse as Germany's Weimar Republic, the post-war German Democratic Republic, the post-war Federal Republic of Germany, France, the United States, and India. Bryant-Bertail attempts to lend the book a greater coherence by choosing plays that fit the Brechtian model of journeys and political resistance. However, romantic dramas such as Ibsen's *Peer Gynt* and classical plays such as Aischylus's *Oresteia* do not automatically become epic plays because they share an expansive narrative structure. Finally, considering Peter Stein's strong engagement with Brecht's theater and the political involvement of his Schaubühne am Halleschen Ufer during the 1970s, this major director probably deserves his own chapter instead of being sandwiched between the U.S. premiere of *Peer Gynt* and Bharucha's Indian version. Generally the choices of performances are too few and too selective to justify the book's subtitle "the Brechtian legacy." Neither does the book capture the historical, geographical, and theoretical breadth of Brecht's influence nor does it devote extensive space to any of the represented directors. The book's most important contribution is to suggest the geographical and historical force of Brecht's theater.

In contrast to Bryant-Bertail's book, Peter Yang's *Play is Play* is neither an engaging nor an enlightening contribution to the discussion of Brecht's theater. Yang aims at showing "that the characteristics of the 'epic' plays have been misunderstood and misinterpreted" (15). He wants to shift the focus toward the "conscious theatrical performance on stage and the conscious spectatorship offstage" (15). To achieve this goal he proposes a "formal-aesthetic comparison" between plays from different literary and theatrical cultures: Max Frisch's *Chinese Wall*, Brecht's *Caucasian Chalk Circle*, George Hazelton's and Harry Benrimo's *The Yellow Jacket*, Thornton Wilder's *Our Town*, and Li Xingdao's *The Story of the Chalk Circle*. Yang sees his contribution as the first comparative analysis of this particular group of plays, but he does not articulate the advantage to be gained from grouping these particular plays, besides the fact that they share formal characteristics such as storytelling and manipulation of the performer-spectator relationship. Furthermore, he claims a methodology which is "experimental" and "incomplete," again without explaining or showing in his argument which methodology he follows, why it is incomplete, and wherein the experiment lies.

Much of Yang's discussion centers on issues that have been explored elsewhere in more depth and with more clarity. In the introduction Yang leads the reader through the history of theater, pointing to the existence of earlier forms of epic theater from ancient Greece to the twentieth-century avant-garde, recognizable by their use of nondramatic devices. In a brief chapter called "conceptual foundations" Yang uses Frisch's play *The Chinese Wall* to introduce the reader to three ideas that seem to be his yardstick for discussing epic theater: the stage as a closed world, audience interaction, and the play's potential power for effecting political change. In the following chapters Yang examines issues such as the distinction between the dramatic and the theatrical and strategies for making the audience conscious that the play is only a play such as different levels of time experience within the prologue or audience address, differentiation between actors and their characters, and the acknowledgment of the physical stage as a theater. None of this is new, and the bibliography and argument show little awareness of two decades of performance theory which would have helped the author develop his ideas. In particular Yang misses the opportunity to follow through on what he considers the innovation of his study: the comparison of authors from many cultures. This exploration suffers exactly from the formal-aesthetic method: while pointing out the various functions of epic strategies in the plays, Yang does not allow the cultural context and complex processes of the plays to enter into his discussion of performer-spectatorship communication as, for example, Erika Fischer-Lichte recently attempted in her analysis of Hazelton's *The Yellow Jacket*. The upshot of the formalist argument seems to be that "the theatrical staging and acting devices creates [sic] their own illusion" (133). Yang's methodological approach is unsuitable for untangling the complex issue of interaction between actor and spectator consciousness, as recent phenomenological approaches have demonstrated, and for gauging the political effect pursued by directors like Brecht. If there is more to Yang's argument, it fails to emerge owing to serious stylistic and editorial problems.

Both Bryant-Bertail and Yang are interested in reinvigorating the discussion of epic theater. Based on recent performance theory, Bryant-Bertail has developed a concept of performance which offers a thought-provoking reading of the political dynamic of Brecht's theater. In contrast, Yang becomes entangled in the formalistic explorations of epic devices, narrative strategies, and theatrical illusion which Brecht tried to leave behind in favor of the political dynamic between stage and society.

Klaus van den Berg
University of Tennessee

* * *

Manfred Wekwerth. *"Erinnern ist Leben": Eine Dramatische Autobiographie.* Leipzig: Faber & Faber, 2000. 461 Seiten.

As anyone who is familiar with the history of the Berliner Ensemble knows, Manfred Wekwerth was one of Brecht's closest collaborators during the last five and, in some ways, most productive years of Brecht's life. Wekwerth then became the longest reigning artistic director of the Berliner Ensemble, first as Helene Weigel's associate director (1961-1969) and later as the Ensemble's "Intendant" or manager (1977-1992). His memoir was anticipated with considerable expectation, since he is more familiar than anyone else with the Berliner Ensemble's inner workings during the decades when it was the GDR's most prestigious theater as well as one of the few companies whose practice enduringly influenced twentieth-century world theater. Wekwerth also occupied high-ranking positions in the GDR's cultural and political hierarchy: he was elected President of the Academy of Arts in 1982, and became a member of the ruling party's (SED) Central Committee in 1986. Consequently, he gained intimate knowledge of the complicated, not to say convoluted, cultural politics of the GDR, as he was continually involved with the problems of artists and intellectuals who had to suffer a bureaucratic system's rigid yet often amazingly ineffectual ideological control.

As the tale of an exceedingly successful and multifaceted creative life, the book is a good read, rich in anecdote and trenchant views of events that molded society in East Germany since World War II. It is also somewhat disappointing. "Remembering Equals Living"—that is the title's claim. Yet Wekwerth appears to exclude quite a number of recollections from those he subsumed in his text under the rubric "Living." While providing many insights, the text is withholding others one would have wished to read about, and thus its value as a historical document is somewhat limited. Nonetheless, it offers an engaging narrative of one gifted person's voyage through the vicissitudes of political and cultural German history during the second half of the twentieth century. Having been a stage director and dramaturg under Brecht's tutelage, Wekwerth structures his book, tongue-in-cheek, according to a strictly non-Brechtian principle: Gustav Freytag's five-act rule of drama. After a prologue about his youth—the only concession to an epic dramaturgy, one might say—four chapters are devoted to his artistic life in theater and television, while the fifth takes stock of his experiences as an academy president, theater administrator, and top-ranking member of the GDR's ruling party.

The incidents that Wekwerth cares to recount from his early years are at times a bit meager, if not evasive. For instance, a young person born in late 1929 did not have to fear the draft until the very last months of the war in 1945, when the so-called "Volksturm" was called to serve. At the age of fifteen avoidance of the draft would hardly have been the incentive to attain the rank of "Fähnleinführer" and be in charge of more than a hundred boys, as Wekwerth claims it was. Such a position was not granted to anyone who had not convincingly demonstrated his commitment while serving in the "Jungvolk," the Nazis' equivalent of the Cub Scouts (28). There were quite a number of ways to dodge involvement in the Nazi system, as I well remember from having grown up in Germany during the war. Wekwerth did not choose them, it seems. His account of the early post-war years in his hometown of Köthen indicates that he picked political affiliations according to the benefits they offered, moving from an outspoken "social free market" party, the LDP, to the Communists, who were to become the ruling party of the young GDR.

Of course, one should not blame Wekwerth for decisions he made when he was in his teens and still searching for a purpose in life and also a career. What becomes evident throughout his memoir, though, is a rarely faltering instinct that enabled him to play off competing political pressures (such as the GDR government and the ruling party) and economic forces (such as those of the Brecht heirs) in ways that mostly appear to have worked to his advantage. Yet for every defeat he seems to bear an unforgotten grudge, even if it seems barely important from today's vantage point. For instance, when he had reason to believe he was considered as a Candidate for the Party's Central Committee but was not chosen, he blames this outcome with some bitterness on an argument with the Party's leader, Walter Ulbricht. In a way he is right: Hans Dieter Mäde (at the time the Intendant of the Karl-Marx-Stadt—now once again Chemnitz—theater), the person selected in his stead, to general surprise, as Wekwerth implies, was certainly less qualified except for an adeptness at toeing the Party line and delivering theater productions that were politically correct (208).

Wekwerth's narrative of the years when he emerged as Brecht's preferred assistant and eventually as a director in his own right at the BE does not tell much that is new. The reader will discover amusing anecdotes about Brecht's womanizing and about the love of food and especially drink shared by most members of the Ensemble, quite in contrast to Brecht's own somewhat abstemious attitude, which Wekwerth rightly attributes to his fragile health rather than to principle. The text also reveals the often quite serendipitous ways in which decisions concerning repertoire and casting were made. Wekwerth treats as well Elisabeth Hauptmann's influence on the Ensemble's repertoire during and after Brecht's time and her not unusual disagreement with options considered or actually implemented.

There are, however, a number of inaccurate recollections from the years between 1951, when Brecht invited Wekwerth into the Berliner Ensemble, and 1961, the year he joined Helene Weigel in the Ensemble's artistic leadership. A few of these inaccuracies demonstrate either a surprising neglect of available information or a quite selective memory. For example, he reports on the 1953 Vienna production of *The Mother* with Helene Weigel and Ernst Busch as guests from the Berliner Ensemble, where they had been playing the leads in Brecht's own staging since 1951. Brecht had entrusted Wekwerth with conducting rehearsals at Vienna's New Scala Theater for a production based on the Berlin model until he himself would arrive to direct the last two weeks of rehearsal. As Wekwerth recounts it, he alone was responsible for the production and its remarkable success, due to his creative fusing of Brecht's practice with performance modes that were more familiar to the Viennese actors (91). It is true that Brecht was very pleased with Wekwerth's work; I remember that he said so and, chuckling, called Wekwerth a "veritable Genghis Khan of directing." Nevertheless, the production was supervised and completed by Brecht, a fact at which Wekwerth does not even hint. Similarly, he leads the reader to believe that he was the main, if not sole directing assistant of Brecht and merely concedes that during the rehearsal of *Caucasian Chalk Circle* Käthe Rülicke, Isot Kilian, and Hans Bunge were also present (119). In fact, Brecht had a number of other assistants, and I was one of them. Coincidentally, a photo shows Wekwerth sitting next to Brecht in rehearsal, and I can be seen on Brecht's other side (98), since I was an assistant during all rehearsals of *Chalk Circle*, as I had been for Brecht's *Katzgraben* production, when I wrote many of the rehearsal notes which, edited by Brecht, were included in his *Katzgraben Notate* (41).

There are other trivial errors that would be too tedious to enumerate. Suffice it to remind the reader that the memoir sometimes treats facts and dates quite nonchalantly. For instance—and this surely is a minor point, yet illustrates a penchant to exaggerate even quite insignificant facts—it did not take two days to go by train from Berlin to Paris in 1954 (129); one left Berlin around noon and arrived in Paris the next morning, a travel time of about twenty hours. Or Nicolay Erdmann's play *The Suicide* is misdated in 1938, at the height of Stalin's purges, instead of 1932, at the time of their beginnings (342). Furthermore, I was quite surprised by Wekwerth's predilection to somewhat depreciate the work of coworkers such as Peter Palitzsch and Benno Besson. Judging from the memoir, there were no other directors at the Berliner Ensemble whose work truly equaled his own. An early example is his remark that Therese Giehse's production of *The Broken Pitcher* was "jammervoll" (miserable) in spite of Brecht's efforts to improve it (106). Presumably it succeeded only because Wekwerth was asked to direct a partly recast company for the Ensemble's guest performances in Paris in 1954. In fact, Brecht was supervising his rehearsals as he had those of Giehse, and the production toured Poland as early as 1952, long before Wekwerth became involved.

After 1961, the events and encounters Wekwerth recalls from the long years he was at the helm of the BE provide an impressive examination of the company's successes and failures as well as of the political environment in which it had to survive until the Cold War ended and the GDR imploded. Moreover, he includes many well-told recollections of his life and work outside the GDR borders—especially anecdotes about the productions he directed in Zurich, Vienna, and at London's National Theater—while also commenting on the successful films he directed for GDR television. Wekwerth sketches a sobering portrayal of a so-called socialist state that deeply distrusted the arts and always seemed to fear their subversive potential, notwithstanding the mantra-like claims that culture with a capital C was one of the GDR's most important endeavors. His memoir is an exceptional, if very personal, account of the role performance media played in the GDR. It offers a treasure-trove of facts and observations that no future cultural history of post-World War II Germany—before, during, and after the German partition—can afford to ignore. This being said, I would have wished to read more detailed information about several of Wekwerth's stagings, in the way he recounts the production history of *Coriolanus* and the process of its creation. After all, a number of the performances he directed have become landmarks of European theater during the second half of the twentieth century. They were and will remain his historic achievement.

The book's last chapter (Act V, according to Freytag's Arsitotelian scheme) consists of a conversation with Ulrich Dietzel, his former collaborator at the GDR Academy of Arts. Here Wekwerth comments, in retrospect, on that estimable institution's role in the GDR's cultural and political life, its manifold conflicts with political authority, and the events and actions that shaped his own presidency of it. He recounts a number of skirmishes he fought in defense of censored artists or works of art, and he discusses his efforts to enhance cultural latitude and intellectual integrity within a socialist system that became increasingly paranoid and sniffed subversion everywhere. Wekwerth remained loyal to the socialist state until its very end, though he also criticized, albeit in circumspect ways, the abuses and deficiencies which disfigured the East German version of socialism and finally destroyed it. His loyalty has since been used as a transparent pretext to attack him, to question his probity, and to chase him from office. His memoir understandably devotes much space to the defense of his actions and conduct during the years he worked in the GDR. Even if one might be inclined to dispute some of his assertions, he has written the narrative of an exceptional and, at times, controversial creative life, a life that was guided by a sharp mind and sincere convictions. That he did stick to his convictions and kept trying to implement them, often in conflict with the ever more depressing reality the Party liked to label "Real Existing Socialism," should be regarded not as a fault but rather as one of his accomplishments.

Carl Weber
Stanford University

* * *

Antony Tatlow. *Shakespeare, Brecht, and the Intercultural Sign.* Durham and London: Duke University Press, 2001. 297 pages.

Antony Tatlow's *Shakespeare, Brecht, and the Intercultural Sign* is an exemplary comparatist study whose importance lies in the way it links Brecht to wider theoretical issues such as globalization and interculturalism. Tatlow brings to the study of Brecht the kind of literary and cultural training that characterized scholars in the heyday of Comparative Literature: classical training in languages as well as in the Western traditions of literary history, here broadened to include Japanese and Chinese philosophical, historical, and aesthetic traditions. Eclectic in the best sense of the term in its historical and theoretical rigor, the study is constantly provocative, renewing the most valuable kernel of Brechtian theory: its ability to provide an *activating*, rigorous critique without sacrificing the formal and aesthetic dimensions of analysis. While acknowledging a debt to Adorno, Tatlow makes critical theory and materialist understandings inseparable, arguing that Brecht deflected "the energy of metaphysical thinking...into the reimagining of nontranscendental relations." In constantly shifting constellations, European texts and historical contexts are brought into contact in new ways through an ongoing study of Brecht's plays; the revisionary dialectical approaches of the Frankfurt School; Levi-Strauss's and Clifford Geertz's work in anthropology; Foucaultian, Derridean, and Lacanian poststructuralism; and discussions of Aristophanes, Aristotle, and Kott, among others. But these simultaneously enter a comparatist, mobile, and shifting framework in which they are made to interact with Asian traditions, all of which are carefully historicized: Shakespearean performances in East Asian settings; East Asian performances; Buddhist metaphysics; Zen koans; Confucian ideology; Akira Kurosawa, to name only a few. (As an aside, Tatlow's work might provide a way to assess Buddhist and Asian conventions in Brecht that can counter New Age misappropriations of Eastern thought in US culture.)

Tatlow bases his methodology on two notions of the foreign: the cultural Other and the past as Other, a methodology that shows the impossibility of Brechtian analyses *not* to be comparative. The defamiliarization of the past, in this sense, is also a defamiliarization of the present, including the familiarity dramatic scholars come to assume about our subject matter when we fail to historicize, as Tatlow insistently does, the specific conventions of interpretation that constructed *this* Shakespeare or *that* Brecht, especially our "own." Of particular concern is the Shakespeare whose presentations have achieved what Tatlow calls an "aesthetic state of grace," which legitimate a suspension of thought because of that familiarity. His attempt, at least in this second notion of the foreign, is not to fetishize history or to imagine that one could ever see it just as it was or as it was experienced, but to assess the relation of aesthetic form to the debates and ideologies of the day. Of primary importance in relation to the cultural Other is Tatlow's notion of dialectical acculturation, a highly fluid yet historically careful, theoretical prism through which he critiques traditional notions, not simply of Shakespeare, but of intercultural studies of influence, many of which, he argues, remain locked into a unidirectional, static, or debt model. Dialectical acculturation can show us something called interfiliation, which is not a static focus on differences and transmissions that travel only one way but instead reveals how a second culture "absorbs, transforms, and then retransmits" the first culture back to itself so as to foreground its own lack or foreignness to itself, the lack revealing the repressed in its own self-knowledge.

Tatlow carefully revises attempts to historicize the unconscious, continuing a project familiar from the long tradition of both Frankfurt School and Structuralist efforts to bring together Marx and Freud. He does so not only by reclaiming the possibilities of the Freudian notion of the unconscious (in particular, even though indirectly, the phantasm) but by thoroughly wresting the unconscious away from the ahistorical universals of the discipline of psychoanalysis in order to resituate it within the much more loosely disciplined field of ethnography. Hence, he not only retains the indispensable insights into the relation between signs and bodies available from Freud and Lacan, but his refusal to honor the disciplinary and historical boundaries of psychoanalysis means that he can also reject its historical limitations as a theoretical concept limited to the nineteenth and twentieth-century history of the European bourgeois subject. Similarly, he retrieves, by way of the Brechtian dialectic of acculturation, the possibilities available from discourse and textual analysis, which have been limited in the West by mimetic concepts of language, thus opening language up to the far more materialist, semiotic notions of languages, of gestural and analogical analyses informed by poetics and theories of performance.

In developing the concept of dialectical acculturation, Tatlow relies on the concept of repression. Yet, by this point the concept has become thoroughly "strange" through his comparative historicizing. His notion of the social unconscious intervenes in earlier discussions of the political unconscious by making Brecht and dramatic form central to such a concept of the unconscious, thus ensuring that aesthetic form and the body are there from the beginning and obviating speculation about where "reality" lies. Reality is now located squarely within process, relationality (not relativism), the dialectic between sign and body, and the contradictions of materialist history and signification. Though he calls his methodology textual anthropology, it might better be called textual ethnography, given his distrust of the historical foundations of anthropology in the tradition of the sovereign subject, and he ultimately describes what he is doing as a materialist ethnography of the imagination, though every one of those terms has to be "made strange" or reconsidered so that we readers do not assume we know what they mean; they must first be made foreign to us by being circulated through the past, through other cultures, and through the social unconscious.

Through such a methodology Tatlow finds the "foreign" of contemporary theory as he constantly unearths its past. In fact, one of the pleasures of reading this book is the way it interrupts an overly "familiar" theoretical chronology that is constantly shaken up and estranged in quite remarkable ways. In this vein his concept of the unconscious, informed by Freud, is nevertheless also informed by Foucault's use and critique of Freud, his argument that Freud's model of repression did not account strongly enough for the productive mechanisms of the unconscious. Here Tatlow renews our interest in *The Order of Things*, which might be seen as the companion volume to Freud's *The Interpretation of Dreams*, at least in the sense in which Tatlow reconceptualizes the unconscious both positively in terms of its productivity and negatively in terms of its blockages, which lead to "the steady acquisition of knowledge." Foucault here provides the critique of a static model of unconscious structures by way of a counterscience of psychoanalysis and ethnography in which "moments of apparent arrestation [occur] where a dynamic concentration pulls together psychic states that are normally compartmentalized and so kept apart, and then we are simply forced to examine the connections between them." As the historical psyche of the character is taken apart, "in a flash of unforgettable insight" the "repressions lodged in the social unconscious" are uncovered. Freud gives us back the formal depth that Foucault's dialectical engagement with Freud seemed to repress.

Tatlow's revisionary notion of the unconscious and aesthetic form is an invaluable intervention, along the lines of Pierre Macherey's *A Theory of Literary Production*. One only wishes that his review of contemporary psychoanalytic studies had not been quite so idiosyncratic as to omit what was perhaps the most important shift in Freudian psychoanalysis of the war period, its circulation through women—Melanie Klein, Anna Freud, Joan Rivière, among others. Neither does Tatlow acknowledge the powerful contemporary revisions of sociopsychoanalytic theory that might have informed his study, such as the work of Julia Kristeva, Jacqueline Rose, Teresa Brennan, Kaja Silverman, Anne Ubersfeld, and Elizabeth Grosz; Arianne Mnouchkine is the only woman whose work he treats here. Similarly, though he devotes a good deal of space to the concept of Don Juan, he also argues that speech act theory has no way of talking about the unconscious, in spite of Shoshana Felman's brilliant study of Lacan and speech act theory, *The Literary Speech Act: Don Juan with J.L. Austin, or Seduction in Two Languages*, and Judith Butler's work. A part of Tatlow's own "theoretical unconscious" thus remains remarkably unanalyzed here, though he does give a very fine reading of gender in Plautine comedy.

Disagreements aside (and one might have wished that Tatlow did not have such a propensity to footnote himself), this is a very important book precisely because it intervenes in contemporary theoretical and historical discussions in order to allow entry for readers like me who are unfamiliar with East Asian texts and contexts. His first three chapters show the interfiliations of Western theory and exposes their lack; his fourth chapter returns to the genre of farce to argue that it can best provide the formal methodology to trace the workings of the social unconscious (calling farce the "logic of the unconscious"). Revalorizing Plautine comedy in relation to Shakespearean comedy in order to reveal an épistème "facing two ways" while escaping the Western hierarchy of tragedy over comedy, he then links that characteristic culled from the past as Other to Brecht's discovery of the genre's fecundity through his encounter with East Asian dramatic traditions as cultural Other. Tatlow then follows the genre of farce through the performance traditions of Japanese Kabuki, the comic kyogen plays of the Noh theater, and the Chinese traditions of Kunju opera.

Ultimately his analysis of Brecht and farce links the conventions of physical farce to the conventions of philosophical interpretation, countering the binary coding of process as nothingness and linking farce to Eastern metaphysics and Western dialectical critical theory in which nothingness is not empty but full, even if fluid. Because farce is "more immediately associated with social incoherence and less with universal meaninglessness, loss of hope, or intellectual incomprehensibility" and because physical farce functions as "comic meditation" on the way language and representation attempt to produce reality as their effects and the inevitable mismatch when they are taken for reality, its conventions also externalize the comic mediations of philosophical farce. This is true, in particular, of the traditions of Buddhist and Confucian metaphysics and the humor Brecht identified in Hegel's dialectics. In each of these, nothing ever stays the same but constantly turns into its opposite. Here Tatlow has finally given us a methodology informed by poststructuralism, "post-Marxism," and a newly revised interculturalism, along with a practical methodology that demands cultural specificity, reclaims process from accusations of nihilism, and decenters the West by making it Other to itself.

Linda Kintz
University of Oregon

* * *

James Fisher. *The Theater of Tony Kushner: Living Past Hope*. New York and London: Routledge, 2001. 274 pages.

B ased on the publisher's name (Routledge), the series' reputation (Studies in Modern Drama, edited by Kimball King), and the author's background (multiple publications, including articles on Kushner, and a directorial stint for the Indiana premiere of *Angels in America* in 1996), I expected a scholarly treatise founded upon an original critical analysis, which in turn would extend the existing scholarship on Tony Kushner. Moreover, since Kushner is widely considered the most important American heir to Brechtian theater, I looked forward to an exploration of this component of Kushner's theatrical universe. The scholarship on Kushner and his work is not large, and hence these expectations did not seem extraordinary. Unfortunately, my expectations were not met. Fisher's volume is a disappointing work of scholarship but not an unsalvageable one.

A weak critical argument dooms Fisher's monograph. He wants to provide the first examination of Kushner's extant oeuvre, from the first major work, *A Bright Room Called Day*, through the two-part *Angels in America: A Gay Fantasia on National Themes*, to adaptations of Corneille and Brecht and the lesser-known one-act plays. In the process, he seeks to confirm Kushner's status as a major American playwright who has produced more than the iconic *Angels in America*. This in itself is an important statement and a necessary project. Yet the argument Fisher pursues to weave Kushner's oeuvre together is not commensurate with the stated task: "Belief in progress, in compassion, in the transformative power of love, in true community is the religion Kushner offers for the new millenium" (13). Perhaps if he had developed this thesis beyond its yawning banality, the volume would stand as a work of credible scholarship. The lack of an organized and analytical introduction, coupled with little or no new critical insights in the individual chapters, and cemented by the lack of a strong and formal conclusion sabotages any recovery from this initial weakness. Fisher seems content to provide extensive summary and description of the individual works as well as what amounts to mere citation of Kushner's theoretical statements and scholarly secondary literature. Critical analysis is present, but for the most part derived from secondary sources; Fisher's own original insight is largely absent. When it is present, for example in the chapter on *Angels in America*, where the author contextualizes Kushner's work within the history of Gay American Theater, especially in relation to Tennessee Williams, the analysis is excellent but frustratingly brief. To glean critical knowledge about Kushner's work, it is far more efficient to examine the primary and secondary source material. This includes the plays and adaptations themselves, Kushner's essay "Notes on Political Theater," his "Afterword" to *Angels in America*, and secondary source material such as the 1997 anthology *Approaching the Millenium: Essays on Angels in America* (particularly the essays by David Savran, Janelle Reinelt, and Art Borreca) and the 1998 anthology *Tony Kushner in Conversation* (especially the dialog between Kushner and Carl Weber).

Yet, after such scathing criticism I would still not discard this volume. While it does not offer much critical analysis, it is entirely necessary on the level of bibliographic information. In a handy, one-volume reference, the reader is provided a general understanding of Kushner's life and entire theatrical and literary output. An appendix includes a complete production history of Kushner's plays, and the bibliography includes, as far as I can tell, almost every single shred of literature written by or devoted to Kushner, including a stunning list of performance reviews from every conceivable source. Finally, numerous photographs from various productions provide an important visual complement to the bibliographical information. From this perspective the volume is an extremely valuable critical bibliography and sourcebook. Furthermore, Fisher's volume is a useful "Denkanstoss" for the Germanist and the Brecht scholar. Without a doubt, Tony Kushner is the most important American proponent of a contemporary Brechtian political theater. *A Bright Room Called Day*, the adaptation of *Good Person of Sezuan*, and "Notes on a Political Theater" are testaments and extensions of Brechtian theory and praxis. Kushner's work provides a useful lens to explore important consequences of Brecht's dramaturgy and philosophy as well as to investigate the nexus of American and German theater. Fisher's volume, despite its deficiencies, makes abundantly clear through sheer information that the relationship between Kushner and Brecht is begging to be explored within the German Studies classroom and scholarship. Moreover, the Germanist will be amazed at the influence of German culture on Kushner's life and work. Beyond Brecht lies the influence of Walter Benjamin (in some ways more important than Brecht), Goethe, Kleist, German history, and, most interestingly, the German language itself.

Fisher's volume is frustrating but it is at present the only work which encapsulates Kushner's entire theatrical output. With a disciplined reading and a bit of dialectical prestidigitation one can draw upon it for useful scholarly purposes.

Norman Roessler
Temple University

Herr Puntila und sein Knecht Matti. Berliner Ensemble, Berlin 1949. Foto: Ruth Berlau. Rechte: Johannes Hoffmann. Bertolt-Brecht-Archiv.

Books Received

Bertolt Brecht. *Ecrits sur le théâtre.* Ed. by Jean-Marie Valentin. Bibliothèque de la Pléiade. Paris: Gallimard, 2000.

Bertolt Brecht. *Collected Plays.* Vol. 4. Ed. and with an introduction by John Willett and Tom Kuhn. London: Methuen, 2001. [includes English translations of *Round Heads and Pointed Heads, Fear and Misery of the Third Reich, Senora Carrar's Rifles, The Trial of Lucullus, Dansen, How Much Is Your Iron?*].

Bertolt Brecht. *The Stories of Mr. Keuner.* Translated by Martin Chalmers. San Francisco: City Lights, 2001.

Sarah Bryant-Bertail. *Space and Time in Epic Theater.* Rochester, NY: Camden House, 2000.

Katharina Ebrecht. *Heiner Müllers Lyrik: Quellen und Vorbilder.* Würzburg: Königshausen und Neumann, 2001.

Neil Edmunds. *The Soviet Proletarian Music Movement.* Oxford: Peter Lang, 2000.

James Fisher. *The Theater of Tony Kushner: Living Past Hope.* New York and London: Routledge, 2001.

Jan-Christoph Hauschild. *Heiner Müller oder Das Prinzip Zweifel. Eine Biographie.* Berlin: Aufbau, 2001.

Günter Heeg. *Klopfzeichen aus dem Mausoleum: Brechtschulung am Berliner Ensemble.* Berlin: Vorwerk 8, 2000.

Jost Hermand. *"Das Ewig-Bürgerliche widert mich an": Brecht-Aufsätze.* Berlin: Theater der Zeit, 2001.

Michael Hofmann, Martin Rector und Jochen Vogt, Hrsg. *Peter Weiss Jahrbuch für Literatur, Kunst und Politik im 20. Jahrhundert.* St. Ingbert: Röhrig Universitätsverlag, 2001.

Keith Holz und Wolfgang Schopf. *Im Auge des Exils: Josef Breitenbach und die Freie Deutsche Kultur in Paris 1933-1941.* Berlin: Aufbau, 2001. [includes many unknown photographs of Brecht and Weigel, including performance stills of Brecht productions in Paris and New York].

Volker Kaiser. *Risus Mortis. Strange Angels: Zur Lektüre "Vom armen B.B." Eine Studie zu Brecht und Benjamin.* St. Ingbert: Röhrig Universitätsverlag, 2001.

Taekwan Kim. *Das Lehrstück Bertolt Brechts.* Frankfurt am Main: Lang, 2000.

Jan Knopf, Hrsg. *Brecht Handbuch. Band I: Stücke.* Stuttgart und Weimar: Metzler, 2001.

Jan Knopf, Hrsg. *Brecht Handbuch, Band 2: Gedichte.* Stuttgart und Weimar: Metzler, 2001.

Kyung-Boon Lee. *Musik und Literatur im Exil: Hanns Eislers dodekaphone Exilkantaten.* New York: Peter Lang, 2001.

Heiner Müller. *Die Stücke 2.* Hrsg. von Frank Hörnigk. Frankfurt am Main: Suhrkamp, 2001.

Cornelius Partsch. *Schräge Töne: Jazz und Unterhaltungsmusik in der Kultur der Weimarer Republik.* Stuttgart und Weimar: Metzler, 2000.

Ekkehard Schall. *Meine Schule des Theaters: Seminare—Vorlesungen—Demonstrationen—Diskussionen.* Frankfurt am Main: Suhrkamp, 2001.

Antony Tatlow. *Shakespeare, Brecht, and the Intercultural Sign.* Durham and London: Duke University Press, 2001.

Ian Wallace, Dennis Tate und Gerd Labroisse, Hrsg. *Heiner Müller: Probleme und Perspektiven. Bath-Symposion 1998.* Amsterdam und Atlanta: Rodopi, 2000.

Manfred Wekwerth. *Erinnern ist Leben: Eine dramatische Autobiographie.* Leipzig: Faber & Faber, 2000.

Hendrik Werner. *Im Namen des Verrats: Heiner Müllers Gedächtnis der Texte.* Würzburg: Königshausen & Neumann, 2001.

Peter Yang. *Play Is Play: Theatrical Illusion in Chinese Wall by Frisch and Other "Epic" Plays by Brecht, Wilder, Hazelton and Li.* Lanham, MD: University Press of America, 2000.